A CONTINENT ASTRAY

A CONTINENT ASTRAY

ASTRAY

EUROPE, 1970-1978

Walter Laqueur

New York · Oxford

OXFORD UNIVERSITY PRESS

1979

Copyright © 1979 by Walter Laqueur

Library of Congress Cataloging in Publication Data

Laqueur, Walter Ze'ev, 1921–
   A continent astray.

   Includes index.
   1. Europe—Politics and government—1945–
2. Europe—Economic conditions—1945–
I. Title.
D1058.L25   309.1'4'055   78-12021
ISBN 0-19-502510-5

Printed in the United States of America

PREFACE

This book is about a crisis in Europe which, for all one knows, may not be over for a long time. "Europe" in this context means the governments and the societies of Europe. A united Europe does not, of course, exist—only a loose functional confederation, meaning an imperfect common market complemented by certain other activities such as communal listening to the traditional Johann Strauss concerts under the able direction of Willi Boskowski each New Year's day. Europe did have a chance to unite, which it missed; there may or may not be other chances but only when there is a political and psychological readiness which clearly does not now exist.

It is the central contention of this book that, to paraphrase Gibbon, if a man were called to fix the period in the history of Europe during which the condition of its inhabitants (with the exception of one or two countries) was most happy and prosperous, he would without hesitation name that that elapsed from Stalin's death to the early seventies. But just as the stability and the prosperity of that period in the history of the Roman empire referred to by Gibbon depended largely on the character of one man, the well-being of Europe depended on a specific set of circumstances: domestic stability, relative security and independence in foreign affairs, economic growth. All this is now changing, not for the better, and in addition there are the general perils increasingly threatening not just Europe but all mankind. These perils have been widely discussed for a number of years and sometimes in a spirit of exaggeration, but for all this they are quite real.

During the period that is now drawing to a close there was more freedom in Europe than at any previous age in its history. The authority of the state, and indeed all authority, grew progressively weaker; it is quite likely that this was part of the charm of the period. There were, of course, even during that period, problems and "crises" of sorts, and since human memory is notoriously short, many contemporaries were not even aware that they never had it so good. Of late it has become obvious that the pendulum is about to swing in the other direction, towards greater state control and a strengthening of authority, or perhaps a new form of authoritarianism. The belief that the "system" is no longer capable of coping with the problems facing it may be exaggerated, but it is the belief that counts, and in any case, even if exaggerated, the belief is not altogether unfounded. Whether this process will be quick or slow, and how far it will go, no one can say, for the simple reason that it is not foreordained. Partly, it is the result of neglect, the lack of psychological preparation for a new historical period; partly, it is the inevitable reaction against the state of semi-anarchy now prevailing in some European societies in which it has become seemingly impossible to overcome even minor difficulties. It is, of course, quite likely that this process would have occurred in any case.

It is true that the old authorities have been discredited, but historical experience teaches that when authority is needed it usually appears—sometimes provided by the anti-authoritarian forces. That this process may vary greatly from country to country goes without saying; in some societies there is greater social cohesion, discipline, and maturity than in others, and democracy has not equally deep roots in the countries of Europe.

But all this does not make for a vision of the future that is one of unrelieved gloom and doom; I do not share the pessimism of some observers who see nothing ahead but disaster and catastrophe. The reassertion of authority may be brutal, far-reaching, and costly, but it is equally possible that societies facing a crisis of survival will voluntarily surrender some of the freedom to which they have become accustomed and that gradually a new equilibrium will emerge between the rights of the individual and the interests of society. If the general direction of development seems fairly clear, there still is an enormous span of possibilities, ranging all the way from a relatively humane and civilized new order to a new totalitarianism. To this extent human beings still are, as they always were, masters of their own destiny.

A new ice age, in brief, is not a foregone conclusion. But it seems quite likely that recovery will be preceded by a further deterioration in the state of Europe. It is difficult even to envisage the emergence of a new sense of purpose until the societies of Europe awaken from their present stupor and unless much that is rotten will be swept away. This will not be accomplished as the result of friendly persuasion. May the ordeal be not too protracted and not too painful.

I am grateful to my friend Dr. Herbert Block for his advice all along. Dr. Block, until recently of the Department of State, is the author of the annual *Planetary Product, Political Arithmetic of the World Economics*, and other works. Chapter Two in the present study was written by him.

A research grant by the National Endowment of the Humanities has greatly helped me to continue and complete this study. The views expressed here do not necessarily represent the views of the Endowment.

Washington, D.C.   Walter Laqueur
December 1978

CONTENTS

Però, se 'l mondo presente disvia,
in voi è la cagione, in voi si cheggia.

(Therefore, if the present world
goes astray, in you is the cause,
in you let it be sought.
Dante, *Purgatorio,* Canto XVI)

A CONTINENT ASTRAY

ABULIA[1] OR THE STATE OF EUROPE

Arduum res gesta scribere—to write history is difficult; to write on contemporary Europe may even be a disturbing experience. For the subject is of more than academic interest; it directly affects every single one of us. Nor is it obvious whether to write in the past or present tense in dealing with a subject as yet unfinished. The history of these last years is the history of a crisis, mainly political in character, even though it was triggered by an economic recession. If its origins and causes are obvious, its outcome is, of course, uncertain. At a time of crisis in the life of individuals as of nations, balance sheets are drawn and future perspectives are considered and the results are usually dispiriting. There is a temptation at this stage for the historian to turn prophet, or at the very least, philosopher. The reaction is all too understandable, even though it may not contribute a great deal to the understanding of our present predicaments. Guiccardini once noted that since all kingdoms, states, and cities are mortal, the citizen who happens to live when his country is in its decline should not lament over its unhappy fortunes, but over his own. Such advice, however, is not really very helpful, and the assumption of the inevitability of decline is of doubtful validity. That kingdoms and states have come and gone has been apparent for a great many years, but usually there has been nothing inevitable about these developments. With the benefit of hindsight it is only too easy to see how almost always both rise and decline could have been arrested or even reversed.

---

[1] The term "abulia" was coined by Charcot, the great French neurologist, or one of his collaborators in the 1860's. Charcot had observed that patients suffering from Parkinson's disease frequently showed a paralysis of will and could not engage in any kind of activity, even though they were physically capable of doing so following an outside stimulus or command. Charcot mistakenly believed that this paralysis of will was neurotic in character. See also page 263 ff.

That Europe is at present in a state of decline cannot be seriously disputed. But this has been the case, according to Nietzsche for almost five hundred years, and while history indeed is full of examples of countries, states, and societies suffering eclipse and ruin, for every such case there have been several predictions of impending downfall that were belied by subsequent events. While what we know of the past does not necessarily inspire optimism, it does teach us caution. The sense of decline and decadence, the prophecies of doom, can be traced back to the beginnings of history, and it is probably true that the feeling of pessimism has been on the whole more dominant than the so-called optimistic ages. Thus Rousseau saw *tour les états de l'Europe courir à leur ruine,* and this at a time when the rise of modern Europe had hardly begun. Gibbon considered the possibility of the victorious barbarians carrying slavery and desolation as far as the Atlantic Ocean—but they have not arrived yet.

The optimistic nineteenth century, and even more the twentieth, produced prophets of doom in unprecedented numbers. A great many studies entitled *Finis Galliae* or *Finis Germaniae* were published and all argued convincingly that the end was at hand. Although arguments were irrefutable, they were not quite borne out by subsequent events. France during the last quarter of the last century provides a good example. The effects of the disastrous defeat by Germany in 1870 were felt for more than three decades, and the manifestations of the *fin de siècle* spirit were unmistakable. Friends and enemies of France alike pointed to the decline in the birth rate, economic stagnation, growing alcoholism, decrease in church attendance, irrationalism in philosophy, decadence and eroticism in literature. Others referred to the lack of patriotism and national self-discipline, the excessive pursuit of pleasure and the spreading anomie, the social disorganization.[2] There were apocalyptic predictions from Léon Bloy on the extreme right, who thought the French nation more corrupt than any people had ever been, to the economist Charles Rist on the left, who wrote that France was an islet of sugar dissolving in the water. As Taine said to the young Paul

---

[2] If French political science had been more developed than it was at the time it would have produced, no doubt, a great many books on the "governability crisis," referring either to the growing search among the masses for instant gratification or, alternatively, to the severe and sharpening contradictions inherent in late capitalism.

Deroulede: Young man, France is dying—leave it alone in its agony.[3]

This mood prevailed until about 1905, and then suddenly, almost overnight and for no apparent reason, the mood changed. Defeatism gave way to a new spirit of self-confidence and even aggressive nationalism. There was a transformation of values as the young people of 1905 discovered new preoccupations, such as sport; individualism and self-analysis became outmoded and new trends asserted themselves in literature and the arts. Somehow the national will, believed to be dead and buried, reasserted itself, and France "was herself again." There are no obvious explanations for this change, for neither the birth rate nor church attendance had risen; alcohol consumption certainly continued at the old level. There had been no major upturn in the business cycle, no new industrial revolution. Perhaps it was just the violent reaction of a new generation repelled (or bored) by the pessimism and cynicism of their elders; perhaps it was the fact that the mood of decadence had been restricted to a small elite and that the real France had not been all that much affected by it. Whatever the cause, the change of mood is an historical fact and it is by no means an isolated case in the annals of history: if a miracle, it tended to recur quite frequently.

Carlo Sforza had begun his career in the Italian diplomatic service well before World War I, and he lived to serve as foreign minister in five consecutive Italian governments after World War II. Living in exile, he was one of the most astute observers of the European scene between the two world wars. In a book published in 1936, when the lights were about to go out again over Europe, he reached conclusions that sound uncomfortably familiar today. Referring to a nationalism running amuck and suicidal tendencies brought on by short-sighted selfishness, he wrote: "Either we shall serve the European ideal or we shall perish." Writing at a time when there was precious little ground for optimism, Sforza nevertheless refused to give in to utter despair. For he knew that there were numerous examples of what he called "sudden readjustments." But he also noted that such "miracles" were more likely to occur after periods of social anarchy.[4]

---

[3] The French mood is described in painstaking detail in a fine study by Koenraad W. Swart, *The Sense of Decadence in Nineteenth Century France* (The Hague, 1964).

[4] Carlo Sforza, *Europe and the Europeans* (London, 1936).

Among the nineteenth-century pessimists it had been the fashion to believe in the impending ruin of the Latin nations; they still had high hopes for the Germanic and Slavic races, and some pointed specifically to America and Russia as the coming great powers. Spengler and Moeller van der Bruck, proclaiming the decline of the West in the 1920's, likewise thought that the future belonged to the "young peoples," as did, after World War II, a whole galaxy of thinkers ranging from Arnold Toynbee to Sartre and G. Barraclough. For them, politically and economically, the European age was over, and with it the predominance of European values; culturally, too, Europe had had its day, new peoples were arising, new energies seeking expression—a positive view of life set against the weary disillusion of Europe. How could one be blind to the wave of the future personified by Mao and Sukarno, by Nkrumah, Nasser, and Ben Bella? Only two decades have passed and the new light from the East and South has very much dimmed. Whatever the state of Europe, only a few enthusiasts still believe that the salvation of mankind will come from the third world. The same is true for communism; even though some Communist parties in the West still have many supporters and in a few cases have even been gaining ground. But this is due to the domestic political situation in these countries. The faith in the Soviet Union (or China) as a new Jerusalem, such as existed in the 1920's and even the 1930's, has faded; Russia as a model is of no great attraction even in the third world, and for the Western Communist parties Soviet realities have actually become an embarrassment. To despair of Europe, in short, is to despair of mankind.

But Europe has given much cause for despair in recent years. Not because the age of European domination has ended, nor in view of its failure to become one of several superpowers. But it was not unrealistic to expect that the European will would reassert itself after a period of physical recovery and prosperity unprecedented in its history, i.e., the will not to dominate others but to be masters of their own destiny, to stand on their own feet, to be strong enough to withstand outside pressures, to protect their freedom. Instead, Europe of the 1970's presents a melancholic picture of fragmentation, internal squabbles, and aimlessness.

A review of the European scene in the 1970's is of necessity an attempt to understand the causes of the crisis. Some observers have ready-made interpretations. They refer to the breakdown of the capitalist system evidenced by the intensification of international competition, over-production, decline in the rate of profit, stagnation, disproportions in production and distribution. Struggling through a maze of conflicting evidence one may envy the Marxists for the certainties derived from their credo. On the basis of critical analysis, it is less easy to accept these certainties. The political crisis of the 1970's was triggered by an economic recession—but it can hardly be claimed that the emergence of OPEC was foreseen by Marx and Engels. True, there was a cyclical downturn but not, as will be shown, of particular severity. Capitalism may be doomed, not because of a lack of achievement, but as a result of the unlimited expectations it gave rise to and cannot fulfill, the hostility it engendered among intellectuals, the fact that it was *mal aimée* from the very beginning. Whoever went to fight for capitalism on the barricades? Capitalism, as Schumpeter noted long ago, was far more likely to be destroyed by success than by failure, because it created an "atmosphere of almost universal hostility to its own social order." One should not forget, however, that when Schumpeter wrote about socialism as the "heir apparent" of capitalism he simply meant "the migration of people's economic affairs from the private into the public sphere,"[5] or, as he put it elsewhere, "an institutional pattern in which control over means of production and over production itself is vested with a central authority." He did not argue that such a system was bound to be democratic in character, and that the huge bureaucratic apparatus managing the economy would be controlled by organs of political democracy. Seen in this light, "socialism" has already won, for control over means of production is an established fact not only in the communist countries but throughout the third world, and to a considerable extent even in the industrialized countries. But the kind of state and society that has emerged corresponds far more with the vision of a Prussian socialism such as advocated by Gustav Schmoller—a nationalized (or part-nationalized) economy run by a more or less competent bureaucracy within the framework of an autocratic state—than with the ideas of those who envisage socialism as the liberation of mankind, not just a mode of production. Such a social system may be called socialism by

[5] "The March into Socialism," in *Capitalism, Socialism and Democracy*, fifth ed. (London, 1976), p. 421.

conservatives in order to discredit socialism, or by Communists, to justify their record. Schumpeter's socialism as a mode of production shorn of messianic visions may or may not be inevitable, but it no more generates enthusiasm than capitalism.

If material achievements are the decisive yardstick, of success even ten or twenty years of stagnation would not necessarily invalidate the case for capitalism. Even if it were to appear that it has done less well than communism, it would still have a case, for a great many people do not want to live in a society that is unfree, even if food is plentiful and other supplies abundant. But the whole discussion has been academic for some time. The capitalism of the "textbooks" no longer exists in Europe; the mixed economies are subject to great and growing state intervention and are no longer subject to blind forces of supply and demand. Very much depends on government intervention—investment can be directed, production planned, inflation reduced, order brought into the monetary system. These decisions, political in character, depend on choice of priorities, on the will and the strength to cope. There may be no ideal solutions but the economic difficulties are not intractable, nor are the more troubling social problems. If the road to recovery is blocked, the obstacles may be political or psychological or moral, they are not located in the realm of pure economics.

To dwell too long on the economic manifestations of the crisis is to deal with only one of its aspects, and not the decisive one. With equal justice, the recent history of Europe could be written in the categories of clinical psychiatry; if individuals suffer from mental disorders, so do groups of people. The old textbooks with their clear-cut descriptions, such as provided by Kraepelin, of various neuroses and psychoneuroses, provide ample tools for an analysis of this kind. West Germany, seen in this light would be considered a medium-severe case of free-floating hypochondria, of great anxiety caused by relatively minor setbacks in the economic field and hypersensitivity to attacks whether emanating from terrorists at home or journalists abroad. France would be analyzed a medium-to-severe case of paranoia (complaints about oppression by the United States and West Germany; in the nineteenth century the same complaints were directed against Britain) with occasional fits of megalomania, over-aggressive and defiant behavior trying to assert her individuality against social controls. The case of Britain would be interpreted as a textbook illustration of maladaptation to surroundings combined with the relatively rare symptom of claustrophilia, the wish to insulate herself. Italy is a mixture of severe symptoms of various illnesses, including regression, restless, semi-purposive overactivity with handwringing, and inability to sit or lie still, physical and emotional depletion, and fatigue. Scandinavia displays symptoms of withdrawal, escapism, and the inclination to suppress uncomfortable realities. (In clinical language these are not primary delusions which are completely incomprehensible, but delusional ideas which are demonstrably false but explicable in the light of the patient's emotional state.) As for Europe as a whole, the old concept of *abulia* could be invoked; the term no longer appears in modern textbooks of psychiatry but was earlier used with reference to the loss or lack of will, a condition—fortunately—now known to appear more often than not in a cyclical pattern with many ups and downs, rather than as a permanent affliction.

It is a truism that severe economic crises have had severe political repercussions, but not invariably so. The German inflation of 1921–23 was an economic catastrophe of the first magnitude yet its immediate political consequences were minimal. One could easily point to similar cases. On the other hand, minor recessions have sometimes had political results out of all proportion to the dislocation and the suffering caused. The political outcome of economic crises obviously depends on a great many factors, and in the final analysis it is the perception that counts—a perception shaped by the presence or absence of reserves of strength and the will to recover. The European crisis of the 1970's did not break suddenly upon an unsuspecting continent as the result of the Yom Kippur war and the oil embargo. There were earlier indications, but in the optimistic mood of the sixties there was little inclination to pay heed. My own comment at the time reflected the optimism. In a book on the postwar history of Europe written in 1969, I noted that events since World War II had belied the prophecies of the continent's impending demise. The astonishing post-war economic recovery had resulted in an era of prosperity unprecedented in European history. This affluence was not limited, as so often in the past, to a relatively small section of the population. The welfare state and the rapid spread of higher education had made it possible for larger sections of the populations to participate actively in political and cultural life. The new prosperity had given rise to self-confidence and optimism, even though signs of demoralization and decay were not lacking. But such signs had always been present, just as there had been always political crises. In view of the overall progress made from 1948 to 1972, Europe moved right back into the center of the world stage.

Compared with the crisis facing the United States with its involvement in Vietnam and its domestic troubles, compared with the difficulties facing the Afro-Asian countries, the problems of Europe seemed almost trivial: "Not decay but the resilience, the will to survival, that Europe displayed after 1945 constituted the great novelty, and a source of renewed hope for its future. Far from dying in convulsions as Sartre had predicted, Europe has shown a new vigour which has astonished friends and foes alike. European ideas and techniques have spread to all corners of the earth and European civilization is still the model for the entire world. The age of European predominance has ended but no other centre has so far wrenched from Europe the torch of civilization. In a wider sense the European age has only begun."[6]

These confident lines (to repeat once again) were written in 1969; a series of articles published three years later expressed an acute sense of discomfort and even alarm. There was something profoundly askew about a continent that for the preceding twenty-five years had lived on borrowed time, incapable of mustering sufficient strength to overcome national particularism and establish some form of political unity. As a result Europe in the seventies suffered, as never before, from a large and perceptible discrepancy between economic strength on the one hand, and political and military impotence on the other. Below the surface of relative prosperity. Europe was afflicted by a paralysis of will, all the more dangerous because its progress was gradual. On the one hand, there was the inability to advance farther on the road to political and military integration, and on the other, a series of domestic traumas besetting the individual European nations. Future perspectives gave cause for much apprehension: "While a sudden castastrophe can sometimes release hidden resources of strength that can enable a people to

---

[6] W. Laqueur, *Europe Since Hitler* (London and New York, 1970), pp. 401–2.

cope with and eventually to overcome an emergency, creeping afflictions of the kind now troubling Europe sap the will and make recovery more difficult. In the perspective of the next few years—and few politicians look beyond this span—there is no reason to expect a major breakdown in Europe. Yet if the present state of affairs should continue, the road to recuperation may become hopelessly blocked."[7] The change in mood was so sudden and radical as to raise some legitimate questions. If the pessimism of 1972 was justified, had the hopes expressed three years earlier been unwarranted? Or alternatively, was there perhaps an inclination to take some passing difficulties too seriously? The optimism of 1969 had not been altogether misplaced. True, experts were unhappy about certain trends in the world economy such as the breakdown of the old international monetary system. When the heads of the International Monetary Fund and the World Bank met in Copenhagen in 1970, the central topic of discussion was inflation and how to combat it. But the rate of inflation in the OECD countries at the time was an almost idyllic 4.7 per cent. With the resignation of General de Gaulle the main stumbling block to an extension of the European Economic Community (EEC) had disappeared. When the European leaders met in The Hague in December 1970, George Pompidou, his successor, expressed willingness in principle to expand the Europe of the Six. The year after negotiations with Britain, those with Ireland, Denmark, and Norway got under way. Perhaps even more significant, in the future important foreign political issues were to be discussed on the ministerial level. This was widely considered a first step towards a West European political confederation. France had seemingly overcome the shock of 1968, and a program of social and economic reform was envisaged. Pompidou showed greater willingness to co-operate with France's neighbors, as did Britain with hers, under Edward Heath's Conservative government which, much against expectation, had defeated Labour in the elections of June 1970. In West Germany the grand coalition had broken down, and as a result of the elections of September 1969 a social democratic-liberal government emerged. The momentum of German prosperity continued and there was continuity too in Germany's foreign policy. The

[7] W. Laqueur, "The Fall of Europe," *Commentary* (January 1972); and "The Year of Europe," *Commentary* (June 1973).

opening to the East which had begun under the previous coalition was pursued with more emphasis by Chancellor Brandt; the inviolability of borders and the *Gewalt verzicht* were solemnly affirmed in the Soviet-German treaty signed in Moscow in August 1970. In Italy there were frequent changes of government, and the center-left coalitions headed by Rumor and Colombo had but a narrow parliamentary base. The "hot autumn" and the mass strikes of 1969 reflected a deeper social malaise. But Italy, once one of Europe's most backward countries, had made tremendous economic progress during the previous decade and there was no sound reason to assume that this trend would suddenly be reversed.

Above all, there were the almost messianic expectations connected with that magic term "détente." President Nixon had announced a new era of negotiations as part of his general peace strategy. Discussions on SALT began in Helsinki in November 1969, and the debate about an all-European Security Conference continued. Dr. Kissinger had not yet been to Peking, and the heyday of détente was as yet to come, but there were already unmistakable signals emanating from the world's capitals. There was a feeling in the air of a new stage in international relations ushering in an age of stability and lasting peace. And it was generally believed that Europe would be among the main beneficiaries of this new golden age. There was almost universal agreement that the post-war era had come to an end, that a turning point in world affairs had been reached, that the old bi-polar system (confrontation) had been replaced by a new multi-polar system, and by negotiation, and that as a result there would be greater stability the world over. Among many Western political commentators the general euphoria continued well into 1974. As Alastair Buchan noted in a book entitled *The End of the Postwar Era* (1974): "At the beginning of 1973 the ordinary citizen . . . might pardonably feel that for the first time in forty years (that is, since the Japanese invasion of Manchuria or Hitler's reoccupation of the Rhineland) something that could be called peace had descended on the world. Men must have felt like this when learning of the Treaty of Westphalia." In October 1972 a *Washington Post* columnist announced the arrival of a new "golden age." Let the skeptics scoff, he wrote, ten years hence they will be convinced. The world is moving towards a period of reconciliation, towards generations of peace. The Middle East conflict will be settled within the next three to six months, Middle Eastern oil will bring the great powers together. This messianic vision, it was explained, did not derive from an inherently optimistic frame of mind but from a "cold assessment of the facts of international life."

Similar views were expressed by leading West German students of world affairs. The situation had evolved to a point where relations between the two sides could be put on a qualitatively different level. Hence the conclusion that the next few years could be used to create the conditions for a moderate and peaceful international system in the remaining decades of this century. Professor Johan Galtung, a Norwegian, published a book in 1973 with the title, *The European Community: A Superpower in the Making*—and it does not really matter in the present context that he regarded the new superpower as profoundly reactionary and imperialist, "an effort to turn history backwards." Europeans who still felt a little apprehensive about the future of the continent were assured by George F. Kennan that "Finlandization" was a nonsensical idea. Short of actual occupation, Mr. Kennan said, no nation could fully enforce its will upon another; the smaller and weaker a country, the more sensitive its government to any hint of military pressure being applied against it, and the more ready its resistance to anything that smacks of pressure of blackmail from the stronger power. If these were the analyses based on a "cold assessment of the facts of international life," the futurologists could be excused for painting global landscapes with rivers of milk and honey. The fears I had voiced in 1972 were not shared at the time by many other observers.

And then, quite suddenly the confident mood changed radically. There emerged a vague and persistent feeling that the democracies had become ungovernable.[8] There was talk about a new tragic period of social and political regression and of the possibility that the whole European system might crumble. In 1974, reflecting on the human prospect, Professor Robert Heilbroner in a widely read book noted that there was a question in the air more sensed than seen, like the invisible approach of a distant storm: is there hope for man? M. Giscard d'Estaing thought there was not: "The World is unhappy. It is unhappy

[8] Samuel Huntington, Robert Heilbroner, Daniel Bell, and Michel Crozier were among the first to comment on this; recent contributions include Juergen Eick, *Das Regime der Ohnmaechtigen* (Frankfurt, 1978); and J. Huntzinger, *Europes* (Paris, 1977).

because it does not know where it is going, and because it guessed that should it know, it would be to discover that it is going towards catastrophe." Shortly before leaving office in 1975, Chancellor Willy Brandt was said to have told some of his confidants that Western Europe had only twenty or thirty more years of democracy left, after that it could sink, engineless and rudderless, into the surrounding sea of dictatorship.

The hopes of 1970 suddenly gave way to pessimism, and since the hopes had been so high, the despair was bound to be all the deeper. Seen in retrospect, the years between 1969 and 1973 were wasted years, one of the famous tides in the affairs of men which "omitted . . . is bound in shallows and miseries."

After de Gaulle's disappearance from the political scene, a new beginning could have been made in Europe: there was general agreement to that effect but no sense of urgency. There was no guarantee that Europe united would have been in a better position to face the dangers confronting the individual countries, but there was at least a chance. Closer economic co-operation would not have prevented the recession but it would probably have made its consequences easier to bear. Politically, a united Europe would have been in a more advantageous position to weather the storms of the seventies. It could have been an active participant in the conduct of world affairs instead of being a mere object. It could have made the defenses of Western Europe less dependent on the United States, less exposed to threats and pressures from the Eastern Bloc and the Middle East, correcting the anomaly that had bedeviled European politics since 1945. Greater European unity might have alleviated the domestic problems of some members of the community. Instead of strengthening internal cohesion there was drift, and a fruitless chase after structures of peace and security treaties.

The multiple crisis of the 1970's was a shock, but not a salutary one. It did nothing to strengthen the European resolve to draw closer together.[9] True, the impotence of a continent which had only yesterday

---

[9] "Crisis" is used here for want of a better term. In Greek, the word was mainly used in a legal context, for a dispute, but also a decision. But in the Septuagint and in the Revelation of St. John the Divine, it has assumed an apocalyptic meaning—referring to the day of Final Judgment. In Latin and in the middle ages it was mainly used in medical language, concerning the decisive stage of a disease in which the decision is about to occur but has not

been proclaimed a great "civilian power" became only too obvious. But the crisis created new difficulties on the road to unity, for the growing economic disparity thwarted the schemes for closer co-operation; the European countries became even more absorbed than before in their various domestic emergencies. As for a common defense, the Europeans were told on the authority of a French president that the Russians would not like it—a perfectly true statement and a fine illustration of the progress of Finlandization.

Seen in retrospect it is still correct that Europe made amazing progress in the 1950's and 1960's but the advance was uneven and incomplete. For this reason the achievements were not secure, they were dependent on too many factors beyond the power of the Europeans. Quite likely Europe would have been in a better position to confront the crisis of the 1970's if it had made less economic progress during the previous two decades, but if that progress had been matched by greater political integration—both domestically and between the members of the community. The historian has the duty to ponder the might-have-beens but there is no obligation to prolong the regret and the lament beyond a certain point. He has to accept Europe with its weaknesses and its self-inflicted wounds with the patience of a teacher dealing with slightly retarded students. Constant harping on infirmities will not speed up the process of learning, and, in any case the historian should not even try to act as the preceptor of nations and continents.

fallen yet. Rousseau and his contemporaries introduced the word into the political debate. In English the "politicization" of crisis had already taken place in the seventeenth century: "This is the Chrysis of Parliaments" (B. Rudyard, 1627). Steele published a pamphlet *The Crisis* in 1714 which was considered seditious and caused his expulsion from Parliament. Contemporary readers will find nothing subversive in Steele's pamphlet, but this, I suppose, is true with regard to most of the issues agitating people a long time ago, and it is a sobering thought that it applies, no doubt, also to many of the problems troubling us (R. Koselleck, *Kritik und Krise* [Freiburg, 1959], pp. 189, 211). While crisis is no longer used in medicine and only rarely by economists, except of the Marxist persuasion, and while in political science jargon it has assumed a specific meaning which is of no relevance in the present context, it has been overused by historians, philosophers, and needless to say—critics. ("Crisis" and "Critics" share the same etymological root.)

2

EURO-ECONOMICS

YEARS OF ADVANCE

WESTERN EUROPE NO ECONOMIC UNIT

There was a time when "Western Europe" actually meant Western Europe, namely, the European countries bordering the Atlantic Ocean. Nowadays the term covers all the European members of the Organization for Economic Co-Operation and Development (OECD), i. e. Europe, west of the Communist realm. It even includes millions of Asians, namely, the Turks living in Anatolia (and why not? descendants of the janissaries turned back before Vienna in 1683 have taken over whole neighborhoods in German cities).

The nations of Western Europe have in common their pluralistic societies (presently, at least) with market economies operated by private enterprise, though with varying degrees of state intervention. The governments interfere in the markets (adroitly or clumsily), own a number of large enterprises (money losers, as a rule), and apply, in a more or less pragmatic fashion, the tenets of ideologies such as British or Swedish socialism, French *dirigisme,* the German social market economy, not to mention the Spanish corporate system now in well-deserved liquidation. But the Western European market economies, despite their lively commercial intercourse, do not form a unit; the nine-member European Community—producing 80% of OECD-Europe's output—has not reached unity either. Economically, the countries are separate entities. The economic modes of behavior, policies, and destinies of the UK, the FRG (Federal Republic of Germany), and Italy have probably less in common that those of the United States, Canada, and Australia. A pan-European Hegelian may be tempted to test his dialectical triad: Western Europe is a unit; it is not a unit; it will be a unit (will it be?).

There was also a time when countries were bluntly called "advanced" or "backward"; now the terms are "developed" and "developing." The categories are economic and technological; our "less developed" cousins may be more civilized than highly efficient but ill-mannered and over-specialized meritocrats. In Western Europe, Portugal and Turkey are for all practical purposes less developed countries; Greece and Spain joined the club of advanced nations years ago.[1] Italy, developed as a whole, is by far more advanced north of Rome than in its southern provinces, and other countries have at least some disadvantaged regions (e.g. the Camargue in France, parts of Wales and Scotland, Bavaria's northeastern rim). But all of Western Europe, irrespective of its diversity and developmental stage, has made extraordinary progress since the Second World War and the cleanup in its wake.

QUANTUM JUMP SINCE WORLD WAR II

It is convenient to measure economic progress in terms of the gross national product (GNP), its volume, growth, and structure. Let us look at the performance between 1950, a year when the ravages of the war were largely but by no means completely repaired, and 1973, the year that ended with the "oil crunch." During this period Western Europe as a whole expanded its GNP by an average annual 4.7%. This was one percentage point faster than in United States. Consequently, the Western European-American GNP ratio increased from 77 : 100 in 1950 to 95 : 100 in 1973.

But Western Europe is not a unit; it consists of about two dozen sovereign nations growing rapidly or slowly for different reasons and with changing degrees over shorter periods; moreover, their performance is reflected by statistics of varying coverage and reliability. The least developed members, irrespective of their sometimes problematical regimes, show the fastest growth; they have been able to send surplus labor to more advanced countries while receiving capital and technology

---

[1] To skirt sticky issues as to what the social or political characteristics of developed or less developed nations are or should be, I have used as the dividing line between the two groups a per capita GNP of 1,680 dollars of 1976 purchasing power, close to the average per capita GNP for the world. See the latest issue of my series, *The Planetary Product*, The Department of State, Bureau of Public Affairs, Special Report No. 44 (June 1978).

TABLE 1A   TOTAL GNP FOR SELECTED REGIONS, 1950–1977[a] (in billions of 1977 dollars)

	1950	1960	1970	1973	1974	1975	1976	1977
United States	755.5	1,043.4	1,522.7	1,748.9	1,724.6	1,702.6	1,799.9	1,887.2
OECD–Europe	587.6	916.0	1,480.6	1,687.9	1,726.5	1,699.4	1,771.8	1,808.7
European NATO	484.2	782.5	1,256.0	1,428.8	1,460.2	1,434.5	1,503.4	1,536.5
European Community of Nine	456.4	768.8	1,184.1	1,343.9	1,321.4	1,347.9	1,411.2	1,440.1
Of which: France	105.8	164.3	285.8	335.3	345.0	341.6	357.4	368.1
FRG	114.7	244.2	389.4	435.4	438.4	427.7	452.0	463.8
Italy	53.1	92.9	159.1	178.1	184.2	177.5	187.6	190.8
UK	117.3	153.8	202.1	225.3	225.9	222.4	227.5	231.2
Others: Spain	27.4	33.7	62.9	77.6	81.4	82.1	83.8	85.9
Sweden	29.6	41.5	60.5	64.7	67.3	67.8	68.7	67.0
Switzerland	21.6	30.8	47.6	52.6	53.4	49.7	49.0	51.1

TABLE 1B   GNP PER CAPITA FOR SELECTED REGIONS, 1950–1977 (in 1977 dollars)

	1950	1960	1970	1973	1974	1975	1976	1977
United States	4,962	5,775	7,432	8,312	8,138	7,972	8,366	8,704
OECD–Europe	1,959	2,771	3,990	4,468	4,534	4,449	4,605	4,691
European NATO	1,943	2,815	4,111	4,561	4,689	4,532	4,678	4,781
European Community of Nine	2,115	3,308	4,707	5,191	5,123	5,214	5,453	5,543
Of which: France	2,531	3,595	5,627	6,423	6,573	6,470	6,756	6,906
FRG	2,295	4,408	6,415	7,023	7,067	6,921	7,350	7,554
Italy	1,127	1,847	2,964	3,244	3,324	3,181	3,338	3,371
UK	2,318	2,923	3,641	4,023	4,040	3,971	4,063	4,138
Others: Spain	947	1,108	1,408	2,225	2,312	2,306	2,330	2,363
Sweden	4,234	5,531	7,560	7,988	8,246	8,268	8,378	8,171
Switzerland	4,542	5,746	7,682	8,177	8,287	7,754	7,717	8,124

TABLE 10   ANNUAL AVERAGE GNP GROWTH RATES FOR SELECTED REGIONS, 1950–1977[a] (in per cent)

	1950-60	1960-70	1970-73	1974	1975	1976	1977
United States	3.3	3.8	4.7	-1.4	-1.3	5.7	4.9
OECD–Europe	4.5	4.9	4.5	2.2	-1.7	4.4	2.1
European NATO	5.2	4.8	4.4	2.2	-1.8	4.8	2.2
European Community of Nine	3.4	4.4	4.0	1.7	-2.0	4.7	2.0
Of which: France	4.5	5.3	5.4	2.9	-1.0	4.6	3.0
FRG	7.8	4.9	3.8	0.7	-2.5	5.7	2.6
Italy	5.8	5.6	4.4	3.4	-3.7	5.7	1.7
UK	2.7	2.3	3.7	0.3	-1.6	2.3	1.6
Others: Spain	3.6[b]	6.4	6.4	5.0	0.8	2.1	2.5
Sweden		3.6	1.9	4.0	0.8	1.3	-2.5
Switzerland	3.6[c]	4.5	3.4	1.5	-7.4	-1.3	4.3

[a]GNPs for 1974–77 are converted into dollars not with average annual exchange rates for those years—which do not reflect purchasing power equivalents—but, though this is not an ideal solution, by extrapolating 1973 exchange rates. For details see *The Planetary Product*, quoted on p. 17, footnote 1.

[b]Figure refers to 1954.

[c]Figure refers to 1951.

Early data for European NATO and the European Community refer to the present membership of those organizations.

from abroad, not to mention remittances from emigrants and payments from tourists. The average annual GNP growth of Spain was 6.9% (1954–73), of Greece 7% (1950–73), of Turkey 6.2% (1950–73), of Portugal 5.9% (1953–73). Italy's 5.3% (1951–73) is evidence of postwar recovery as well as developmental progress. West Germany's 6.2% between 1951 and 1973 was heightened by reconstruction; it was 4.7% from 1960 to 1973. France, on the other hand, managed 5% from 1950 to 1973 and 5.6% from 1960 to 1973. The two oases of peace and quiet, Sweden and Switzerland, show an annual increase of 3.8% (1951–73), a touch above the US record. Of the larger nations in Western Europe, the British are a special case. The average 2.6% growth annually between 1951 and 1973 is evidence of the *mal Anglais*, a puzzling affliction, because, whatever the specific causes (they will be discussed presently), a stout and gallant people should not be expected to put up with a self-inflicted condition that hurts their welfare, strength, and pride.

It is illuminating to compare Western Europe's overall performance since the Second World War with that of preceding periods. It would have taken Western Europe half a century to achieve the 1950–73 progress per capita of the population in the peaceful and progressive times before the First World War.[2] The period that followed, that is from the eve of the First to that of the Second World War, was dismal. Not counting some oases (like Switzerland) and disregarding a few flourishing years, there were hostilities between and within countries, revolutions and strikes, deprivation, pronounced or even wild inflations, and commercial crises leading up to the Great Depression. Between 1913 and 1939 the average annual GNP growth was only 1.9% in Germany, Italy, and Switzerland, 1.3% in the UK, 0.9% in France. (It was 2.2% in the US.)

Thus in the years after the Second World War, Western Europe made a quantum jump. The period was by no means free of political tensions, social conflicts, and economic difficulties; yet, under a *pax*

[2] In those days GNP growth *per capita* averaged around 1.5% annually, rising to 1.7% in Germany and in the UK only 1.3%. Did the *mal Anglais* begin at the height of the Victorian Age? The US had an average annual growth per capita of 2.2%. For these and the immediately following rates see Angus Maddison, *Economic Growth in the West* (New York, 1964), and *Economic Growth in Japan and the USSR* (Reading, Mass., 1969) (in the latter: Table B-1) and also Simon Kuznets, *Modern Economic Growth* (New Haven and London, 1966) (Table 6.6).

Americana, the Western European nations expanded rapidly and, in the process, transformed their economies thoroughly. Since the US was, and in many respects remains, the country leading in technology, organization, and attitudes to match, modernizing has meant Americanizing.[3] Western Europe, ascending to a much higher level of income and wealth, has changed its ways of production and consumption. We will adduce a few facts and figures, not in an attempt to write an economic history of Europe but to place the less prosperous years of the 1970's in a long-range perspective and to explain how extraordinary expansion has produced stress and strain in societies much more traditional than the American. Not that growing pains are limited to Europe; they afflict the entire world. Nations economically less advanced than Western Europe and less rooted in Western civilization are endangered by more severe tensions than is the European-American realm.

BRANCH STRUCTURE MODERNIZED

Our survey of Western Europe's progress as reflected in its national accounts will begin with data on output by branches of industry, showing the characteristic shift from agriculture to manufacturing, from manufacturing to services; it will discuss the sources of the progress achieved, namely growing application of labor and capital with productivity gains on top, i.e. increasing output per unit of input; it will finally examine how the GNP was used, either in consumption or investment. Here the circle—a benificent circle—closes because producers shape their supply in accordance with expected final demand.

Everywhere in Western Europe agriculture has declined as a con-

---

[3] The task on hand was clearly stated by the Economic Commission for Europe in its *Economic Survey of Europe in 1948* (Washington, 1949), p. 159: "The more fundamental problem of the European economy is the increase in the productivity of European industry and agriculture which alone could satisfy the universal desire for better standards of living. . . . While the superior productivity of the United States may, to some extent, be explained by its abundant supply of natural resources . . . the bulk of the difference was not due to such 'natural' factors but to its higher standards of capital equipment and the use of more efficient techniques in production. These differences, therefore, may provide an indication of the extent to which the productivity of European labor could be raised through the adoption of superior techniques requiring both more capital equipment and more efficient methods of organization."

tributor to the national product and as a claimant of labor. But this comparative shrinkage has been accompanied by great progress in productivity and also a moderate increase in physical output—often beyond the call of duty as evidenced by the mountains of butter and meat stored by the European Community or the wine war between France and Italy. The smaller share of agriculture in the economy has not notably diminished the clout of the farming communities with their by and large protectionist demands, but the political reality is slowly catching up with the facts of economic life (a step in this direction was the failure of the American "farmers' strike" in the winter of 1977/78). In sociological terms the peasant, a type with a history of millennia, has been fading away; he is replaced by a rational agricultural businessman working with up-to-date information and equipment. The result is, first, an increased efficiency in farming itself. Second, large numbers of laborers have been freed for more effective work outside of agriculture; this shift has contributed to the extraordinary rise in productivity in the economy as a whole. In each country the size and direction of the labor shift influenced the efficiency boost. It was stronger in France or Italy, which entered the second half of this century with large peasant populations, small in the UK with its already reduced agricultural sector. In Great Britain not much labor was left to move from agriculture into manufacturing or services; this was one of the many facts responsible for its failure to expand the economy more rapidly.

The share of industry is affected by the country's stage of development. Italy and Ireland built up their industries after the war and thus increased their share in the GNP and in employment. In the already industrialized FRG the share has remained more or less stable. In the UK, Belgium, and the Netherlands the share has declined. These three countries, following the lead of the US, are developing toward "post-industrial societies" with a heavy share of services. In industry and also in a number of services, modernization and Americanization has meant the liquidation of under-sized and outmoded stores and workshops (in the early 1930's Switzerland still featured a "railroad" run by the owner and his family without further help). As in agriculture, labor has moved out of such dwarf outfits into more efficient enterprises with a net gain in productivity. While the trend has favored larger and larger firms, it has decidedly not ended small business; it has simply modernized antiquated forms of doing business.

"Service" is a catchall encompassing transportation and communications, wholesale and retail trade, finance and insurance, restaurants and hotels, domestic aid, personal services from massage to funeral parlors, as well as community and social services. Most of these services are marketed; dominant among those not selling their products at market prices but covering their costs through taxes (inflation is also a form of taxation) is Big Government. The example of the US, the world's most advanced economy, illustrates the growth of the service sector. In 1950 it employed half of the American labor force; in 1976 two thirds. In a stimulating essay on "America's Third Century,"[4] *The Economist*'s deputy editor, Norman Macrae, expects the share of the US labor force in manufacturing, currently close to 20%, "to drop to below 5% over the next few decades." If this were to become true—such extrapolations are dubious—America would be one vast service station around the turn of the century. The following table assembles data on the labor force by sector of activity in important countries of Western Europe:

TABLE 2   SHARE OF AGRICULTURE, INDUSTRY AND SERVICES IN CIVILIAN WORKING POPULATION (in per cent)

		US	FRANCE	FRG	ITALY	UK
Agriculture	1950	13.7		23.8		5.5
	1960	9.1	22.4	13.8	32.8	4.8
	1970	4.7	14.0	8.6	19.5	3.2
	1976	3.8	10.9	7.0	15.5	2.7
Industry	1950	35.3		42.7		47.7
	1960	34.2	39.1	48.2	36.9	47.6
	1970	31.3	38.8	49.3	43.8	44.8
	1976	27.0	38.1	45.1	43.5	40.0
Services	1950	51.0		33.5		46.8
	1960	56.7	38.5	38.0	30.2	47.6
	1970	64.0	47.2	42.1	36.6	52.0
	1976	69.2	51.0	47.9	41.0	57.3

SOURCES: Social Indicators for the European Community, Luxembourg, 1977, Table II/1 US Department of Labor, Bureau of Labor Statistics

[4] *The Economist,* London (October 25, 1975), p. 15 of Survey.

Occupation groups always have their admirers and detractors; since the Industrial Revolution the respective merits or demerits of agriculture, industry, and services have been judged from political, military, medical, aesthetic, even from economic angles. The physiocrats considered only agriculture "productive." Adam Smith extended the compliment to all producers of material goods. Marx followed him, and to this day Soviet bloc statistics exclude most services as "unproductive" from national income calculations. The USSR is strongly goods-minded; services occupy only one-third of the labor force, even though there is no want of bureaucrats and soldiers. In the advanced West opinions are divided. Environmental enthusiasts applaud the trend toward services. They oppose not only "these dark satanic mills" of William Blake's malediction but also shiny nuclear plants; nor do they mind a shift of smoky and noisy factories to backward nations still eager to industrialize. There are, on the other hand, critics who—without going back to the outdated notions of Adam Smith and Marx—warn that the modern democratic state has expanded its own service establishment beyond the taxpayers' circumstances. Two distinguished Oxford economists, Walter Ellis and Robert Bacon, have tried to show "How Britain Went Wrong" by pointing to the increasing numbers of "civil servants, social workers, and most teachers and medical workers" who "rely on others" to "supply the total private consumption, investment and export needs of the whole nation."[5] In other words, the labor demand for public service stands accused of shortchanging manufacturing and also the market-oriented service sectors. This diagnosis of the *mal Anglais* is reminiscent of past times in which the huge number of clerics was blamed for the poverty of peasants and townsmen who, willy-nilly, provided their upkeep.

The question may be asked whether in pre-industrial societies, beliefs and behavior apart, people became monks and nuns because there were no better employment opportunities and, passing to present-day Britain, whether it has not been a slack labor demand for manufacturing purposes that induced job seekers to join the public services. A dynamic industry finds the labor it needs by absorbing the unemployed

[5] Robert Bacon and Walter Ellis, *How Britain Went Wrong*, Center for the Study of American Business, Publication No. 16, p. 13, reprinted from articles in the *Sunday Times*, November 1975. See also the authors' *Britain's Economic Problem: Too Few Producers* (London, 1976).

and attracting workers from either other sectors or other countries in addition to using labor-saving methods. In Norway services have grown to an even higher GNP share than in the UK, yet investment, industrial growth, and GNP have developed at greater speed than in Great Britain.

LIFE STYLES AMERICANIZED

The changed structure of the economies in Western Europe is both cause and effect of a revolution in economic and social values and attitudes. Following American life-styles, Europeans have turned to the market place or public agencies for goods and services that once were produced in the household by family members or domestic servants. Foods formerly laboriously cooked at home are now bought more or less ready-made with an array of mechanical gadgets speeding their preparation; lunch is usually taken at a cafeteria or restaurant. Money management has moved from cash hoards to bank accounts. Instead of exposing themselves to risks, people buy insurance privately or through the government. Sickness formerly treated at home is now handled by medical specialists and hospitals full of costly equipment and eager to let it depreciate at the expense of the health insurance. Social security payments have to quite a degree replaced personal charity, and even philanthropy has become a large-scale service industry. All this has transformed age-old relations between Upstairs and Downstairs. Moreover, it has freed women from domestic chores and has enabled them to seek gainful employment with controversial effects—good and bad—for the family. If the new life-style requires many more service jobs, it is the women who fill them. The UK, to give an important example, employs a larger share of its labor force in services; at the same time, however, the share of women in the overall labor force exceeds in Great Britain (43.4% in 1975) that of France (39.7%) or the FRG (35.5%); moreover, the share of women with service jobs as part of all British women with a main occupation (71.6%) is higher than in France (66.2%) or Germany (60.3%). In other words, services do play a great role in the UK, but at the same time the participation of women in the labor force and service force is above average. The figures provide an additional argument against the hypothesis that British services have been staffed at the expense of manufacturing.

The shift from household-produced goods and services to the market place or public suppliers has a counter-current: the trend toward do-it-yourself activities. This refers both to regular chores (e.g. washing at home instead of calling the laundryman) and to repair jobs. Well-to-do Western Europeans were rarely American Jacks-of-all-trades; but now, with hired help costly or unavailable, they have begun to learn how to fix things with their manicured hands without mechanics or domestic servants (formerly a well-to-do European without a chauffeur was unthinkable).

The transition from time-consuming traditional ways to large-scale production and streamlined distribution is one facet of the more efficient organization and technology that has accelerated GNP growth in past decades. Downstairs has benefited from the change, the very rich are enjoying the best of two worlds; for the middle classes the shift may in some respects have lowered the "quality of life." Cooking, to give an example, was probably tastier in the days before frozen foods and high-speed ovens. Let us hope that, as income and leisure increase (and assuming the world remains at peace), all consumers will become gourmets; we might then witness a Golden Age of the culinary arts.

The changes just described have also affected the "quality of statistics." The GNP concept is by and large limited to goods and services exchanged on markets; those produced at home remain unrecorded. As a result, the statistics of countries with a rapid shift in production from the household to enterprises or agencies make GNP growth appear slightly faster than reality warrants. This should be kept in mind in comparing growth rates of Germany or Italy in an early post-war period with the more advanced US of that time (the warning applies even more to comparisons between advanced and less developed countries).

By another quirk of GNP statistics, rapidly expanding public services make for some understatement of economic growth. In the private business economy output means sales (net of purchases from other firms to avoid double-counting the costs of materials, and so on), and this output normally rises faster than the input, i.e. the outlay for labor, capital, and land services. The difference is a gain in productivity. But governments do not sell, they tax, and the value they add to the GNP is in practical statistics determined by only one of their inputs, namely the salaries and wages they pay their employees. Neither are the services of government-owned capital imputed nor is a presumable productivity gain calculated. In the UK the value added by government increased between 1964 and 1975 from 9% to 14% of the gross domestic product (in the US it is about 12% with little change). Insofar as the British Civil Service improved its productivity (let us give them the benefit of doubt), the UK's GNP growth during this period (2.2%) might have been slightly higher. Under no circumstances, however, would a correction have raised the rate to a level remotely comparable with other European performances.

DIFFERENCES IN INPUT OF LABOR AND CAPITAL

What did go wrong in Britain and why did most other European nations develop more rapidly than the US, at least up to the "oil crunch"? We may rule out cyclical fluctuations with different impact on different countries. It is true, GNP growth in 1960 was only 2.1% in the US but 8.9% in the FRG and an unusually lusty 4.8% in Great Britain, while in 1966, using the same order of countries, it was 6%, 2.9%, and 2%. Such ups and downs in resource utilization affect output per unit of labor and capital employed. But on the whole, progress was quite even in the thirteen years before the "oil crunch," generally poor in the UK, good in the US, and excellent in OECD-Europe excepting the UK.

Given a fairly steady business activity, economies grow as they put more labor and capital to use. Land is, of course, a third factor of production, but its contribution to growth is usually small. Much depends on how effectively labor, capital, and land are combined. Factor productivity may actually decline (as in the USSR since 1974) or grow by leaps and bounds as in Europe during the period under review.

During this long period of prosperity some European countries were able to use increased employment as an important engine of progress. In West Germany in 1950 the unemployment amounted to 11% of the labor force; twenty years later the figure was 0.7% in other words, there was a shortage of labor. Natural population growth was low (recently it has declined), but net immigration led to an overall increase of the population by 1% per annum in the 1950's and 1960's. Until East Germany built the Berlin Wall in 1961 and fortified the Elbe frontier, large numbers of Germans crossed from the GDR (German Democratic

Republic) into the FRG; they were later supplemented by millions of guest workers from Yugoslavia, Turkey, Italy, and other Mediterranean countries. In 1974 7.1% of the FRG's inhabitants were aliens (not counting illegal immigrants). In that same year Switzerland, once so allergic to foreigners, estimated that aliens made up 16.6% of its population.

The recession of 1974/75 induced thousands of guest workers in the Northern tier of OECD-Europe to go home, and their departure has caused their erstwhile hosts little unhappiness. Millions remain, many as permanent residents or citizens. Their work is useful, it is even indispensable in occupations the natives are no longer willing to perform, but the host countries are not the United States in the Frontier days. The presence of foreigners, usually crowded into the shabbier sections of large cities and with the high birth rates of their home countries, has created social as well as national tensions. An "external proletariat" (to use Toynbee's expression) has been internalized and adds to the present malaise. (There exist similar problems within countries with migration from less to more developed provinces, e.g. in Italy.)

Labor input is not identical with employment. The input depends on the number of hours worked—the work week was everywhere reduced: in manufacturing between 1958 and 1973 by 6.3% in W. Germany, by 5.8 in the UK, by 3.9% in France—and the composition of the labor force by age, sex, and also nationality. After taking account of such particulars, the FRG remains among the larger countries the one with an above-average labor input contribution to its economic growth (Switzerland may be percentage-wise in a similar situation).

Capital as a factor of production is as much a composite as labor input. Its contribution to growth depends on its age and model as much as the labor force on its structure by age, sex, and so on. Capital stocks of equal value yield services of different value in different branches of industry as does labor in different employments. International capital migration has to be taken into account as is the case with labor migration, except that capital tends to flow from more to less advanced nations, at least until the advent of petrodollars, and labor the other way around. In the post-war period Western European capital resources were replenished by American funds, first under the Marshall Plan, later in the form of loans and risk capital.[6] Since American investment in European corporations was embodied in advanced technology, it not only increased the quantity of capital available to European recipients but also improved the quality of capital (a term which points to another statistical conundrum). There has also been a lively flow of intra-European investment, partly induced by the Common Market but going beyond its confines. Thus on the 1966–68 average foreign sources (including, of course, American) supplied Spain with 8.7% of its investment funds, Greece even with close to 18%.

The contribution of capital input to economic growth differs from place to place, and in major countries of Western Europe it has been far from the average, higher in Germany and France, lower in the UK.

West Germany's industry emerged from the war (believe it or not!) with a capital stock larger than before the war; investments during the war exceeded destruction and dismantlement (the latter a minor loss).[7] The FRG increased its fixed capital formation between 1950 and 1965 by 9.1% in the annual average; in the end it reached 26.8% of the GNP. After 1960 France began to out-invest Germany. A rising capital stock is by no means the only source of economic growth but it helps if it is of good quality and well utilized.[8] The West German GNP increased from

[6]US direct investments in Western Europe increased between 1950 and 1977 (end of year) from $1.73 billion to $60.6 billion or in monetary terms 35 times, in real terms about 14 times. Western Europe's share in all direct American investment positions rose from 14.7% to 40.7%, understandably considering the solidity of Western Europe as a place for investments. Western Europe's direct investment in the US was $2.2 billion in 1950, $22.7 billion at the end of 1977.

[7]Capital stock within the boundaries of the FRG gross (in parentheses: net) in bill DM of 1950 purchasing power.

January 1, 1935, all industries 50.4 (25.0),	capital good industries 10.6 (5.0)
May 1, 1944	61.8 (37.2)	12.7 (7.9)
July 1, 1948	57.3 (32.2)	11.4 (6.6)
January 1, 1950	61.1 (34.2)	12.3 (7.1)

Ratio of net to gross stock 1935: 49.7%, 1945: 61.3, 1950: 56.0%.

See: Rolf Krengel, *Anlagevermögen, Produktion und Beschäftigung der Industrie im Gebiet der Bundesrepublik von 1924 bis 1956*, Deutsches Institut für Wirtschaftsforschung (Berlin, 1958), pp. 16, 23, 79.

[8]Japan is the most sensational case of rapid capital formation, its rate growing in the annual average by 14.1% between 1960 and 1973. During these years the GNP increased by an annual 10.3%. In 1973 gross investment absorbed 37% of the Japanese GNP.

1950 to 1965 by 7.4% per annum. France expanded its capital formation 1960–73 by 7.9% per annum and scored a 5.6% GNP growth. The
Germans were miffed some time ago when Herman Kahn's Hudson Institute predicted that by 1985 France would be "Europe's leading economic power." In 1977 the German-French GNP ratio was still
125 : 100. Messieurs, Mesdames, faites votre jeu!

Even those who hope for an oil-borne British economic miracle do
not expect the UK to catch up with and overtake France and Germany
(but then who, several years ago, expected Saudi Arabia to reach the
level of the Swiss GNP and Iran to draw even with Sweden?). Between
1950 and 1973 Great Britain's gross fixed capital formation increased in
the average year by 4.7%, its capital stock by 2.9%, its GNP also by
2.9%. These are low growth rates for capital input compared with most
other European countries, but during the same period the US managed
to achieve a GNP growth of 3.9% per annum with private fixed investments rising by only 3.7% and a capital stock increasingly by 3.2% per
annum. The American stock has obviously developed a more effective
composition than its British counterpart; it has provided a faster-rising
flow of capital services. To be sure, the American economy did not grow
as fast as that of Germany or France or continental Western Europe as a
whole. This was due to many factors: several minor recessions in the
US, which might have been more effectively countervailed; the American burden for national defense and international affairs; last but not
least, Western Europe's ability to Americanize. This leads to the important issue of output per unit of inputs, in short, productivity.

PRODUCTIVITY SPURT
ON THE AMERICAN MODEL

Judging by Edward F. Denison's seminal work on the sources of
economic growth and on factor productivity, in particular,[9] factor in-

[9] The literature on this issue is rich and sophisticated. Important contributions were Ed. F.
Denison's *Why Growth Rates Differ: Postwar Experience in Nine Western Countries*
(Brookings Institution, 1967) and *Accounting For United States Economic Growth
1929–1969* (Brookings, 1974), Simon Kuznets' *Economic Growth of Nations* (Cambridge,
Mass., 1971), and Abram Bergson's 1974 Wicksell-Lectures *Soviet Post-War Economic
Development*. For basic issues using the U.S. as an example see John W. Kendrick's writ-

puts, i.e. labor and capital contributed in Western Europe from 1950 to 1962 between one-half and one-fourth of the national income growth rate. Output per unit of input accounted for the by far larger inverse percentage (the US ratio is given as 59 : 41). If we look upon the educational progress of labor as a productivity gain and transfer its contribution to growth from input to output per unit of input, the share of productivity rises in important areas to between ⅔ and no less than ⁴/₅ of the growth (the US ratio changes to 44 : 56 in favor of productivity). The ratios prevail whether a particularly economy is consistently fully or under-employed (FRG 37 : 63 and UK 36 : 64 with productivity the larger contributor). But an economy fully employed and modernizing has a high overall growth rate and therefore also a high growth rate for output per unit of input compared to economies either not fully employed or at the technological frontier: increase of the output per unit of input 1950–62 was for Italy 4.7%, the FRG 4.6%, the UK 1.5%, the US 1.9%. These figures are dated. Recent calculations by Christensen, Cummings, and Jorgenson (see previous footnote), though not strictly comparable, show what might be expected when 1947–60 and 1960–73 are compared: a significant slowdown of productivity gains in Italy and Germany as both nations are catching up with superior economies, an increase in France with its accelerated growth in the later period, and less productivity progress in (alas!) the UK and also the US.

The elements that are responsible for productivity gains vary from place to place and period to period, and with increasing detail the picture gets very complex. It appears that everywhere the autonomous or imitative advance of knowledge was a major force, followed in the US by the educational upgrading of the labor force. Labor has, of course, also improved its quality in Europe, more in the less advanced countries such as Italy, and *vice versa* in Germany and the UK. The shift of resources away from inefficient farms and small firms to where they could be more effectively employed was of great importance in Italy and

ings (such as the recent statement "Productivity Trends and Prospects" in the Joint Economic Committee's *US Economic Growth from 1976 to 1986*, vol. 1 (October 1, 1976). The National Bureau of Economic Research will soon publish *An International Comparison of Growth in Productivity, 1947–1973* by L. R. Christensen, Dianne Cummings, and D. W. Jorgenson; this study uses in part a different methodology, in particular in regard to the quality of capital.

also in the FRG and France, much less significant in the UK and US which had progressed further on this road. Italy, France, and to a lesser degree Germany benefited from economies of scale, less so again the UK and US.

These economies of scale have, in turn, many facets. The national markets have been growing, even though the demographic increase per annum is small (total population in all countries of OECD-Europe 1950: 306.7 million, 1978: 391.4 million). Cities have not only grown in population (and pollution) but have merged into a continuum of urban landscape (names have already been invented for future conglomerates such as Central European Megalopolis extending from Bonn to Rotterdam or Parihavre for an urban stretch from Paris to the Atlantic). As transport and communications have gathered speed, existing markets have become denser. With rising incomes, mass production has proliferated, particularly in consumer durables. Foreign trade liberalization in Europe under various agreements has created markets of international scope (see below). All of this has enabled enterprises to produce with diminishing costs. There are, of course, also diseconomies of scale; bigness may degenerate into elephantiasis not only in government but also in business, though in market economies there is usually a healthy ascent of efficient smaller firms into the big league. The list of the world's fifty largest corporations, which *Fortune* magazine publishes, was once overwhelmingly American; nowadays it includes twenty-eight enterprises with headquarters outside the US, among them twenty in the European Community and Switzerland. Formerly, multinational enterprises were American with branch offices in Europe; there are now numerous Europeans firms with dependencies in the US.

While it is illuminating to define and quantify the economic sources of GNP growth, the issue transcends the dismal science. It confronts the even more dismal discipline that probes the undisciplined behavior of groups. What explains the lethargy of British industry, which had shown its mettle by inventing and commercializing radar and jet propulsion, not to mention that costly Franco-British gadget, the Concorde? What enabled the West Germans to transform the immigration of compatriots into massive growth instead of massive idleness? Why has the European space program fizzled despite its large endowment of money and talent? No psychoanalyst's couch is large enough to accommodate a whole nation; moreover, the individual soul is also unfathomable.

CONSUMPTION PATTERNS
CHANGE WITH RISING INCOMES

The modernized branch structure discussed above is the correlate of a modernized demand pattern. Roughly 60% of Western European social product is used by way of private final consumption expenditures (slightly less than in the US); these outlays increased between 1950 and 1973 in real terms by an average annual 4.5% in toto and by 3.4% per capita; the rates were more than twice as high as in the good old days before the First World War. Differently expressed, in 1973 the average Western European consumed two-and-a-quarter times as much as in 1950. Let those intellectuals who bewail modern "consumerism" (their consumption is high!) ponder this progress.

Equally important is the increase in savings. Savings rates go up with incomes. This is true even at a time when all-embracing social security systems reduce the individual's need to provide for a rainy day and when social grants—whose recipients save less than income earners—gain in importance. (Transfer payments as a share of gross domestic product amounted in recent years 27% in the Netherlands, 21% in France, 20% in Italy, 17% in the FRG, 15% in the UK, 10% in the US.) To give a concrete example: between 1966 and 1976 households of German workers and employees increased their savings from 11.4 to 16.3% of their incomes. Their financial assets—not counting social and private insurance claims—more than tripled in current DM; after deflation, assets still doubled in only ten years (and these financial assets exclude, of course, physical belongings such as consumer durables). Today there are few people in the advanced world "who have nothing to lose" and many who loathe the savings-eroding inflation as much as unemployment.

Rising incomes change the structures of expenditures according to a so-called law first formulated in 1857 by the German statistician Ernst Engel. As a share of income, household outlays for food decline as the income grows. Engel calculated that in the Saxony of his time the family of a comfortably situated worker spent 62% of all outlays on food, a middle class family 55%, and a well-to-do family 50%. In the US of 1973 the overall budget share for food was 22.4%. In Ireland it was still 44.1% (1973) and in Italy 37.3% (1974). From the angle of Engel, the Northern tier of Western Europe, Ireland excepted, comes close to

American conditions (Great Britain 31.1%, France 25.9%, the FRG 22% in 1974, with no judgment implied on the quality of the food). For shelter Herr Schwabe formulated a similar law, but rent is a complicated matter; expenditures for rent (and utilities) have actually been rising everywhere (UK 18.4%, West Germany 15.5%, Italy 13.9%).

It is clear that the share of service-intensive outlays has gone up sharply, even though some of them are government-subsidized. Outlays for health and hygiene as a share of the average household budget have increased between 1953 and 1973 in the US from 5.1 to 8.3%, in Scandinavia and Benelux from 3.4 to 7%, in France, West Germany, Italy, the UK, and three smaller countries from 2.2 to 4.8%. Expenditures for education and leisure rose, in the same regional order, from 6.4 to 8.4%, from 6 to 7.2%, and from 5.3 to 7.3%. Finally transport and communication: US from 12.7 to 13.7% (approaching saturation), Scandinavia and Benelux from 7.4 to 11.7%, in the third group from 7 to 12.1%.[10]

MORE HAPPINESS?
CERTAINLY A MORE COMFORTABLE EXISTENCE

The question whether the change reflected both in the consumption pattern and in the output by industry has increased the happiness of Western Europeans is improper, to begin with. Happiness is a perishable good; it sours quickly. Moreover, many Europeans have a penchant for self-pity; at the least, they enjoy grumbling. Perhaps they are afraid of provoking the envy of the gods were they to express their satisfaction with existing conditions. But, whatever they feel or say, who could deny that they are better off than in 1950 with a per capita consumption of 2¼ times as large? With very few exceptions none of them would like to have his or her consumption cut back to 45% of the present level.

Thus life expectancy has gone up, e.g. for French men from 62.9 years in 1950 to 68.7 years in 1974/75 (measured at birth), for French women from 68.8 to 76.7 years (nature denies man equal opportunities). Responding to the requirements of modern work and taste, nu-

---

[10] Data from UN Economic and Social Council publication EC.AD. (XV)/R.4/ Add.3, *Overall Economic Perspective for the ECE Region up to 1990*, Part II, January 20, 1978.

trition has shifted from starchy to protein-rich foods. In Germany, for instance, in the few years between 1966/70 and 1975 consumption per capita per annum of potatoes changed from 107 to 92 kg, of meat from 80 to 90 kg, of citrus fruit from 19 to 22 kg.

The number of consumer durables, rented or owned, has increased greatly. In 1950 for every hundred Germans there were 5 telephones, in 1976, 31.7. This is a sixfold increase, though the number is still less than half that of the US (66.5 telephones) or Sweden (66.1—the Swedes took early to the telephone; Strindberg's plays already feature telegraph and speaking tube). And there is, above all, the automobile. In the FRG, car registrations (all types) rose between 1950 and 1976 from 1.05 million to 20.5 million, in Italy from 577,000 to 30.07 million, to mention only two countries. This is still less per 100 inhabitants than in America (29.4 in the FRG, 26.9 in Italy, 51 in the US). But passenger cars provide Europeans with the fun of fast speed and free movement (traffic permitting); facilitate tourism (and terrorism): take, e.g. in West Germany (1975), 58.2% of all employed men and 33% of all employed women to work; disfigure beautiful old cities; increase the revenues of OPEC (between 1972 and 1976 the value of the FRG's petroleum imports increased 4.2 times and doubled to 16.4% of total imports); and account for 45.3 out of 100 persons killed in traffic accidents.

Hospital admissions per 1,000 population rose in West Germany from 116 in 1956 to 162 in 1975, in Italy from 88 in 1960 to 162 in 1975, while the hospital stay of patients declined in the FRG from 31 to 22 days, in Italy from 29 to 19 days on average. This indicates not an increase in illness but the shift from home to hospital care and also a more efficient, i.e. rapid treatment. From cradle to grave, life has become more efficiency-oriented, more time-conscious, more skill-demanding, more congested, and people are also instantly informed about all the thrills and disasters that occur daily in Europe and on the shrunken planet.

FOREIGN TRANSACTIONS
EXPAND EVEN FASTER THAN OUTPUT

In previous sections an attempt was made to show, with figures from several European countries, how in the decades after the Great

War supply and demand patterns changed. Each economy has modern-ized according to its own efforts and fortunes, but all have come under the influence of the American example. The US has also made a strong impact on relations among countries and has forcefully contributed to an extraordinary expansion in the international exchange of goods and services, financial funds and labor in Europe as well as in the world at large.

Let us compare the average annual growth rates of GNP at market prices and of exports of goods and services as reflected in the national accounts (this is a broader measure than merchandise trade alone). We limit ourselves to the years between 1958, when most currencies had become convertible and the European Community began its activity, and 1973, the year beginning with Great Britain, Ireland, and Denmark joining the Community and ending with the oil crunch. During these fifteen years the GNP rose by 4.9% both in OECD Europe and in the Community of the original six members (France, FRG, Italy, Benelux). Exports of goods and services increased by 9% in OECD Europe, by 10.2% in the Community (imports by 9 and 10.6%, respectively). The rates show, first, international economic relations growing faster by far than output and, second, the trade-promoting effect of the Community (it is worth noting that in the mid-1960's the six original members provided about 60% of OECD Europe's GNP).

To place these figures in a worldwide historical context, let us re-member that in modern times a similar rate of trade and output growth was experienced only once, namely in the mid-nineteenth century. At that time world GNP grew by 3%, world trade by close to 5%. The 1950–73 rate for the planetary product was 5.1%, for world trade 8.3%, both rates in real terms. The higher level of the two rates show that in the third quarter of the twentieth century the world economy had a greater capability for well-organized sustained growth than in the past. The faster trade expansion in both periods points to the presence of spe-cific trade promoting factors. They can be described as follows:

SIX REASONS FOR TRADE EXPANSION:
PEACE AND TECHNOLOGY . . .

First, "peace;" or conditions peaceful enough to carry out interna-tional transactions of all sorts. There was great power rivalry in both periods (the Crimean War, the Italian wars, and other wars that engulfed Denmark, Austria, Prussia, the smaller German states, and France). There was no lack of local and civil wars, and Russia, called the "gendarme d'Europe," occasionally felt the need to intervene with force. After the Second World War both superpowers maintained peace in their respective spheres, despite the Cold War and several confrontations between themselves. While there were local hostilities in Asia and Africa, Western Europe, under the protection of NATO, remained at peace.

Second, technology is constantly increasing the speed and reducing the cost, of transportation and communication. In 1873 Jules Verne's Phineas Fogg went round the world in eighty days; our rockets require only minutes. Moreover, modern technology has begun to miniaturize products. Thus they can be shipped, for processing or final use, over long distances in little time and at little cost.

METHODS OF PRODUCTION, TASTES, MULTINATIONAL FIRMS

Third, all over the world the methods of production have become similar as have the tastes and the behavior of consumers. This facilitates the international exchange of both producer and consumer goods. The process began with the Industrial Revolution but is by now much more dramatic (one need only think of consumer behavior under the impact of radio and television). However, let us not imagine that people like each other more because they are more like each other; not even within the European Community.

Fourth, a few enterprises with branches abroad existed in the nineteenth century and even before (chiefly financial institutions). Our time is the age of the multinational corporation. It is a powerful and efficient tool for moving not only goods and money but also technology and labor (above all managerial and engineering labor) from country to country. In the early post-war years these firms were almost entirely America-based. Slowly European firms ventured abroad, within the European Community and beyond, and now there are numerous European (and Japanese) multinational corporations. Moreover, the Community attempts to create a common legal framework for its firms and a "European joint stock company."

TRADE LIBERALIZATION

Fifth, the recent past has not been a free trade era as was the mid-nineteenth century; nevertheless, trade has been significantly liberalized. The US has led this movement. America has a long protectionist tradition, moderated temporarily between 1833 and 1860 but then continued until the days of Franklin D. Roosevelt and Cordell Hull. In 1934 Cordell Hull initiated the reciprocal trade program and the Trade Agreement Acts which, adapted to changing times, are still operating. These autonomous measures have been supplemented by US international initiatives aimed at establishing law and order in the world economy after the war. They brought about the UN, the World Bank, the IMF, the OECD, and GATT. After the Marshall Plan the Organization for European Cooperation (OEEC) came into being and, among other tasks, worked for trade liberalization, while a European Payments Union helped overcome the monetary disorganization of the 1940s. OEEC was later broadened to include the US and other Western nations, changing its name to Organization for Economic Co-Operation and Development (OECD). The General Agreement on Tariffs and Trade (GATT) was concluded in 1947. Since that year Gatt has conducted seven rounds of Multilateral Trade Negotiations (MTNs); the sixth of 1964–67, called the Kennedy Round, reduced average tariffs on trade by roughly one third in the US and in Europe. A seventh round started in 1973; it was not called after Nixon, as the president had hoped, but the Tokyo Round, and it concentrated on the numerous non-tariff barriers which have been erected since tariffs lost some of their bite.

Trade liberalization has not prevented the Cold War. Its diplomatic and ideological aspects apart, it was the longest commercial war in history. Remnants of the Cold War remain in order to deny the Soviet bloc strategic products—a cause of frequent US–Western European disagreements. Otherwise, East-West trade has made a comeback, particularly trade between the Soviet bloc and Western Europe. It has been financed with large Western credits (including Euro-money), again with Western European banks, firms, and governments the chief lenders. The credits may be on the high side; warnings can now be heard that Poland, Romania, the GDR, and also the USSR may have difficulties servicing their obligations. But despite the increase in imports from and above all in exports to, the Soviet bloc, none of the Western European countries (leaving aside the special case of Finland) have extended their East-West "interdependence" to a limit implying economic or political vulnerability. In the early 1960's the share of the USSR in the total trade of either OECD Europe or the Community or the European Free Trade Association (EFTA) ranged from 1 to 1.6%, the share of Eastern Europe (the USSR's six associates) from 2.2 to 2.6%. Since Western Europe's trade has expanded so much, the percentages have moved up only slightly, namely (using 1976 figures) the Soviet share from 1.3 to 2.1%, the Eastern European share from 3 to 3.3%. There are a few countries with higher percentages: West Germany shipped 2.6% of its exports to the USSR and 5.1% to Eastern Europe (imports: 1.9 and 4.4%); the special relation between West and East Germany—their trade is included in the Eastern European figures—explains the somewhat higher level of its rates.

The movement towards freer trade has not precluded lapses into old-fashioned protectionism, either among Western countries in general— the US by no means excepted—or within the European Community (which will be discussed presently). Every country has pressure groups with enough clout, often out of proportion to the number of their members or their economic significance, to obtain protection against imports or subsidies for their exports; the prime example is European farming protected by the Community's wasteful Common Agricultural Policy (CAP). Also within the Community each government sees to it that the overwhelming bulk of its purchases benefits its own nationals. Protectionism increases every time resources become idle, i. e. in recessions, and every time a specific commodity, whether oil or foodstuffs, becomes scarce. It has therefore increased in frequency and intensity during the past several years.

REGIONAL UNIFICATION

Sixth, in the period since the Second World War the US has pressed not only for trade liberalization but also for regional unification. These two objectives are sometimes in conflict with each other: a unified region may turn protectionist. Only eight years after Germany had finally established a single market in the newly founded Reich, the Bismarck government abandoned free trade. In the 1880's it even conducted something of a Cold War against Russia with special tariffs on grain imports from the East and a credit embargo. Behind the tariff walls big corporations and cartels sprouted, and some used their high profits to underbid on foreign markets. The British, with some of their previous drive already lost, complained about the "German blight." This would not have triggered the First World War, but it helped sour the atmosphere.

Purely political quarrels aside, free trade and unification are in harmony in periods of strong economic growth; when practically everybody thrives, few clamor for protection. It is the other way around when growth is sluggish or worse, and emergency measures, themselves in favor of strong claimants, contribute to the contraction. This was the case in the downturn that began in the early 1870's and explains why an almost universal free trade policy came to an end.

In the third quarter of this century Europe and the world at large prospered; growth and a freer trade reinforced each other. The atmosphere was bracing; sometimes the optimism turned into hubris. In past years the vigor has declined, at least temporarily, and if the present minipause in the world economy should be the beginning of a climacteric, the nations will resort to protectionist stimulants and tranquilizers.

When the US exhorted Europe to unify, the European economies were still in acute postwar difficulties. America's interest in again making Europe a going concern economically and financially was obvious but political considerations were primary. The US, having been drawn into two world wars by overseas quarrels, feared that one day the eternally bickering powers of Europe would start another conflagration or, a more immediate concern, would succumb to Soviet domination. Faced with such eventualities, other nations might have opted for different policies but, at that time at least, the United States had a penchant for uniting everything else. It would never have occurred to a Roman to propagate a Gallic-Teutonic community or—Jove forbid!—a congregatio gentium where Parthians, Dacians, Cherusci, Pannonians, not to forget those stubborn Hebrews, could gang up against SPQR, with the Romans even defraying the expenses. Such a dreamer would have been thrown to the lions.

In the Old World the Russians knew what they wanted: an empire (it was to include even Libya). They got much, if not all, of what they wanted, and they acquired a strong position, for defense if needed, for attack if so desired. The West Europeans were past empire-building; those with colonies left had at best illusions about holding on to some of the remnants of their empires. Aghast at the holocaust they had either kindled or not prevented, Europeans evoked old and noble visions of a continent united in peace. The United States of Europe could also be expected to overcome an outdated fragmentation (*Kleinstaaterei*) and develop into a power center not much inferior to the two superpowers. At the minimum a large integrated market (a *Grossraumwirtschaft*) would promote everybody's welfare through the benefits derived from specialization of industries and economics of scale.

Each nation had valid reasons of its own for favoring unity. The Germans wished to regain a voice in world affairs as good Europeans. The French and smaller members of the Grand Alliance thought of keeping the Germans in check in a united Europe. Italians looked upon a helpful Europe as a means to escape communism. (Communism pure and simple, not yet its Eurological variety.)

At that time Europe had the good fortune to be led by a group of truly great statesmen: Schuman and Monnet in France, Adenauer and Hallstein in Germany, de Gasperi in Italy, in the smaller countries Spaak, Beyen, and Becht, but let us not forget Winston Churchill who so powerfully voiced his hopes for Europe. Through their endeavors France, West Germany, Italy, the Netherlands, Belgium, and Luxembourg (the latter three with a customs union of their own since 1948) created step by step the European Economic Community (EEC; the second E was later dropped). Its constitutive document, the Rome Treaty of 1957, promised "to establish the foundations of an ever closer union among the European peoples." This body politic (an entity all of its own in international law [11]) was to transcend economics and embrace political, social, legal, and other affairs.

[11] Walter Hallstein, as an eminent legist, explains the nature of the Community as against state, federation, and confederacy in the second chapter of *Europe in the Making* (New York, 1972).

THE EUROPEAN COMMUNITY
AS A TRADE-CREATING FORCE

Viewing European unification from the year 1978 may be more a handicap than a vantage point; this is a time of disenchantment and malaise. In the first fifteen years of its existence the EC, even though its development encountered obstacles from the very beginning, provided Europe with an effective tonic. The Community was and remains an enterprise "of great pith and moment." It is a civilized and rational movement, epithets that honor it but also imply that it does not incite the frantic fervor of national unification movements. Europe with its national and regional traditions and antagonisms is not easy to unite; it took Italians and Germans, even with all their passions aroused, many decades of the nineteenth century to achieve unity, decades filled with strife and turmoil.

Since its foundation the Community has expanded geographically. One of the first chain reactions it set off was the establishment of the European Free Trade Association (EFTA) in 1960. Originally, its seven, later nine members (the UK, five Scandinavian countries, Switzerland, Austria, Portugal), had in mind to include the Community in a Europe-wide free trade zone, i.e. an association with no tariffs in internal dealings but without the common tariff that characterizes a customs union like the Community. The proposal failed at that time, and in subsequent years EFTA often felt discriminated against by the Community. In the end, in 1973, the UK and Denmark were able to join the Community (likewise Ireland), while at the same time the remaining EFTA countries succeeded in establishing special free trade arrangements with the Community. Portugal wants to become a full member of the Community and so do Greece, Spain, and Turkey, all of them presently "associates" of the EC. Preferential agreements exist between the Community and about fifty countries, chiefly bordering the Mediterranean or in Africa (many of them former colonies of Community members). These associations or applications show the effectiveness and attractiveness of the EC or the inadvisability for trading partners to remain complete outsiders.

There exists a sophisticated literature on the trade-creating and trade-diverting effects of the EC; the findings are not unanimous.[12] Inevitably some deviation of trade flows has occurred but the vitality of the Community's economic growth during those years, its increasing requirements for investment and consumer goods, over-compensated for diversions; its existence was beneficial all-around and not only for its members.

Looking only at the Community of the original six countries and comparing 1960 with 1973 at current (i.e. rising) prices, total exports increased in the average year by 13.3%, exports within the EC by 16.1%, and exports to outsiders by 11%. The rates for imports were somewhat lower (12.8, 14.1, and 10.5%). The booming intra-Community trade shows the effect of a step-by-step removal of industrial tariffs between 1958 and 1968 (agriculture is a different story), but the growth of the EC's trade with outsiders was also remarkable.

As mentioned before, the Community was founded with Europe as a whole in mind and with integration extending far beyond a customs union. The purely political and the military aspects need not concern us in this context. It suffices to note that politically there is no united Europe, only separate states. As allies of one superpower and antagonists of the other, the countries will inevitably stick together—to a degree. Thirteen European nations are members of NATO, which makes for neighborly relations stretching from the Benelux Economic Union to Greek-Turkish fraternity. But a common political environment or an alliance is not a federation or confederation. It only means close ties, frequent consultation, some neighborly ties, and of course military cooperation within NATO. This symbiosis is not determined by power alone—the nations share cultural traditions and have similar economic systems—but power does weigh, and circumstances have operated in such a fashion that the FRG is now the strongest of all European states. A European Defense Community drafted in 1952 came to naught, chiefly because the French and also the British objected to German rearmament; in the end the West Germans were not only permitted but induced to create their own military establishment, which is now sec-

[12] For a brief survey see OECD, *The Growth of Output 1960–1980* (Paris, December 1970), pp. 64–66.

ond only to NATO's protagonist, the US. The FRG has only 24% of the Community's population but close to one third of its national product; the Community could be called the Holy Common Market of the German Nation. The mark is one of the strongest currencies in the West, and what is left of the Joint European Float (see next paragraph) is the DM-backed snake. Various Community-wide endeavors to integrate and unify corporation law or the anticartel and antitrust legislation—all very much in the beginning—are influenced by German law and procedures (antitrust moves also by US practice). Which brings us back to economics.

YEARS OF FALTERING
TURBULENCE WORLDWIDE, NOT LIMITED TO EUROPE

Most of the facts and figures adduced in previous sections led up to 1973. This was a year of a worldwide boom, but its end was anticipated even before the oil crunch reversed business conditions dramatically. If our topic were the US, the divide would have been the end of 1969; at that time the country entered a recession with a real decline in GNP. Inflationary policies increased prices, an overvalued dollar brought about balance of payments difficulties, and an international public began to sell dollars and buy first gold, then foreign currencies. In 1971 the dollar had to be devalued. Western currencies began to operate under an interim regime, the Smithsonian Accord, which extended the permissable limits of exchange fluctuations somewhat. At that time, a number of European countries formed the European Joint Float (called, for reasons which are now history, the snake). Its purpose was to restrict the ups and downs among their exchange rates even further.

The Smithsonian Accord subsisted for two years; then the turbulence began anew. The dollar underwent another devaluation, and the Great Float began. The monetary system established in 1944 at Bretton Woods had disintegrated. The snake developed troubles of its own. The UK, France, and Italy sneaked out, and by now the group has in reality become a DM-area. It is not coextensive with the Community: the FRG,

Denmark, and Benelux belong to the EC, but Norway and an informal member, Austria do not.

Current arrangements on the international currency markets cannot be called a "system." Numerous summit meetings and IMF conferences have not put together a new order determining what should be the West's monetary standard (it is still the dollar despite its precipitate fall in relation to important currencies), how the currency float should be managed (or not managed), and so on. There exists at this moment a pitiful lack of leadership. Since the US is by far the strongest economic power of the advanced West (embodying in terms of GNP two fifths of Western economic capabilities), it is difficult not to fault its government for want of judgment, want of willpower, or lack of concern. The result is that, despite all the great words about "trilateral" friendship, ill feelings have arisen among those who should and could cooperate closely, with deplorable economic and political effects.

These international happenings were sketched in order to show that Europe's turbulence (it is not a "crisis" in the strict economic sense) is not a specific European phenomenon. It is either universal, with Europe one of its foci, or national with special problems besetting countries like Great Britain or Italy or Portugal.

FOREIGN TRANSACTIONS ECHOING
OIL CRUNCH AND RECESSION

The recession that engulfed Europe was worldwide and its severity the result of an event outside Europe's control: OPEC's oil embargo and price quadrupling. As Table 1c shows, the combined GNPs of OECD Europe rose in 1974 by only 2.2% (with a range from minus 3.7% in Greece and plus 8.5% in Turkey). The average rate for the EC was 1.7% (from 0.1% in Ireland to 3.4% in Italy). The American GNP declined by 1.4%. In 1975 results were worse: GNPs dipped by 1.5% in OECD Europe, by 2% in the EC, by 1.3% in the US (in that year the range extended from Switzerland's minus 7.4% to Turkey's plus 9%). In 1976/77 the American economy recovered strongly (plus 6% and 4.9%), while OECD Europe and EC had less of a recovery (roughly 4½ and 2%). The discrepancy in recovery explains to a degree—but only to a degree—

why Europe's demand for US export goods has disappointed the Americans (in constant prices exports to Western Europe have stagnated between 1974 and 1977), why the American trade deficit was large, even disregarding costly oil imports, and why the dollar has weakened alarmingly.

The industrial nations of the West as a whole have a deficit in their current accounts with OPEC (these accounts measure the balance of trade in goods and services including earnings from investments; they exclude capital inflows or outflows). But the structure of the balance of payment varies greatly from country to country. In 1977 OECD Europe's current accounts combined had a deficit of $17 billion, i.e. one billion less than the US alone. Up to now Europe has had to import practically all its oil (the UK and Norway have begun to benefit from their off-shore drillings, and the Netherlands has exported natural gas); nevertheless, it withstood the oil crunch fairly well. The chief deficit countries in 1977 were Norway, Sweden, France, and Spain—their deficits totaled up to $25 billion; the principal surplus countries with a payment excess of $8 billion were Switzerland and West Germany. These two last-named countries, despite their high-priced currencies, managed to earn on balance through export of goods and services (Switzerland above all through profitable banking services). The European Community as a whole balanced its current accounts, but then, as we shall see presently, the Community as such does not count much in matters of money and balance of payments. It is true that the FRG has extended financial aid to weaker members of the Community, Great Britain as well as Italy, but it also helped Portugal and its government beleaguered by communist forces.

It was noted in an earlier context that up to 1973, world trade expanded even faster than the rapidly growing planetary product. This ratio continued after 1973 despite the severe recession. The statement applies also to Western Europe. In the annual average of the three years 1974 to 1976, using current prices, i.e. without deflating, OECD Europe's combined GNPs increased by 10.7% (pure inflation!), its exports to the entire world by 15.7% and its imports by 17.3%. The higher rate for imports is, of course, the result of higher prices for oil and several other materials and foodstuffs. Western Europe's ability to generate exports was certainly remarkable. For the EC an inflationary GNP growth was 9.2% per annum, exports 15.5% and imports 16.8%. Because of the oil crunch and similar price developments, the Community's nine members reversed the ratio of trade with members and outsiders: imports within the Community increased only by 15%, exports by 14.7%. Deflating all these rates would not only reduce them considerably but would also lower the growth of trade as against the growth of GNP because the GNP deflators rose less than the unit values in foreign trade; still the ratio would favor foreign trade over GNP growth.

Another consequence of the described development is the mounting ratio of foreign trade volume and GNP. In the US this ratio has grown from 3.1% in 1965 to 7.3% in 1976 for imports and from 3.8 to 6.7% for exports. Such ratios increase, the smaller the economic unit. In 1976 the ratio in OECD Europe was 24.6% for imports, 22.2% for exports. In the Community the ratios were slightly higher (25 and 23.7%). In a still smaller unit such as the Netherlands imports represented 45.8% of the 1976 GNP, exports 44.4%. It is obvious that this dependence on foreign trade makes European countries with appreciated currencies sensitive to the decline of the dollar, since its current undervaluation puts their firms at a disadvantage vis-à-vis the US and countries with currencies pegged to the dollar.

EMPLOYMENT PICTURE
RANGING FROM MEDIOCRE TO GOOD

Since the recent recession has affected the whole of Europe, unemployment has become a problem practically everywhere. There are, however, differences between countries suffering from a chronic labor surplus and others which in good times or even in mediocre years have not enough indigenous labor. During years of full employment, regions with manpower scarcity attracted guestworkers. Migrants streamed chiefly from the Mediterranean belt to the Northern tier of Europe (in Sweden also from Finland). As mentioned on p. 28, the recession induced at least some of the foreigners to return to their native lands. This shifted the burden of providing employment or relief back to countries with endemic unemployment. However, the return track is slowed by two circumstances.

Many guestworkers and their families have acquired a right to stay or have been naturalized. Within the European Community, blue-collar migrants from other EC members must be given the same employment opportunities as citizens of the host country. There are also large numbers of illegal migrants who may choose to remain.

Second, despite a degree of unemployment in the native labor force many workers in the advanced countries are inclined to shun dirty or otherwise unpleasant work as long as they receive unemployment benefits, possibly supplemented by some surreptitious "black labor." For example, the *Frankfurter Allegemeine Zeitung* reported on February 22, 1978, that a spinning mill in Germany's Ruhr district was about to hire fifty guest workers from Southern Italy because none of the city's 6000 registered unemployed was willing to accept employment. While reports of this kind may occasionally be exaggerated, there are too many of them to disbelieve them entirely.

Unemployment statistics must be taken with a grain of salt, particularly in international comparisons. Statistical definitions vary. Registration practices vary. Worker behavior varies: people may quit the labor force because they are discouraged hunting for a job (which they obviously do not need urgently), or they may count themselves as members of the labor force in order to receive unemployment benefits. The following OECD figures refer to registered unemployment as a share of the civilian labor force towards the end of 1977. A few countries have extremely low rates: Sweden and Norway 1.9%, Switzerland 0.4%. One cannot speak of cyclical unemployment in these countries. The figure for West Germany was 3.6% (but in the FRG's own definition 4.7%). This is a moderate unemployment except for young people (double their share in the population) and for persons in some groups with academic training. They require special programs to put them to work; otherwise the rates will decline soon after the economy begins expanding (there exists a time lag until part-time is eliminated).

France, Benelux, Denmark, and Finland have unemployment rates fluctuating around 6%. Spain's 5.2% would be higher without large numbers of Spaniards in Northern countries; the same is true of Italy's 7.9%. It is alleged that in Italy, with about 1.2 million registered unemployed, 5 million people are working on the sly, either moonlighting, i.e. holding a second job without paying taxes on such earnings, or drawing both unemployment money *and* wages. In these Mediterranean countries the employment problem is structural as well as cyclical, and it will have to be tackled nationally, since the outlook for mass emigration is no longer as good as in the 1960's. The UK is a case by itself, the OECD estimate is 8.1%, the British figure 5.9%. Unemployment coexists in the UK with lack of skilled labor, with an egalitarian wage policy discouraging the acquisition of skills.

However, the rate of British unemployment (if we accept the OECD definition) is not much worse than that of the US and Canada, and Europe as a whole has a smaller percentage than North America (OECD Europe without Portugal and Turkey in 1977 5¼% of the civilian labor force compared with 7% in the US). This is not an attempt to disparage the misery of income loss and idleness but to stress that, some pockets of unyielding unemployment excepted, the affliction is moderate in Europe and the relief measures are by and large adequate. The situation would otherwise have incited by far greater political unrest. It has invoked here and there nationalist sentiments against foreign residents or imported goods, but up to now there have been no riots due specifically to unemployment. This is remarkable at a time when violence and contempt for authority are widespread and on a continent with stronger ideological commitments than is the case in America.

GREAT ASPIRATIONS,
LESS OUTPUT, RESULT INFLATION

Inflation is as little a specific European phenomenon as sluggish output or unemployment. In the course of the 1960's it accelerated everywhere, became rampant in 1973 even before the oil crunch and worse thereafter. In 1976–77 inflation abated somewhat but it is still excessive. The degree of inflation differed and still differs greatly, the worst cases being Italy, the UK, and Ireland, the mildest West Germany and Switzerland. Switzerland shows how a small economy (1% of the developed West's GNP), which is highly dependent on foreign economic relations in goods and services, is capable of accelerating its economic growth (4.3% in 1977) with the hardest currency of all, with hardly any inflation 1.3%) or unemployment (0.4%) and a surplus on current account of $3¼ billion (equaling 5¾% of its GNP).

The widely differing inflation rates attest to the fact that in monetary matters there is no Europe, not even a European Community. In the EC an economic and monetary union was discussed at length throughout the 1960's.[13] A plan bearing the name of Raymond Barre (later to become Prime Minister of France) was elaborated in the 1960's; Pierre Werner of Luxembourg was the guiding spirit of another plan in the following years. Werner's proposals were adopted by a Ministerial meeting of the Community in June 1970. The final report, dated October 8, 1970, proposed that by 1980 the EC should achieve economic union and develop a single monetary personality within the world monetary system. The document concluded with the resounding statement: "Economic and monetary union works like yeast to bring about political union, without which it cannot be permanent."[14] Seven months after the October report the Bretton Woods system broke down.

In the 1970's each government, whether part of the EC or not, has managed its monetary policy sovereignly. How it has fared has been dependent on its wisdom and energy (energy *sub utraque specie!*) and on the pressures it has faced from domestic and foreign quarters. Pressures are exerted by sellers of goods and services, labor included, who insist on higher incomes (cost-push). The government may be forced into a more generous fiscal and monetary policy to endow specific social or defense programs or to generate demand in a search for fuller employment (demand-pull). Prices for imported goods may rise sharply without a chance to offset the effects through deflationary measures in general; foreign currencies (say: dollars) may have to be bought with money reserves created for this specific purpose (say: in the FRG) in order to prevent a further appreciation of the country's own currency (imported inflation). These pressures arise in part from basic social and political facts of life in our time. They too vary from country to country but are noticeable everywhere and operate as follows:

While the GNPs grew little or not at all in the recession years, consumer expectations have remained high. The public has been conditioned by two decades of increasing affluence, new technical devices, social progress, and a fair degree of leisure and job security—an experience unique in history but now taken for granted. Consumers expect

[13] For a detailed description see Walter Hallstein, *loc. cit.*, pp. 124 ff.
[14] *Ibid.*, p. 146.

more goodies every year, their anticipations have hardened into aspirations,[15] and their claims are bolstered by parties and other organizations serving group interests. As inflation becomes endemic, the groups set their sights on income increases discounting the expected rate of inflation and insofar as they are able to realize their claims, their prognosis of more inflation becomes self-fulfilling. In the process the share of labor in terms of wages and salaries appears to have grown at the expense of profit margins in important European countries as well as in the US.[16] This, in turn, discourages the investment of capital. Since OPEC will continue to exact danegeld, and substitutes for OPEC oil are costly, since defense expenditures rise in a time of mounting international tensions, since, finally, measures to enhance the "quality of life" are expensive,[17] the way back to increasing affluence requires a spurt in productivity and capital formation. The task for the authorities is to create a climate favorable to investment in producer goods and research without re-inflating an inflation constantly anticipated by the public.

FORCES SHAPING THE FUTURE

It demands a healthy optimism to disregard political dangers threatening the future of the West and of Western Europe in particular. Movements hostile to the present economic system may either overthrow it or disfigure it to such a degree that it becomes unworkable. The peace that has precariously existed up to now may crumble, should local conflicts deteriorate into superpower confrontations. Such calamities would change the economic situation thoroughly. In their absence—his-

[15] See Herbert Block, *The Role of Aspiration and Anticipation in Price Developments,* Center for Strategic and International Studies, Commissioned Papers on Inflation/Recession, Energy and the International Financial Structure, ed. P. Hartland-Thunberg (Washington, D.C., February 1975).

[16] See Citibank, *Monthly Economic Letter* (January 1978), p. 10.

[17] Edward F. Denison, in a new study published in *Survey of Current Business* (Department of Commerce), January 1978, pp. 21–44, has measured for the US the effects on the output per unit of input of environmental expenditures. They include protection of the physical environment and of the safety and health of workers as well as the costs of crime and dishonesty. These outlays combined detracted in 1975 roughly 0.5 percentage points from the growth of output per unit of input; since the latter grew by 2.1% from 1948–69, the reduction amounts to one quarter. Conditions in Western Europe are hardly different and the same is true of other industrial nations such as Japan or the USSR.

tory is as unpredictable as man—we may expect three forces to operate:

First, it is one of the saving graces of a decentralized market that the producers, individuals or firms, know how to function even under trying conditions (though it is inadvisable to test their endurance beyond a certain—or rather uncertain—limit). In past years European and other Western economies, despite the rigidities engendered by monopoly-minded organizations and the interference of governments, have been able to cope with "slumpflation," the oil crunch, the onrush of petro-money, currencies floating irresponsibly, capital flights from countries politically threatened, the restlessness of the Third World, and last but not least, the Soviet menace. Once the severe recession of 1975-75 was overcome, Europe's output grew again, not by the remarkable long-term 4.5% of the average year 1950-73 but by 4.3% in 1976 and about 2% in 1977. The rate may be higher in 1978 than in the preceding year, a prognosis based not on an econometric model but on a hunch (hunches are less expensive but not necessarily less reliable). Normal trade and capital flows have remained vigorous, despite protectionism of all kinds. Technology is anything but stagnant. The energy situation is more relaxed than a short time ago; it has begun to generate a helpful investment activity. OPEC members have been spending their lucre in Western Europe and America (partly recklessly) or are investing it in western countries—while Europeans are making use of the cheap dollar to buy themselves into American enterprises. Unemployment is not as low as desirable but has been borne with patience in view of quite effective welfare payments. There is no reason why Western Europe as part of the advanced world should not escape the present turbulence.

Second, among the Western and also among the European governments there exist considerable differences on economic issues, and the experience following the oil embargo has shown that under heavy pressure a *sauve-qui-peut* panic may occur. A similar disarray in a future political crisis is not out of question, and yet there exists a good chance that the Soviet threat, the insistent demands of the Third World, and the danger of internal radicalism will induce the Western governments to keep their disagreements within manageable limits. Economic differences, unless they are elevated into the realm of national prestige or personal ego, have the advantage of inviting and admitting old-fashioned haggling leading to compromise much more easily than political and, particularly, ideological conflicts. There is no economic problem at issue among Western nations that could not be solved by some rational compromise.

Third, Europe has already been integrated to an impressive extent through trade, financial transactions, migration, and tourism. It has not been unified as the Community's creators had hoped but there now exists much more of a Europe than in the first half of the century. Maybe, one day, another group of leaders will arise who will see an advantage in unification.

In the meantime Europe will have to content itself with the present dispensation. Coming at a time when a boom turned into recession, the inclusion of the UK and two more countries has probably done the Community more harm than good. If one day Portugal, Spain, Greece, and Turkey should be admitted as full members, the Community may lose a cohesion which is not too firm anyway. It could be in danger of becoming a glorified free trade zone (with many qualifications and exceptions to prevent an onrush of surplus labor and confusion on the markets for Southern agricultural produce). But unforeseeable political developments may bring about different solutions. One would be the confederation of a few economically and politically compatible countries. Such a Little Europe might be surrounded by *zugewandte Orte* (associated districts), to borrow a term from the history of the old Helvetic Confederacy. Some countries now loosely tied to the Community might enter into alignments with powers outside of Western Europe. We are thinking not only of a North Atlantic community or, *horribile dictu,* an enlarged Soviet empire, but also of, say, a Portuguese-Brazilian economic union or some arrangements stretching across the Mediterranean. In history anything is possible.

3

EUROPEAN POLITICS 1970-1978

European history during the 1970's is largely about a sequence of economic emergencies and the ways in which governments, parliaments, and experts tried to cope with such problems as inflation and unemployment and crises in balances of payments and investments. Only at rare intervals in Spain, in Portugal, and in Greece when the regimes changed, were the countries of Europe deflected from their preoccupation with economics; elsewhere this occurred under the impact of some spectacular terrorist operation. That European economics dominated European politics is a fact that hardly needs further elaboration, but since, as shown in the last chapter, the recession was of only minor dimensions it is not at all clear what caused this relentless preoccupation with economics at the expense of almost every other issue. It would have been understandable if hordes of starving children and haggard beggers were swarming over the cities of Europe in search of crumbs of bread or if Europe had been reduced to a state of abject poverty and hopelessness. Yet this was clearly not so; shops were full, the consumption of non-essential goods continued as before. Had the proverbial visitor from Mars descended on the streets of London or Paris, of Hamburg or Milan, of Amsterdam or Madrid, he would not have been aware of a recession unless, of course, he had read about it in the newspapers. If he saw drawn, haggard faces the reason, more likely than not, was medical or psychological rather than want of food. If he met people in shabby clothes these were not the poor and deprived, but usually young men and women following the most recent sartorial trends.

Unemployment and inflation, it has been noted, constituted serious problems, and it could also be plausibly argued that Europe as a whole had lived beyond her means and had now to face the consequences. But there still was the striking fact that even at a time of recession the great majority of Europeans had enough money to buy non-essential goods, and that, by and large, they were better off than at any other period in the past, and of course, still much wealthier than the rest of the world with the exception of the U.S., Canada, and a few oil-producing countries.[1]

And yet there was a feeling of gloom and doom, of the center coming apart, of an end of stability, of the bankruptcy of the system, to mention only some of the clichés most widely used at the time. Such reactions seemed, at first sight, paradoxical, but it was, after all, the perception that counted, not objective realities. Even millionaires may suffer from a feeling of relative deprivation. It is certainly true that measured against the expectations of the 1950's and 1960's, of steady growth and constantly rising living standards, the feeling in the 1970's was one of disappointment. Elsewhere, as in Britain, there was dejection because the country had been doing badly in comparison with others. The GNP, output of manufactured goods and exports, had grown much faster between 1950 and 1970 than during the first half of the century. Yet the mood in Britain was certainly not one of self-congratulation, for achievements were compared not with those of a past age but with the performance of other countries, and there was no denying that Britain was steadily falling behind. No country remained immune to the revolution of expectations, and the more the consumers' mentality spread in the societies of Western Europe, the

---

[1] Anthony King quotes a British factory worker telling his member of parliament: "If this is an economic crisis, I like it." (*Why Is Britain Becoming Harder To Govern?* (London, 1976), p. 5) The "relative poverty" was an abstraction; in Italy during 1977 prices went up by 18 per cent, wages increased by 28 per cent. But there was the problem of unemployment: there were at the beginning of 1978 1.7 million unemployed in Italy, 1.4 in Britain, and one million each in West Germany and France. Even more worrying perhaps was the high unemployment rate among young people. Unemployment was only in part the result of recession; it was at least equally the consequence of technological advance. But this was of little comfort to those affected, and the state was still expected to create employment for those who could not find it on the labor market.

But the heavy, almost single-minded concentration on economic factors as the explanation for the "crisis" is puzzling for yet another reason. As Mr. Patrick Hutber and others have noted, the question of effect and cause is by no means clear with regard to adverse economic trends: "The nature of my job . . . means that week by week I have to focus on this or that aspect of Britain's economy, and it is a natural temptation for me to seek the cause of the trouble in the economic field. But the more one focuses on Britain's economic problems the clearer it becomes that the difficulties Britain suffers from are not economic alone." (P. Hutber, ed. *What's Wrong with Britain* (London, 1978), p. 12.)

greater the importance attributed to the production and distribution of goods, essential and non-essential. What made the recession appear so formidable was not however its magnitude but a feeling of impotence. Yet even such serious problems as youth unemployment or the energy crisis were by no means intractable. The know-how, the technical means to cope with the issues existed. But the political will to deal with them, the solidarity, the leadership, were in short supply and consequently there was a fear that the countries of Europe were becoming, or had already become, ungovernable.[2] The deeper reasons for this crisis were widely and heatedly debated, and if classical scholarship had not gone out of fashion Titus Livius would have had a revival, for his appraisal of Roman history seemed apposite to the state of Europe in the 1970's: "With the gradual relaxation of discipline, morals gave way, then sank lower and lower, and finally began the downward plunge which has brought us to the present time, when we can endure neither our vices nor their cure."[3] But since the days of Livy there have been many ups and downs; few periods in human history have been altogether free of crises, political, economic, cultural and moral, and a crisis has indeed been defined as a period between two other crises.

A great many causes have been adduced to explain the European crisis of the 1970's. Yet in the final analysis the basic roots were not hidden. Firstly, the weakness of the political system, unable to resist the conflicting demands of various sections of society, and secondly, the clash between the urge for more freedom on one hand and the need for more order on the other. Never before in its history has Western Europe been as free, yet there is a strong urge for even greater liberty, for more participation in the policy making process, for doing away with the last vestiges of repression, real or imaginary. But again, never before had the necessity been greater for a strong executive, for long-term planning, social and economic, to cope with the growing complexity of modern society, and the difficulties connected with the shrinking base of material resources. The post-war period had witnessed a steady erosion of authority—partly as a consequence of, and in deliberate reaction against,

---

[2] I am dealing elsewhere in this study with the proposition that the crisis is insoluble within the present system inasmuch as it reflects the internal contradictions of "late capitalism."

[3] *Ab Urbe Condita* (Loeb ed.), vol. I, 7.

the evil-doings of the fascist dictatorships of the 1930's. This anti-authoritarian urge was not only intelligible but in many respects admirable, and it corresponded with a deep-seated human longing for freedom. But it began to interfere more and more with the effective conduct of affairs of state and society on many levels. This would have mattered less if the critics of authority had been willing to pay the inevitable price. But this they were quite unwilling to do, and through their libertarian excesses they did about everything in their power to provoke an authoritarian reaction. For it is surely one of the few indisputable lessons of history that while societies can exist without freedom, they cannot exist without a minimum of order, and that given the choice in an emergency, they will usually opt for order. All this is not to say that the dilemma of freedom and order is insoluble within the framework of a democratic society. But there are certain pre-conditions for the functioning of such societies such as leadership, a basic consensus on common aims and values, and active co-operation as well as the acceptance of democratic rules. The basic problem of the 1970's was not the intractability of the issues but the absence of the qualities needed to confront them. There was no strong leadership. European governments were headed more often than not by mediocrities, pragmatic politicians lacking strong character, firm beliefs, and on the whole, superior intellect. But this, after all, has been the case throughout most of recorded history; charismatic leaders have been the exception, and their presence has not always been a blessing. It is doubtful, furthermore, whether, given the suspicion of and the prevailing bias against authority, such leaders would have had the chance to rise to the top in the first place and to stay there—except perhaps in an acute emergency. The qualities needed to provide farsighted and responsible leadership in politics are not necessarily those likely to succeed on television. Thus politicians ceased to be leaders and began to engage in popularity contests, taking refuge in half measures dictated by public relations considerations rather than objective need. Authority that did not dare to assert itself became vulnerable, and the more vulnerable it became the more it generated blackmailing group pressure, the less margin it retained for more responsible longer-term actions and the less chance it stood to regain legitimacy (Michel Crozier). In democratic societies a national consensus is usually achieved for any length of time only in war or when facing a threat of similar magnitude. A war constitutes a clear and visible danger, whereas in an economic, social, or political crisis there is hardly ever the same overriding sense of urgency, the same dramatic feeling of the need to act together for the common good, or for survival. Creeping crises produce no great tensions and generate no great passions; there is always the hope that the threat may suddenly go away. There is nothing more difficult than mobilizing a democratic society for an all-out effort in the absence of a demonstration effect comparable to a war. It has been said that nothing clears the mind of a person as wonderfully as the certainty that he will be hanged within a day or a week. But if a person, or a collective, faces a fate of this kind only in a perspective of a year or a decade, and if, furthermore, the catastrophe is not absolutely certain but only highly probable, the result is not concentration of mind, but on the contrary confusion.

Lastly, free societies have been weakened as the mistaken belief gained ground that in such societies one may get something for nothing by right. The old idea that the survival of a free society depended on the civic virtues of its members, on their active participation, on their acceptance that there could be no rights without duties, was considered outmoded. Such abdication of responsibility reflected a state of intellectual anarchy; intellectual anarchy, as Comte observed, is the main factor behind all the great political and moral crises; he could have added that this is the case also with regard to economic crises. But anarchy does not last forever: it usually passes through various stages, and once the situation has deteriorated beyond a certain point the recognition gains ground that authority—any authority—has to reassert itself. The awareness of the necessity for an all-out effort spreads, the political will reawakens, powers that were denied leaders and governments in the past are now thrust at them. Such emergency measures may or may not lead to a lasting recovery, that is, to the reemergence of effective institutions capable of coping with the challenges facing society. There is, in brief, the possibility of a democratic solution, or something akin to it, but there is no such certainty. The political will, or the social cohesion of a nation, may have been eroded to such an extent that there is no alternative but dictatorship, the dismantling of democratic institutions and the abolition of basic freedoms. Whether a dictatorship will succeed any more than democracy in solving the crisis is by no means certain; decrees and rigid controls may bring temporary alleviation, but even if they provide a lasting cure, the price that has to be paid is not commensurate with the gains achieved.

This in briefest outline is the background to the crisis facing the countries of Western Europe, and also the democratic societies outside Europe. Some of them have faced more acute problems than others, some proved to be more resilient than others. The basic problems were remarkably similar, but there was still a great deal of variation in their respective misfortunes, and this will now be examined in some greater detail.

ENGLANDITIS

During the 1970's Britain became the "sick man of Europe." The headlines of the London newspapers on any given day during the period presented a fairly full and realistic picture of Britain's problems and preoccupations: the story of a few dozen workers engaged in a demarcation dispute incidentally paralyzing a whole industry; the British foreign secretary dealing with problems such as Rhodesia or the Cod War against Iceland; the British army command involved in Northern Ireland; political philosophers such as Keith Joseph and Wedgwood Benn making programmatic speeches. Britain in foreign eyes was the most striking case of the sad decline that a mixture of bad luck and incompetence had visited upon a once powerful, self-confident, forward-looking nation. Yet this perception of England, coupled with predictions about its impending demise, was based on misconceptions partly perhaps because an exaggerated notion of British wisdom, or, at the very least, its ability to muddle through, had prevailed in the outside world long after it should have been clear that the country was in very serious trouble indeed. This in turn was connected with recollections of Churchill and Britain's finest hour, the "special relationship" between London and the rest of the English-speaking world (and also some of Europe), the quality of British theater, radio, and television as compared with America's, the image of "Swinging London" as a trend-setter. Britain's image, in short, had little in common with British realities, and as this fact became known with some delay, there was a tendency to overreact; England was written off. But predictions of this kind again failed to take into account certain specifics of the British situation. Some of the very features of national character which had caused the crisis acted at the same time as something of a brake, or safety belt, preventing total disaster. Britain had become one of the poorest nations of Europe and also one of the least productive, but it had the capacity to put up with incompetence and inefficiency with a stoicism inconceivable elsewhere. Those who had conjured up the spectre of "suicide of a nation" were of course wrong: phlegmatic and conservative people seldom, if ever, commit suicide; in facing hardship they are fortified by indifference, and the failure to recognize their own plight. But it is certainly true that much that had made Britain great, and in some respects an example to other nations, was rapidly disappearing; if life went on as usual, the quality of life had certainly changed to an alarming extent.

In June 1970 Mr. Heath won the general election, much to the surprise of his own party, and became prime minister. The inheritance he had received from the Labour government was, to say the least, not a happy one, as sterling had steadily fallen, and prices had risen; in 1973, a boom year, British industrial production had risen by 7%, but the overall record of the British economy was still bad. A great many reasons have been adduced to explain this; lack of professionalism in management and the cult of the amateur, inept bureaucratic involvement, inadequate investment, industrial conflict produced by a multiplicity of craft unions, overmanning, resistance to technological progress by trade unions, and unwillingness on the part of the management to learn from the example of others. Above all perhaps, the proportion of work force employed in manufacture declined far more rapidly in Britain than in any other major industrial country. The service sector rose more sharply (from 47% to 55% between 1960 and 1974), without however improving the quality or the extent of the services. There were, in short, fewer people to generate greater income.

The industrial climate deteriorated very badly; if some two million work days were lost in 1964, the figure had risen to 24 million in 1972—not to count the work-to-rule, ban-of-overtime, and go-slow strikes. British productivity became a topic of greater interest to humorists and gag writers than to economists and statisticians, let alone foreign buyers. The Conservative government tried to remedy the situation by introducing a new Industrial Relations Act in 1971. This measure had broad popular support, but the trade unions rejected it outright, and they ultimately brought about its repeal. This reflected what was no doubt the most important feature of British political life during the 1960's and 1970's—the rise to power of the unions. Parliament would debate new laws and vote on them, but as far as industrial relations, income policies, and related issues were concerned, the ultimate decision lay with the union leadership. So the leaders of the important unions became far more important than any member of Parliament and indeed most ministers. Having been elected, sometimes for life, by a handful of people, frequently not more than 10% of the membership of the unions, their position was unassailable and they were accountable to no one. The role of the unions was considered harmful by the great majority of the public, including almost half of the union members—but this detracted in no way from the power of the unions. It was symbolic that the overthrow of the Heath government in March 1974 was brought about by a strike (or to be precise, an overtime ban) by the Miners' Union, and this at a time of national emergency following the energy crisis.

The Tory government, to be sure, had been quite unpopular, and Mr. Heath had been even less popular than his party; according to all political logic Labour should have won by a landslide in February 1974.[4] Yet Labour was no more popular than the Conservatives, even though its leader, Harold Wilson, in contrast to Ted Heath, attracted more support than his party. Neither of Britain's two major parties succeeded in winning 40% of the popular vote. Dissatisfaction with both Tory and Labour performance manifested itself in a massive vote for the Liberals, who attracted six million voters—but given the inequities of the British electoral system, this resulted in a mere fourteen seats in Parliament. Scottish and Welsh nationalists, though far less numerous, were more successful, gaining nine seats. Thus, the results of the February 1974 elections were altogether inconclusive; Labour had only five more seats than the Conservatives and after some defeats in Parliament, it was fairly obvious that a new election would take place within a few

---

[4] An excellent analysis of the British elections of 1974 is H. R. Penniman, *Britain at the Polls* (Washington, 1975).

months. Having settled the miners' dispute and promised to restore social peace by means of a "social compact" Labour seemed in an excellent position to win convincingly. It did, in fact, increase its share of the poll in the October elections, but again it had only a majority of two over all other parties. As the result of the defection of some of its members and the defeat of others in by-elections, this majority disappeared in 1975/6 and an uneasy alliance with the Liberals became a pre-condition for the survival of the Labour government. Following the second Tory defeat, Edward Heath was replaced as Conservative leader by Margaret Thatcher; two years after the elections Wilson resigned, and James Callaghan became prime minister in his place.

Labour had fought the elections with the slogan to "get Britain going again." But the party, a house divided, was not in a position to inspire even its own members with much confidence. The swing to the left which was apparent in the party manifesto of 1973 and the growing left-wing pressure on the part of some of the big unions had antagonized the Social Democrats, once the backbone of the party; their voice was not a very loud one, but without them Labour was bound to lose much of its electoral support. The economic malaise did not improve, inflation continued at the previous rate. In October 1975 the number of unemployed exceeded the one million mark for the first time since the war—it continued to rise to 1.4 million the year after. In October 1976 sterling had fallen to $1.57; altogether between 1972 and 1976 sterling fell by about 40% in comparison with other currencies. The country was kept afloat only through the massive help of the International Monetary Fund. 1975/6 was the nadir in the fortunes of the country and the party ruling it, and credit is due to Callaghan, Healey, and the others who refused to admit defeat in a seemingly hopeless situation. There were admittedly faint signs of improvement. The increase in prices and wages, and with it the rate of inflation was halved and fell to 13% in 1976; the number of working days lost fell to 2 million—less than in any year since 1967. Sterling slightly recovered, and with the influx of North Sea oil, foreign investments in Britain, many of them admittedly "hot money," also increased. The despair of 1974/5 gave way to cautious optimism in 1977, even though the recovery was modest and based on too many uncertainties such as the uneasy and reluctant understanding with the unions who had promised to exercise restraint temporarily. All that need be said about the situation in Northern Ireland is that it did not deteriorate. A basic solution was no more in sight in 1978 than five or six years earlier, but terrorist operations continued on a reduced scale. There was no progress on the other hand in the attempts to find a new status for Scotland and Wales; the devolution bill introduced in Parliament by Labour without much enthusiasm was not passed.

There was still the question of EEC membership which had preoccupied (and split) the country for years. While the parliamentary faction of the Labour party had voted in favor of staying in, the party executive had opposed it. Wilson opted for a popular referendum, a measure unprecedented in British political history. It took place in June 1975 and the result was decisive: 67% of the voters opted for Europe. As the decade drew to its close, it became clear that the worst fears of the pessimists, of whom there had been a great many, had not materialized. Britain, as so often in its history, managed to muddle through. The policy of buying time combined with a minimum of economic self-restraint had averted a total disaster. But the Cassandras had not been decisively refuted by the course of events. No essential changes had taken place; if the rate of inflation had fallen, there was always the danger that it would again accelerate with the next downturn in the business cycle. Unemployment remained high and investment and productivity low; government spending still exceeded revenue. The country, in brief, cheerfully continued to live beyond its means.

Developments in Britain were by no means unique, but some observers have argued that the particular case of "Englanditis" was caused by weaknesses and pressures specific to Britain.[5] The majority of Englishmen rejected both the extreme conservative cure (monetarism) and the extreme Labour panacea (wholesale nationalization and the radical abandonment of the market mechanism). Both these cures have been tried elsewhere, but the social and political cost seemed quite unacceptable—even had there been greater certainty of their effectiveness. There was only one other cure, the one of democratic compromise, but this involved a measure of wisdom and resolution on the part of the leaders, and of maturity and self-restraint on the part of individual

---

[5] Samuel Brittan and Peter Jay in R. Emmet Tyrell, Jr., *The Future That Doesn't Work* (New York, 1977).

members of society, rarely found in the annals of history. That England would not go under could be taken for granted; on what level of prosperity and happiness it would continue to exist remained uncertain.

FRANCE: THE POST-GAULLIST ERA

General de Gaulle had called a referendum on regional reform which took place in April 1969. It was not at all clear why such a referendum was needed, and when it appeared that de Gaulle had been defeated, he announced his immediate resignation in the briefest of communiqués. He had visibly aged over the last few years and become markedly more pessimistic; perhaps he had not quite overcome the shock of the events of 1968 when the Paris students' demonstrations had triggered off a mass movement that had almost overthrown his regime. De Gaulle was succeeded by a man who was not scheduled to be his heir, though he had served for six years as his prime minister. A *bon vivant* rather than a passionate politician, Georges Pompidou was suspect to the diehard Gaullists, and there is no doubt that he was clearly not one of them. Some of these suspicions were dispelled when he appointed Jacques Chaban Delmas prime minister. Chaban Delmas, a man of charm and dynamism, had played a prominent part in the wartime resistance; he was closer to the mainstream of Gaullism and incidentally also more eager to engage in social and economic reform than the president, who felt that most of France's ills stemmed from her poverty and backwardness and that economic progress would provide the solution to most of her problems.

Pompidou was a shrewd politician and appearance notwithstanding could be as ruthless as his predecessor. Without much fanfare he did away with some of the extravagances of the Gaullist regime. The franc was devalued to make the French economy more competitive, some of de Gaulle's more costly prestige projects were discontinued, the veto against Britain's entry to the EEC was dropped, and while France did not rejoin NATO it inclined towards a looser form of co-operation. But there were narrow limits beyond which Pompidou could not move; he seemingly could not even restrain Jobert, his foreign minister, a little man as successful a diplomat as a novelist who, playing up to domestic xenophobia, clearly gave higher priority to annoying France's friends and allies than to improving relations with them. More decisively still, while Pompidou was willing to placate the workers through some form of participation (the *contrats du progrès*) he opposed basic economic and administrative reforms, he feared major changes in the educational system as much as in local government.

During its first three years the reputation of Pompidou's government soared on a wave of success and some foreign observers predicted a glorious future for France. Economic progress continued, the left was split, and the regime faced no major challenges. But even before the full effects of the economic recession were felt in 1973, public support began to vanish. Increasingly there was talk about the shortcomings of an aimless and weak regime. Chaban Delmas had to resign following some minor financial scandal; he was replaced by Pierre Messmer, a well-meaning and loyal but colourless personality. Meanwhile the left, having agreed on a common program, gathered strength whereas in the government camp there were visible signs of tiredness and internal divisions. Pompidou's grave illness further weakened the resolution of his government at a time when it was most needed. It engaged in conflicting half measures, trying to counteract inflation without affecting economic growth. It attempted without success to stem the rise of prices and floated the franc without any visible benefit to the economy. The country sank into an economic recession and the political effects soon followed. France was divided into two camps of more or less equal strength; as the left moved towards unity, and the center and right towards division, and as the party in power got the blame for the deteriorating economic situation, the ruling coalition's base of popular support continued to shrink. Giscard d'Estaing, who became the new president of the republic after Pompidou's death, scraped through by a mere 300,000 votes in the elections of May 1974.

The obvious economic grievances apart, the basic complaints against Pompidou's administration and that of his successor focused on the absence of change, and this at a time when the demand for change was no longer confined to revolutionaries on the left. France, it was argued, was a blocked society, it was ruled by a bureaucracy, octopus-like ("tentaculaire"), ineffective, and out of touch with the people. Technocracy, it was said, was no answer to social and political ills, and people had no feeling of active participation, the rigid social structure did not correspond with the exigencies of a modern society. The government simply did not dare to do away with the archaic procedures, prerogatives, and privileges (sometimes of medieval origin) of small groups. These complaints were by no means groundless, and it was also true that differences in income were greater in France than in almost any other advanced society, that taxation was often ineffective. When Giscard tried to push through a modest capital gains tax, he encountered stiff resistance from the rich. The French right, which had never been distinguished for its social consciousness and far-sightedness, was clearly in no mood for concessions, and as a result all the latent conflicts became even more acute. Lastly, there was the growing complaint that successive governments, sold on the idea of economic growth, had neglected the quality of life. This was not really true with regard to Giscard's policy, but again, it was the perception that counted, and the perception gave rise to an ecological movement which became a major force in French politics.

This then was one side of the picture, and there was a strong tendency to forget that there was another side to it. France had made progress during the preceding two decades over and above the expectations of even the most sanguine observers. In most respects France had become a modern country, some of its key industries were again able to compete on the world markets, its agriculture had become more productive, and the average Frenchman was far better off in 1975 than he had been in 1955. Social mobility had increased, and with all the criticism of the bureaucracy, there was no denying that its leading "cadres" were as good, if not better, than any in Europe. Within a relatively short time France had acquired a system of social services equal to that of her neighbors. Those advocating radical and immediate change too often tended to forget that despite all the popular demands and protests French society was still conservative with its heart on the left but its purse (or checkbook) on the right, and that there was much instinctive opposition, not just among the wealthy, to any radical changes in their daily habits, customs and way of life. In short, while a majority of Frenchmen was in favor of reform, there was no enthusiasm for drastic change. Confusion, in other words, was not a monopoly of the government; the opposition also, in its program, combined mutually exclusive demands.

Giscard introduced a new style, partly on the Kennedy pattern, and there was a great deal of idealistic speech-making during the early days of his rule about a new society and a new democracy. But the new president, neither earthy politician nor charismatic leader, found the going rough from the very beginning. To the Gaullists he was even more suspect than his predecessor; while Jacques Chirac served as his prime minister criticism was muted, but after Chirac had been replaced by Barre, an economics professor, the right as well as the old Gaullists, who still formed the core of the government coalition, were up in arms and only fear of the left prevented a total breakdown. The left had made considerable gains in the local elections of 1976, and in the municipal elections of March 1977 they obtained some 52% of the vote. Their progress seemed irresistible, their rise to power only a question of time.

Of Giscard's promised reforms only a few materialized. The right to vote was given to those over the age of eighteen. Similar reforms had been made by the British Labour government in the late 1960's and in West Germany in 1970. There were some concessions to the environmentalists and to those pressing for reform in education. But in the economic field the immediate pressures were such that the government was altogether preoccupied with coping with the most urgent problems. It did not use the opportunity to carry out more far-reaching changes which precisely at a time of crisis might have been accepted. The recession reached its climax in late summer 1975. Industrial production had fallen by more than 10% during the preceding year, price controls were no longer effective, and more than a million Frenchmen were out of work. Then improvement set in: Professor Barre, sometimes compared to the friendly family doctor, had a plan (September 1976), and he managed to bring the inflation rate down; industrial production rose by 10% in 1976, and the GNP by about 5%. But the franc remained under strong pressure—it decreased in value in 1976 by some 17% against the more stable European currencies, foreign trade still showed a deficit (six billion dollars in 1976—the same as in 1974), and the rate of unemployment showed no sign of falling. As in Germany, there was no major industrial unrest, but some of the reforms were strongly disliked by the students and there were renewed stirrings in the universities. There were no more major foreign political initiatives of the kind that had been so dear to the heart of de Gaulle. What rays of hope then remained for poor Giscard, who had entered his office with so much confidence?

That the Communists tried their best to dispel any illusions about an alleged change in the character of their party was welcome to their government, but it hardly provided the guidelines for an alternative policy. Some optimistic observers detected the birth of a new civic spirit of trust and co-operation, and a decrease of old tensions and conflicts between social groups. But against this there was still the old inertia and suspicion and a deep-seated negativism, the lack of positive involvement in public affairs. French *morale,* in short, remained low and even France's admirers thought that it would improve only as the result of a gradual process over a long time, or less likely, following some unpleasant shock therapy.[6]

The elections of 1978 did not provide a shock of this kind, though it had seemed at the time that the victory of the united left was virtually assured. Perhaps the defeat was a blessing in disguise for the left, because it could not have possibly carried out its promises, and there is much reason to assume that the united front would have fallen apart after several months. As it happened, French voting patterns showed remarkable consistency. *Il faut que ça change* had been the main slogan of the election campaign, but all the polls paradoxically showed that dissatisfaction with the present state of affairs was by no means as deep as commonly assumed. Distrust of the Communist party and the dependence of the Socialists on the PCF (French Communist party) was probably the main obstacle on the road to a victory of the left. But the result of the elections which had been considered the most important in the post-war history of France—if not of Western Europe—was not a clear mandate for the Center-Right forces. France remained deeply divided into two more or less equally strong camps, and the long term survival of the government coalition still depended on its ability to over-

[6] More instant history is written in France than in any other country and this refers in particular to domestic affairs. The essays of Pompidou, Giscard, Mitterand, and many lesser figures have been published, and there are several biographers of these figures as well as of Chaban Delmas and Chirac. All major and minor French political parties have been described and analyzed in considerable detail.

A good survey of the Pompidou period is R. C. Macridis, *French Politics in Transition* (Cambridge, 1975). The standard works on the contemporary French political system are Henry W. Ehrmann, *Politics in France,* third ed. (Boston, 1976); and on social life John Ardagh, *The New France,* third ed. (London 1977). The newer French political literature (up to 1975) is reviewed in J. Chapsal and A. Lancelot, *La Vie Politique en France, Depuis 1940,* fourth ed. (Paris, 1975).

come its internal splits and the paralysis of will it had shown in the previous years. A narrow election victory was by no means a guarantee for political success, it did not spell the end of the era of uncertainty and turbulence.

GERMANY

When the Social Democrats took over the reins of government in 1969 almost a quarter of a century had passed since the end of the Second World War and Germany had emerged as the richest and most stable country in Western Europe. Germany's post-war economic recovery had been one of the miracles of the century, but there were not a few observers outside Germany and inside the country who expressed misgivings about the durability of the prosperity and the stability of the new political structures. The real test could come only at a time of crisis. Only then would it be clear whether the new state was a fair weather democracy or whether it was more firmly rooted, whether in fact Bonn was not Weimar.

Such a test did not occur under the First Brandt-Scheel administration. True, the Social Democratic-Liberal coalition had only a tiny majority, true again, that there were quarrels on such technical issues as whether the mark should be allowed to float; Schiller, the finance minister, resigned in July 1972 because his advice had not been taken. Some of the more important intended government reforms, such as the one concerning the future of workers' co-determination (*Mitbestimmung*), were postponed; it did not go far enough as far as the unions were concerned, whereas the right wing regarded it as both revolutionary and damaging. But by and large the left-liberal coalition justified the hopes of the electorate. This was the period when relations with the Soviet Union and the other East European countries were normalized, and when massive trade surpluses continued. In the general elections of November 1972 the Social Democrats became the strongest party in the land; the future of the coalition seemed assured for an indefinite period. But the year after, the first signs of the recession were felt, and almost immediately the boisterous mood gave way to a feeling of dejection, difficult to explain in rational terms but nonetheless quite real and tangible. In May 1974 Chancellor Brandt resigned after it had been discovered that Guillaume, one of his close assistants, had been an East German spy. It was a personal shock to the former chancellor, and at the same time provided food for thought for those advocating radical improvement in relations with the communist states. Helmuth Schmidt succeeded Brandt, and since Walter Scheel was elected President the same year, Genscher, another Liberal, became the new foreign minister. Schmidt, more pragmatic and in some ways less hesitant and less given to moods than his predecessor, had fewer enemies than Brandt, but also fewer friends, especially in his own party. The tasks that faced him were unenviable. The effects of the depression became even more acutely felt, and tensions appeared in the coalition with the Liberals. There were no Nobel prizes to be won in German politics.

Germany's economic woes were not remotely comparable to those facing the other European nations. Its inflationary rate—about 6% in 1975—was the envy of all other countries. If the German GNP was stationary in 1974, and if it fell by 3% the year after, there was again 5.5% growth in 1976. Unemployment reached and then surpassed the one million mark, and some branches of industry such as building and even the car industry were severely hit. But the visible trade balance continued to be positive even during the height of the recession, and the mark showed almost embarrassing strength. If there were reasons for concern these were long-term rather than immediate—the decline in investment and in the rate of profit. German uncertainties and fears in the face of comparatively minor problems can be understood only in historical perspective. The fact that other European nations were faring much worse did not impress the average German citizen that much nor did the fact that his per capita income was among the highest in the world and social services among the most extensive. Germany was psychologically less resistant than others to any setback because the inflation of the 1920's and the depression of the early 1930's and their political consequences were seemingly part of the collective unconscious; these specters were likely to be conjured up at the slightest sign of economic stagnation. This is not to say that there was no reason for concern: the job of one worker out of five did, after all, depend on exports, and what if world trade should contract as a result of a lasting depression?

Germany in the middle seventies suffered from a mild attack of hypochondria which in turn influenced, at least in part, the outcome of the elections of 1976, when the Social Democrats suffered a painful rebuff. The Christian Democrats reemerged as the strongest party with more than 48% of the vote; the old alliance polled just enough votes to scrape through. The image of the SPD as a "responsible" party had been damaged by the activities of its left wing, whose extreme demands were grist to the mills of the Conservatives. If the CDU (Christian Democratic Union) had not done even better, the main reason was that they too had their internal problems. No leader had emerged of even remotely the same stature as the late Konrad Adenauer. Franz Josef Strauss was the strongest personality by far, but what his rivals lacked in temperament he had in excess; furthermore he had moved too far to the right from the center of the party, his main base was the Bavarian CSU (Christian Social Union); elsewhere in Germany he was respected or feared, but not liked or trusted. Relations between CDU and CSU were far from cordial, to put it mildly. The other leaders of the party, such as Kohl, Biedekopf, or Carstens, were men of undoubted competence, but they lacked in one way or another some of the qualities likely to attract those extra voters that they needed to give them victory.

The Schmidt-Genscher government succeeded at long last in steering through parliament the industrial co-determination law which gave workers the right of participation in all industrial enterprises with more than 2,000 workers. It also initiated a marriage reform law and made abortion easier. In other respects it ran into difficulties; for example in its attempts to expand the use of nuclear energy for industrial purposes. Quite a few government initiatives were blocked by the *Bundesrat*, the second German chamber constituted by the representatives of the various Laender, in which the opposition had a majority.

Post-war German recovery had been so spectacularly successful because it had been based on consensus politics, on the realization that a common effort was needed. Italian and British union leaders pointed with pride to the greater militancy of their unions which fought for and obtained huge pay raises, and they had nothing but contempt for the docility of the German unions. But at the end of the day the members of the German unions were far better off, much to the bewilderment of the Italians and the British. By the middle seventies, however, the German consensus came under severe strain. The unions were no longer willing to give priority to investment; they became more insistent on getting their rewards here and now. At the same time there was renewed trouble in the universities: the number of students had trebled within a decade, and as in so many other countries there was a danger, indeed a near certainty, of academic unemployment. There was the threat of the disaffection of the young intellectual elite becoming institutionalized, as in the 1920's not because of events in Iran (which had triggered off the protest movement in 1967) but because of much more immediate and vital problems.

The terrorist campaign of the 1970's preoccupied German society far beyond its intrinsic importance. Perhaps it was only natural in view of the German longing for perfection and their apparent inability to live with a modicum of disorder, something other, more fortunate, nations seemed to relish. Some observers argued that Germany faced a civil war–like situation, for which, above all, the leaders of the SPD and the left-wing intellectuals bore the responsibility. Some felt inclined to brand everyone as a "sympathizer" who was not altogether happy with the status quo in Germany. But neither was Germany threatened by a civil war nor was it at all likely that anyone had ever turned to terrorism as the result of reading the novels of Heinrich Böll or Günther Grass. There were some equally disingenuous arguments on the other side. They saw no evil, they heard no evil, as if there had not been a massive attempt to indoctrinate German students by some who should have known better; as if the present German state was either already fascist or about to become so soon, and that it was merely a tactical problem whether one decided to use violence against this state and this society. There was no denying that a certain intellectual climate had spread in some universities according to which democracy was tyranny, with the corollary that any action, even the most brutal, was justified to combat it. A similar climate of opinion after the First World War had provided the background for the murders of Rosa Luxemburg, Walter Rathenau, and many others. Such moral and intellectual confusion was not an act of God; it was aided and abetted by some who may not have been aware of the possible consequences of their ideas.

German prosperity and stability did not necessarily make for popularity among her neighbors. The old image of the brutal, ugly German was again conjured up, the danger of a new German domination was invoked. While German public figures behaved on the whole with commendable circumspection, trying not to antagonize other nations and to re-open old wounds, there were some regrettable slips and blunders. Yet there is good reason to believe that even if they had all behaved like saints they would still have been attacked by some outside critics. There was envy that Germany should weather the economic storms better than the other European countries and that its institutions seemed more stable. Some of the specific charges made against the new Germany were connected with the famous *Radikalenerlass* which made it impossible for members of organizations opposed in principle to the democratic order to enter state service. Legislation to this effect contained inequities, but the basic principle underlying it was, of course, accepted by every democratic society, even though most of them handled it more discreetly or elegantly than the Germans.

If resentment against Germany had been the result merely of fears related to Germany's recent history this would have been understandable. But there was a more sinister aspect: Germany became one of the chief targets of attack not because it was a bulwark of repression, but for the opposite reason, that is, it was attacked just because its democratic "system" continued to work reasonably effectively. With Britain so much weakened, with France and Italy confused and partly paralyzed, Germany had become the main bulwark of reaction. But "reaction" in the new political vocabulary did not mean opposition to political and social innovation, but, on the contrary, the preservation of political freedom and human rights. The new Germany, far from perfect, was by and large as free and democratic a society as any in Europe, and it was attacked, more often than not, for its virtues and achievements rather than for its shortcomings and failures.

ITALIAN TURMOIL

Italy's time of adversity began with the mass strikes of the hot autumn of 1969 and has continued ever since. The underlying reasons have not been in dispute; the "imperfect two party system," the intricate spoils system which undermined confidence in the state, the presence of an inflated bureaucracy and ineffective state sector in the national economy, the unpleasant social consequences of the stormy economic

growth of the 1960's. That the Italian *miracolo* did not last forever was
not surprising, but many of the afflictions besetting Italy could have
been attenuated but for the failure of the political system and the leadership. It was not foreordained that investment in the 1960's should have
gone mainly into the unproductive sectors of the economy, that unit
production costs should have increased in Italy three times as much as
in West Germany or four times as much as in the United States, that
much of the budget should have been spent on running the bureaucracy rather than the country, or that building speculation should have
been unfettered. The economic mismanagement resulted in an inflationary rate which at the depth of the recession was even higher than
Britain's as well as 1.7 million unemployed.[7] If in 1974 the economy still
grew at a rate of six per cent, it contracted the year after by four per
cent and in 1976 it increased again by four per cent. Italy had a trade
deficit of eight billion dollars in 1974, and it managed to survive only by
means of credits from the IMF and Germany. In 1976 there were some
indications of an improvement in the situation, and in 1977 the country
actually had a trade surplus for several months running. But with wage
increases still running at a rate of thirty per cent, the highest by far in
any industrial country, lasting recovery seemed impossible. In Italy,
unlike in Britain, there was no social contract, and one has to turn from
the economic to the political aspects of the crisis to understand its apparent intractability.

The root of the evil was that after three decades of uninterrupted
rule the Christian Democrats were no longer capable of governing and
there was no democratic alternative. The Christian Democrats, to quote
M. Ledeen, were not only the paladin of big business but also the *fau-
teur* of a strong anti-capitalist movement; they spoke for the conservative upper strata of a highly traditional society but also for a working
class ferment; they represented advanced sectors of the industrial north
and Mafia-ridden landed interests in Sicily and Calabria. The result was
not consensus but, paralysis, the inability to break the wage-price spiral
and, generally speaking, to take any effective action. The opening to the
left and the reform policy proposed by some Christian Democratic

[7] It should be noted however that Italian employment figures are notoriously unreliable
and that unemployment in Italy had been relatively high even during prosperity.

leaders was torpedoed by others; in the absence of a strong left-of-center political force the viability of such a policy would have been in doubt in any case. This left the Communists, who had the support of about one third of the electorate—but with two thirds against them. The conviction gained ground that Italy could not be ruled without the Communists, but there was equally no conviction that it could be done with them. Still, as the economic recession deepened, as student unrest, wildcat strikes, and terrorism from left and right threatened a total breakdown of public order, some arrangement with the PCI (Italian Communist party), tacit or open, became an apparent necessity, and the history of Italy in recent years has been the story of the gradual emergence of ad hoc compromises rather than the great "historical" compromise about which everyone talked.

The latent political crisis became acute in 1974 when governments headed by Aldo Moro, Rumor, and again Moro followed each other in quick succession. The Christian Democrats had called a plebiscite for no good reason except perhaps pressure by the Church which brought them defeat: some sixty per cent of those who participated voted against the abolition of civil marriage. In the regional elections of June 1975, the Communists polled 33 per cent; in Milan, Naples, Turin and Florence Popular Front coalitions took over the municipalities, and Fanfani, who was made the scapegoat for the defeat by the Christian Democrats, was replaced as party secretary general by Zaccagnini. Meanwhile Moro's minority government continued to muddle through until, in January 1976, the Socialists decided to withdraw their support. This meant the end of Italy's thirty-seventh post-war government and new elections. Against expectations the Christian Democrats held on to their share of the vote (38 per cent), the Communists made further slight progress (34 per cent), and the main losers were the parties of the center and center left, including the Socialists who had been responsible for calling the elections that did not solve anything. Andreotti, who became the new prime minister in July 1976, headed yet another minority government. The Communists further strengthened their position; one of their leaders, Ingrao, became President of the Chamber, and seven other Communists now headed important parliamentary committees.

Andreotti's government, despite its weak base, lasted longer than generally expected, mainly no doubt because there were hardly any other contenders for this impossible job. His policy was not devoid of ingenuity. While co-operating with the Communists he tried at the same time to out-maneuver them, which was basically the policy the Communists had followed vis-à-vis the Christian Democrats for some considerable time. The Communists were given a say and virtual veto power in running domestic, economic, and foreign policy, and in return for such power-sharing they refrained from overthrowing the government and gave their support to various vague government action programs until, in December 1977, they began to press for their participation in the government following some new *combinazione*. A policy of this kind involved certain risks from the Communist point of view. There was open dissatisfaction among some party militants who argued that it was not their task to prop up a doomed regime. Communist leaders were howled down by students, and there was the danger that the PCI would lose some support in the factories. But, on the other hand, there were important long-term gains; the understanding with the Christian Democrats gave the Communists the legitimacy they needed to be accepted as a fully fledged partner at some future date. They were no doubt aware of the fact that their prospects for further major electoral progress were dim for the time being; on the contrary, there were signs that they might not be able to hold on to all the gains they had made. In the circumstances, the choice was between revolution—not a practical proposition for a variety of reasons, domestic and international—and accommodation with the Christian Democrats, however much some party militants might resent it. The leaders of the PCI frequently invoked the lesson of Chile; they knew that there was little chance that they would come to power heading a minority government and that, in any case, this would be an invitation to disaster.

Some aspects of the Italian situation resembled the state of affairs that had prevailed in the country in the years before the rise of fascism. Terrorist gangs, some of them recipients of foreign help, roamed the streets. Most prominent among them were the *Nap*, closely connected with criminals and the Red Brigades supported by Czechoslovakia; political opponents were attacked or intimidated, newspaper offices were bombed, "reactionary" and "right-wing" judges and journalists were shot.

But "reactionary" and "right-wing" in the Italian context of the middle 1970's no longer meant neo-fascism or even conservatism. It referred to the diminishing number of those opposed to dictatorship who continued to speak up for the virtues of political freedom, men and women who had more in common with the tradition of Mazzini and Garibaldi than those who attacked them.

The situation in the universities was quite chaotic: Rome University, built for some 10–15,000 students had grown to 165,000, following an "open admission" policy. This was an extreme, but by no means altogether untypical case. Officially the universities continued to function, but in practice whole departments no longer provided systematic tuition, standards fell abysmally, and many of the graduates could not find work commensurate with their expectations. They joined the ranks of the demonstrators for whatever cause was put on the political agenda.

Italy has shown in its history a greater ability to live with anarchy than almost any other country. But there are limits beyond which even the most adaptable societies cease functioning; these limits seemed to have been reached in the mid-seventies. The Christian Democratic establishment which had tolerated or abetted the growth of anarchy lacked the stamina, the courage, and the moral standing to cope with a crisis of this magnitude. The indecision and the lack of civic spirit in high places were mirrored in other sections of society. The inability to find in Turin a few citizens sufficiently courageous to act as jurors in a trial against a small group of terrorists was typical of the extent to which the moral fiber of an intelligent, lovable, and industrious people had deteriorated. During the immediate post-war period Italian intellectuals had been in a self-critical mood; never again would they abdicate their responsibilities, never again would they betray the cause of freedom, never again would the time of indifference return. But the good intentions were forgotten with indecent haste once the Communist bandwagon began moving, and the stampede slowed down only when it was discovered that the bandwagon was not advancing as fast as had been originally assumed.

Some observers came to regard Italy both as a microcosm of the European disease and as a harbinger of the shape of things to come. But there were important differences; it was only in Italy that there was no political outlet for many of the country's discontents. Nowhere among advanced industrial societies was the feeling so widespread that the citizen had no means of expressing his views and desires and that the whole system had ceased to function. Nowhere else was there so much pessimism about the future of democracy. Some thought a regeneration possible on a regional basis, removing much of the decision-making from the central authorities to the local level. Others, such as the late Guido Piovene, thought that the lack of civic sense, the failure of the Italian bourgeoisie, the conformism of the intelligentsia could all be traced back to the same source—the failure of the union between Northern Italy and the South: Italian unity had remained a fiction, the Risorgimento was a myth, and the state had virtually ceased to exist. It was not however clear what followed from this analysis; since a new division of Italy, however desirable, was unlikely, perhaps the future of the whole country was with the Khadafis and Boumediens? But Italy had certainly moved beyond the stage of development in which a regression of this kind could still be envisaged. A dictatorship of the right is impossible, one of the left unlikely for the time being. Communist participation in the government remains a possibility in the long run. On the basis of the Andreotti formula agreed upon in March 1978 the Communists received equal footing with the other parties in shaping government policies. In exchange it was agreed that the Communists would vote for the government and not just abstain. The Communists dropped their original demand for cabinet posts (December 1977) and promised support for a national unity emergency government "to get Italy out of the depth of the crisis." The temporary character of an agreement of this kind was clear from the beginning; it was bound to break down if it proved insufficient to cope with the crisis. But even if it functioned well it could only last until it had achieved its purpose. However, since both full success and total breakdown are unlikely possibilities, a provisional arrangement of this kind may well last for years. The outcome of the struggle for power in Italy now depends as much on developments in other parts of Europe and the overall balance of power as on events inside the country.

SPAIN

When General Franco died in November 1975 he had been in power longer than any other chief of government or head of state in Europe.

Few had assumed that he would last that long or that he would die in bed, and hardly anyone had believed that the transition from authoritarian to democratic rule would be relatively short and painless. The fears that had been voiced for the prospects of Spain after Franco had been based in part on a wrong assessment of the character of the regime. Franco's was a brutish dictatorship, but it was neither "totalitarian" nor "fascist," and it was precisely because new political and social structures had begun to emerge during the last years of the regime that a peaceful transition was possible. Important changes had taken place well before Franco's death: economic development had been strong; per capita income had risen tenfold from $248 to $2,865 between 1960 and 1975; and even if the cost-of-living had risen by almost 400 per cent during that period this was commensurate with a very considerable increase in living standards. Spanish export earnings and the number of cars in use, to provide two more examples, had grown at a similar rate. Six million foreign tourists had visited Spain in 1960; fifteen years later their number had risen to thirty million, the largest in Europe. During the same period some five million Spaniards had moved from the countryside to the towns, and several million had gone to work outside Spain. On the surface, Spain had changed more during the last two decades than any other European country.

But there was also political change side by side with the repression that continued through the early seventies. Thus it was clear well before Franco's death that the "Aperturistas" had gained the upper hand, meaning those favoring an opening up of the system, of getting the active co-operation of wider sections of the population. Appearances to the contrary, this was the policy of Carrero Blanco, who was assassinated by members of ETA (Euzkadi Ta Askatasuna) in December 1973, and of his successor Arias Navarro.[8] The concessions were as yet exceedingly modest: Arias Navarro promised some form of democracy on the municipal level, and even before Franco's death something akin to the right to strike was reintroduced. In this respect as in many others it was the first step that counted, for once the sluice gates were opened, "modernization," "liberalization" and "rejoining Europe" became the most popular slogans, very much to the chagrin of the men of the "bunker"—the hard-line Falangists who were firmly convinced that any experiments

[8] R. Tamames, *La Republica, La Era de Franco* (Madrid, 1977), pp. 579 ff.

with democracy were bound to lead to disaster. Political parties and trade unions were in theory still banned, and any open resistance to the regime was still punishable by law. Yet theory and practice were by no means identical; there existed, in fact, workers' commissions and political circles *in statu nascendi* bitterly opposed to the regime. A visit to a Spanish bookshop or a look at the contents of some of the newspapers and periodicals showed that censorship, to the extent that it still existed, was quite liberal, restricted in the main to comment on events inside Spain. The church, once one of the staunchest pillars of the Franco regime, began to adjust itself to the post-Franco era well before his death. Towards the end of its existence, the Franco regime was no more than a loose coalition of a variety of factions and interest groups jockeying for position. It no longer inspired awe, fear, or hate, except perhaps among national minorities. Spain was not a time bomb about to explode, and while the great majority of Spaniards, as it was soon to appear, wanted far-reaching change, they were in no mood for a revolution, let alone a new civil war.

King Juan Carlos, who had been appointed by Franco as his successor, appointed Adolfo Suarez as prime minister, and the two, much to the surprise of left-wing critics, pushed a Political Reform Act through Parliament which within the span of a year was to transform radically the Spanish political landscape. After some hesitation even the Communist party was made legal (April 1977). There was an enormous upsurge in political (as in cultural) activity. In preparation for Spain's first free elections in forty years some two hundred political parties emerged. In view of such internal division there were serious doubts whether Spain was ready for democracy. Yet again, the sceptics were confounded:two-thirds of the votes went to the two major parties—the Union of the Democratic Center (35 per cent) and the Socialist Workers party (29 per cent). Both the Communists (9 per cent) and the right (8 per cent) fared much less well than their well-wishers and many outside observers had assumed; perhaps even more significant was the fact that the Spanish Communists were the most liberal in Europe, and that the right (led by Manuel Fraga) was also willing to abide by the democratic rules. During the election campaign and after, the party leaders showed a measure of maturity and responsibility that no one had expected in the light of Spain's previous experiments with democracy. In a way they were all Democratic Socialists now: the Suarez government's fiscal and unemployment programs were taken almost completely from the Socialist platform, as an observer of the Spanish scene noted, "and it will be difficult for the socialists and the trade unions to refuse wage restraints if the government fulfills its promises about taxing the rich to help the poor."[9] According to the social pact of October 1977, both wage rises and prices were to be held to a maximum of 22 per cent in 1978.

Thus the first stage of the transition period was passed without any major upheavals. But it remained to be seen whether the new democracy would show equal strength and competence tackling the many problems that remained to be solved and the new difficulties that had emerged. The rate of inflation in 1975/76 was between 25 and 30 per cent, the number of unemployed approached one million; some of the leading industries, such as shipbuilding were particularly hard hit, and since no attempt had been made to reduce energy consumption, Spain's massive payment balance assumed dangerous proportions—the foreign debt was twelve billion dollars in 1977. At the same time terrorism, both left- and right-wing in inspiration, increased. Some of it was apparently steered by remote control. On the left there were grumblings, not without reason, that the working people should not be asked to make sacrifices while there was more social inequality in Spain than in any other industrialized country, except France. On the right it was argued with equal justice that there was an alarming increase in crime, that there had been much less pornography, drug trafficking, and juvenile delinquency under Franco, and that there was neither strong leadership nor national discipline. But the main danger came not from the extremes of the political spectrum; the cohesion of the two main parties was still in some doubt. Suarez's party was a coalition of fifteen different groups which began to fight each other the moment the prime minister went on a trip abroad. Equally, the Socialist party and its leaders had yet to show that their electoral success of 1977 had been more than a flash in the pan, that its leaders would continue to work together harmoniously, and that they had the political experience to become a major political factor in a democratic Spain that was to last.

[9] Stanley Meisler, "Spain's New Democracy," *Foreign Affairs* (October 1977), 206.

DEMOCRACY RESTORED: PORTUGAL AND GREECE

When freedom returned to Portugal in April 1974 the country had been under dictatorial rule for a period even longer than neighboring Spain, and the prospects seemed even less promising. The coup was carried out by a group of officers who had been demoralized (and radicalized) by the colonial wars in Africa in which they were not defeated but which, they had learned by bitter experience, the country could no longer afford. Initial jubilation soon gave way to a more sober mood, for it quickly appeared that neither newly won freedom nor indeed the economic survival of the country could be taken for granted. During the first year after the revolution, effective control was in the hands of the MFA (*Movimento das Forcas Armadas*), constituted by several hundred middle rank officers. At first, the more radical elements among them gained the upper hand: they brought about the downfall of Spinola, the moderate head of the junta, and established a close working alliance with the Communists.[10]

The Communists had been the only party to emerge from the dictatorship with an organizational nucleus intact and thus had a head start over all other groups. Their position was reinforced by the support of the officers and their influence in the media, some of which had been taken over by intimidation, other parts of which by force. But they also gained a strong foothold among the poor peasants of Southern Portugal and among the trade unions. The acute struggle for power between the Communists and the democratic parties, much stronger in numbers but poorly organized, lasted for slightly more than a year. In the elections of April 1975 the Socialists, headed by Mario Soares, emerged as the strongest party by far (38 per cent), followed by the PPD (later PSD), a center party which polled 21 per cent whereas the Communists attracted a mere 12 per cent. But the military leadership was not im-

[10] The Portuguese revolution and the struggle for power in 1974/75 produced a great deal of comment and analysis reflecting the views of all parts of the political spectrum. Among the more interesting are the following: A. Rodrigues, C. Borgia, M. Cardoso, *Portugal despois de Abril* (Lisbon, 1976); M. Harsgor, *Portugal in Revolution* (Beverley Hills, 1976); H. Bieber, *Portugal* (Hanover, 1974); and P. Mailer, *Portugal, the Impossible Revolution* (London, 1977).

pressed and certainly had no inclination to be swayed from its course; who, at a time of revolution would pay attention to electoral arithmetic? It was only after the democratic forces inside the junta had asserted themselves that notice was taken of the popular will. The struggle for democracy in Portugal and the attempts to restrict and abolish the newly won freedoms were followed with passionate interest by a great many people outside Portugal. Portugal, when all had been said and done, was one of the smallest and least important countries in Europe, but events there in 1974–75 conveyed some significant lessons for the rest of Europe. The defeat of the Communists and their sympathizers can be explained partly by the Stalinist line pursued by Cunhal, the leader of the party. The Communists faced a genuine dilemma insofar as such policies were indeed quite suitable for attracting some sections of the population in an underdeveloped country; nevertheless a hard-line policy of this kind was a source of weakness in other respects. The Portuguese people in its great majority had the good sense not to want one kind of dictatorship to be replaced by another.

By late 1975 the struggle for freedom seemed to have been won; Soares the Socialist became prime minister. But the fight was by no means over; the difficulties facing Soares were formidable, and the euphoria of victory soon gave way to dejection. In 1976–77 Portugal had the highest rate of inflation in Europe (34 per cent) and the highest per capita balance of trade deficit. Unlike Spain, the Portuguese dictatorship had not laid the foundation for a modern economy, and the heritage of the post-liberation interregnum in which enormous wage increases had been given while productivity was declining had further undermined the Portuguese economy. Lastly, the army of the unemployed was swelled by the hundreds of thousands of repatriates from Africa. Again unlike Spain, the government could not count on the cooperation of the Communists and other opposition parties to help it to pursue an austerity program; on the contrary, they tried to make the most of its economic difficulties. Only through foreign loans was the Soares government able to keep the country afloat, and in January 1978 it had to broaden its basis through a coalition with the center right. But this did not secure the survival of the government for long. When Soares announced in 1977 that it was going to be a "long struggle" he was certainly not guilty of exaggeration; he should have added perhaps that its outcome was by no means certain.

Unlike the Portuguese dictatorship, the Greek military junta was not overthrown, it crumbled and disappeared in late July 1974. This had been preceded by a struggle for power inside the junta and a wave of protest demonstrations. But the decisive factor was the desperate gamble in Cyprus; the colonels had supported a lunatic adventure aimed at overthrowing Archbishop Makarios. The temporary victory of the extremist forces on the island led in turn to the Turkish invasion and a humiliation without precedent for the colonels. Greek defeat in Cyprus also had foreign policy consequences, such as the bitter conflict with Turkey and the tensions with Greece's Western allies. From now on Turkey and Greece were to regard each other as the main enemy; there was a competition in chauvinism in both countries, and both announced that they would restrict their involvement in NATO to less than the necessary minimum. NATO's southern flank continued to exist on paper only. On the domestic scene the transition to democracy went smoothly. Konstantin Karamanlis, who headed the new government received an overwhelming vote of confidence (54 per cent) in the elections of November 1974. There was an even greater majority for the abolition of the monarchy in the plebiscite the month after; King Constantine had to settle abroad permanently. Greece faced the same economic problems as the rest of Europe with a rate of inflation of 30 per cent in 1973/74. But inflation fell to about 10 per cent in 1975–77, and if Greece still ran up a considerable balance of payment deficit, this was to a large extent counterbalanced by invisible earnings. The main economic problem in Greece, as in other European countries, remained the low rate of investment. The main political issue was the instability among the political parties, the constant splits and shifts with new parties appearing, aligning or realigning themselves, or disintegrating rapidly and with monotonous regularity. There was no reason for concern all the time one party had a working majority and the authority of its leaders was not in question. But this had been the exception in the short history of modern Greek democracy, and if the country reverted to the "normal" pattern of unstable coalitions and permanent conflict, there was again reason to fear for the future of the country. The results of the elections of November 1977 in which the share of Karamanlis' party fell to 42% were a warning signal.

The European crisis produced pessimistic analyses and forecasts, but the pessimism on the whole failed to carry conviction. The impression was gained that even most Cassandras believed that the European societies would eventually overcome their present difficulties as they had done so often in the past. One century earlier Jacob Burckhardt had pondered the origin, character, and common pattern of crises of world historical dimensions. He had noted that true crises were exceedingly rare and that more often than not the enormous noise accompanying a political spasm was far in excess of the political and social change underneath. A conservative thinker, Burckhardt noted nevertheless that true revolutions could have positive results or side-effects, releasing energies in individuals and masses, which no one had expected. ("Even the colour of the skies changes.") Such passions could be a good thing insofar as they showed vitality and creativeness, for even fanaticism was a sign that people valued some things higher than material possessions—than even life itself.[11]

Measured by these standards, the European convulsions of the 1970's are, of course, not a "real" crisis, nor did they generate strong passions and fresh energies. The "young peoples" who have been conjured up by Spengler and others, the non-decadent nations and classes about to inherit the earth, are largely figments of imagination. They too are going through crises of their own, unable to solve fundamental problems, even if dictatorial rule may suppress outward manifestations of discontent. But there still remains the question of the deeper causes of the European upheaval in the 1970's. Is it perhaps a case of slow erosion of the political and social base of societies, a crisis of the not-with-a-bang-but-with-a-whimper variety? Around the turn of the century Eduard Drumont wrote that true pessimism was a characteristic of superior races, and that others, in decline, were no longer able to sustain pessimism, but were simply affected by a lassitude which was the

[11] J. Burckhardt, *Weltgeschichtliche Betrachtungen* (Stuttgart, 1969), pp. 157 ff.

prelude to death. Was Europe, in its decadence, no longer able to generate even the hopes, fears, and illusions that according to the philosophers of history had been the concommitant of all major upheavals? Or was it a pseudo-crisis, a false alarm, with the tocsin being rung for no good reason? This crucial question will come up again in our examination of Europe's various misadventures.

4

EUROCOMMUNISM[1]

Throughout recorded history international movements have been subject to splits and schisms, and communism has been no exception. As it spread outside the Soviet Union, tensions among Communist leaders and parties were bound to develop. Even in Stalin's lifetime, Tito defied the Kremlin and was excommunicated. After Stalin's death the great schism with China took place, Albania left the fold, and Rumania showed a desire for more independence. The communist regimes that remained faithful to the Soviet Union were those who were tied to Russia by links of traditional friendship (such as Bulgaria), or were geopolitically not in a position to resist Soviet hegemony (Poland), lacked domestic support and depended therefore on the Soviet Union, or felt themselves threatened by "imperialist pressure" (Cuba). During the 1960's a gradual estrangement between Moscow and several non-ruling Communist parties took place. Over several decades the Soviet leaders had become accustomed to acting as the undisputed leaders of the Communist camp and of all Communist parties. Their agents were everywhere, no important decision was to be taken without their approval, the Soviet model had to serve as the pattern for all other parties. True, in theory, allowances were always made for "national peculiarities" but in political practice this amounted to very little.

[1] The term "Euro-Communism" was first used, as far as can be established by Frane Barbieri, the Madrid correspondent of *Giornale Nuovo* in an article published on June 26, 1975. ("Le scandenze di Breznev"). It immediately gained wide currency joining the long list of Euro- neologisms (Euro-currency, Euro-dollar, Euratom, Eurocrats, Eurostat, Euro-tox etc.). But the use of the term is highly problematical, for while there are certain similarities between the Communist parties of Western Europe, conditions vary from country to country and so does the character of the parties. There are great differences between the policy of the Italian and the French Communist parties, not to mention the Portuguese, the West German, or the Greek party. Thus the indiscriminate use of the term "Euro-Communism" tends to obfuscate the issues involved. But it has been generally accepted and is unlikely to disappear from the political dictionary.

After Stalin's death, and in particular after the Twentieth Party Congress in 1956, Russia's dominant role in the communist world movement was increasingly questioned. Under Stalin there had been a blind belief in the wisdom of Soviet leadership and the greatness of the Soviet achievements among communist militants in West and East. As the real state of affairs in the Soviet Union became known to the party faithful abroad, the attraction of the Soviet Union as a model "socialist" society decreased rapidly, and, to a certain extent, it became an acute embarrassment. Western Communists felt they would be better off with communism as a lofty ideal, as yet nowhere realized, than with basing their political appeal on the achievements of the Soviet Union. This estrangement showed itself in the negative reaction of most Western Communist parties after the Soviet invasion of Czechoslovakia in 1968. But discord does not invariably lead to a break; if there were tensions and conflict, the Communist parties still had a great many interests in common. Many Western Communist parties were at least to some extent materially dependent on Moscow or were exposed to Soviet pressure: even if the Russians could not help them, they certainly were in a position to do them considerable harm by provoking or supporting splits in their ranks. Most Western Communist leaders found Soviet political methods less than admirable. But at the same time they found all kinds of excuses and explanations, and they continued to believe, or at the very least to argue in public, that basically the Soviet Union was a socialist and progressive country and that the political aberrations, caused by historical accident, would in due course be corrected. In these circumstances, a final break with the Soviet Union seemed unwise both politically and ideologically. Politically, because while the European Communists resented Soviet tutelage they still needed the Soviet Union in many ways, nor did they want to be branded as violators of communist solidarity and the sacred principle of internationalism. Ideologically, because it could backfire against their own parties by providing ammunition to those critics who argued that the "distortion" of Communist Russia and Eastern Europe were not an accident of history but that something was intrinsically wrong with communism as a system, and that attempts to realize it would have similar consequences everywhere.

These, in briefest outline, were the limits set to the dispute between the Soviet Union and the major European Communist parties. On one hand there was growing dissension, caused by (to paraphrase a well-known Leninist thesis) the uneven development of Western and Eastern communism; on the other, there were the many ties and common interests still binding the Communist parties together. The Soviet leadership made great efforts to maintain the unity of the camp, and the chosen vehicle to that end, not very wisely as it later appeared, were international conferences adopting solemn and binding resolutions. There were three such world conferences (in Moscow in 1957, 1960, and 1969 respectively) and one European conference (in Karlovy Vary in 1967). For years the Soviet leaders made strenuous efforts to arrange a fourth world conference and a second European conference. They failed to achieve the former aim but succeeded in the latter endeavor. However, the inordinate effort they had to invest and the meager results achieved made them doubt whether the game was any longer worth the candle. It took about three years, countless preparatory meetings and many Soviet concessions to convene a meeting of the leaders of twenty-nine European parties in East Berlin in late June 1976. The result, from the Soviet point of view, was certainly not impressive; not only did the conference adopt resolutions stressing the principles of equality and independence of all parties, it even affirmed that there was room for legitimate criticism among Communist parties. On the other hand it failed to agree on a final communiqué expressing solidarity with all important aspects of Soviet foreign and domestic policies such as the Russian leaders had wanted. There was a growing feeling that meetings of this kind were useless; as George Marchais, the French Communist leader said in a speech soon after the Berlin meeting: congresses of this kind are no longer consonant with the spirit of the times.

The Berlin meeting of 1976 showed, if indeed any further evidence was needed, that most European Communist parties could no longer be counted upon automatically to follow the Soviet lead. This process had not, of course, passed unnoticed in the West: the term "Eurocommunism" was first used in 1975, not by the Western Communists themselves, though some of them declared subsequently that they did not mind the expression. The emergence of Eurocommunism of course predates the appearance of the term by several years. As a definition, the term was not perhaps an ideal choice for a similar process had earlier taken place in other parts of the world—Japan, for instance, and Australia, to provide but two examples.

Historically and culturally, communism in Western Europe is heir to a different tradition from that of Soviet communism; its specific features were suppressed with the Bolshevization of the Communist parties in the 1920's and eradicated altogether during the Stalin period. During the late 1950's and in particular during the early 1960's some of these "Western" elements reasserted themselves in various European Communist parties apparently quite spontaneously and independently of each other. The Italian Communist party (PCI), the biggest Communist party in Europe, was the first, at its tenth Congress in 1962, to make a determined effort to stress its specific Italian features. The progress of socialism in the West would have to proceed, to quote Giorgio Amendola, in forms suitable to the pluralist character of Western society; Togliati in his famous Yalta memorandum (the first formulation of polycentrism) had even earlier emphasized the importance of reducing Soviet influence on the Italian party. Smaller parties such as the Swedish, the Belgian, and the Austrian moved in a similar direction; in some cases, as in Austria, the Russians succeeded in reverting the process, helping to overthrow the "liberals" and reimpose an orthodox, pro-Soviet leadership.

During the late 1960's several regional West European conferences took place dealing with topics of common interest to the Communist parties. But there were few tangible results because some of the major parties, such as the French (PCF), were as yet unwilling to join their Italian comrades in the attempt to modernize the Communist movement. Thus, the Italians were the first to take their seats in the Council of Europe in Strasbourg; it was only after the Spanish, the Belgian, the British, the (inner) Greek, and above all the French party had decided to make common cause with them, that Eurocommunism gathered some momentum in the early seventies.

The causes of this process were not shrouded in mystery: mention has already been made of the different political culture of Western and of Southern Europe, the deeper roots of democracy, the resistance against tyranny. Even a confirmed Stalinist such as Cunhal, the Portuguese Communist leader, had to admit that the slogan of the dictatorship of the proletariat did not go down well in countries that had been subject to dictatorship. There were reasons of a pragmatic character. Unlike the Communist parties of Eastern Europe, those of the West were exposed to the profound economic and social changes taking place around them and they had to adjust their policies accordingly. Between 1959 and 1974 Spain went through a period of stormy economic development, with a rate of growth far surpassing that of the Soviet Union. For several years the Spanish Communist leadership chose to ignore this process, claiming that an economic catastrophe was imminent. Yet eventually they had to take cognizance of the new realities, and this had far-reaching political consequences for their policies. The Italian party, to give another example, announced early on that it would not insist on the immediate further nationalization of big enterprises as a pre-condition for sharing power. The Italian leaders, in their endeavour to create a climate of respectability and responsibility around their party, were, of course, aware that Italy faced a major economic crisis which would not be alleviated, let alone be resolved, by nationalization: many of the big Italian concerns were already owned and run by the state and their performance was poor.

The West European parties all agreed that the transition to socialism should be peaceful. This basic strategy, which in principle was also approved by the Soviet leadership, meant by implication the establishment of a united front and alliances with other parties, and to be credible, such alliances had to be based on concessions and compromises. Lastly, there were the pervasive effects of nationalism. While many European Communist parties benefitted from the nationalist upsurge of the 1960's and '70's, they were also genuinely influenced by it. Once then the first fissures appeared in what had been a monolithic bloc, once China had seceded, and Yugoslavia had been granted autonomy, however reluctantly, by the Kremlin, could not other Communist parties demand similar privileges with equal right? "The left is rediscovering the nation," a radical Gaullist in 1977 jubilantly noted, with the Communists in mind rather than the Socialists, justifying his vote for the new popular front. A demonstrative nationalism was noted by outside observers in Sweden, Holland, and even in far away Iceland, where the most consequently isolationist of all Communist parties boycotted international gatherings. In 1974, at the time of the Norwegian election campaign with the Common Market as the main issue at stake, the Norwegian Communists went so far as to offer the dissolution of their party if this would help the anti-European cause: "They hate Europe more than they hate Norwegian capitalism," Neil McInnes dryly noted. The same seemed to be true with regard to the French Communist party, as shown by its fervent opposition to EEC in the late sixties and early seventies, and when it came to advocate the Gaullist concept of "all round defence" and the *force de frappe* in 1977/78, and this at a time when Britain and West Germany had socialist governments, whereas France had not. It is only fair to add that while West European Communist parties even in their more chauvinist moods had to observe certain limits in view of their international connections, the left wing of the French and British socialist parties faced no such restraints. Hence the virulent attacks of the *Tribune* group against their German and French comrades and the almost racialist views expressed in the writings of J. P. Chevènement vis-à-vis Germany.[2] Another interesting example is Professor Andreas Papandreou, one of the leaders of the far left in Greece, combining social radicalism with the most bellicose anti-Turkish (and "anti-Zionist") views. Such chauvinist slogans were in part a calculated attempt to win over sections of the population otherwise not accessible to Communist or left-wing socialist appeal. But it is equally certain that some of the radical nationalism and the xenophobia was perfectly genuine.

With all the features that were common to the West European Communist parties, there were also substantial differences in outlook among them. Their political importance varied, so did the political problems facing them. Hence the need to examine the policy of the main parties more closely; the Italian party, both in view of its size and its role during many years as the avant-garde of Eurocommunism is the obvious starting point for an investigation of this kind.[3]

---

[2] J. P. Chevènement, *Les socialistes, les communistes et les autres* (Paris, 1977), pp. 282 ff.

[3] There is no comprehensive study of Italian Communism. But see G. Mammarella, *Il Partito Communista Italiano, 1945–1974* (Florence, 1976). G. Galli's study on the PCI deals with the early postwar period, Livio Maitan's *PCI 1945–1969* (Rome, 1969), is a Trotskyite polemic, nor is P. Spriano's *Problemi di storia del PCI* (Rome, 1971), of much help. D. L. Blackmer and S. Tarrow, *Communism in Italy and France* (Princeton, 1976) contains sociological studies. One could also mention M. Padovani, *La longue marche du PCI* (Paris, 1976), A. Levi, *PCI, la lunga marchia verso il potere* (Milan 1971), E. Bettiza, *Quale PCI* (Milan, 1971).

THE PCI

Since its emergence from illegality following the overthrow of the fascist regime, the PCI has been suspected of an inclination towards "right wing deviationism." After Stalin's death, under its long term leader, Palmiro Togliatti, it brilliantly adopted tactics that were independent in appearance rather than in substance. It always tried to keep a certain distance from the Soviet party but carefully never straying far enough to risk an irreparable break. The PCI grew steadily: in the elections of 1946 it polled 19 per cent of the electorate, less than the Socialists. Thirty years later its share had grown to 34 per cent, only a few percentage points behind the leading Christian Democrats. The growth of Italian communism has been explained against the background of increasing social tensions and economic crisis. This is certainly true in part, but it does not explain the fact that at the time of the economic *miracolo,* during the late fifties and sixties, it also continued to expand. More important perhaps for the steady rise of the PCI was the inability of the Socialists to constitute an effective left-wing alternative to communism as well as the internal divisions of the Christian Democrats, whom an "imperfect bipolarism" (G. Galli's phrase) had condemned to be in power ever since the downfall of fascism. The PCI has more members than all other European non-governing Communist parties taken together; at one time it counted 2.3 million members, subsequently this figure stabilized around the 1.5–1.6 million mark. It has a wider social base than the French Communist party; most of its leaders are of impeccable middle class origins, and it has a considerably stronger appeal to the middle class and to intellectuals than any other European party. Its influence spread from the traditionally "Red belt"—Emilia Romagna, Umbria, Toscana—to most other parts of the country. Since 1957 the PCI has favored an alliance with the middle classes, first in theory but later on as a matter of practical policy. More than any other major European Communist party it has been involved in the domestic political process, partly on the municipal and regional level, partly through its active participation in parliamentary committee work, which under the Italian system is responsible for much of the legislation. Thus a working relationship with the ruling Christian Democrats was established, and in many ways the PCI became part of the "system" in 1968–1972 when various left-of-center coalitions ruled Italy. This tacit collaboration with the Communists became a basic fact of Italian politics after July 1973. The Andreotti government in 1977 depended entirely on Communist help (or at least on their abstention) for its survival.

After the elections of 1968 the Communists made it known that they wanted to become a *partito de governo,* hence the insistence of its leader, Berlinguer, on the necessity of a "historical compromise" (first mooted as a slogan in autumn 1973) with the Christian Democrats. Thus in 1974 it came as no surprise that the PCI criticised the intransigence of its Portuguese comrades, causing them considerable embarrassment. They also digested the lesson of Chile which was that, according to Berlinguer, a broad coalition was needed, for even if the forces of the left won 51 per cent of the vote, it would be an illusion to think that this could guarantee the survival and effectiveness of the government.[4]

The PCI tried in many ways to reduce or altogether remove the traditional "anti-Communist prejudices." Having denounced NATO for many years ("Italy out of NATO, NATO out of Italy"), the PCI stopped these outright attacks around 1969 and replaced them with the demand for a gradual withdrawal. In 1975 Berlinguer was reported to have declared that Italian withdrawal from NATO would be not only impractical but also detrimental to détente, and a year later in June 1976 he was even said to have maintained that he would feel safer in NATO than in the Warsaw Pact, a statement admittedly denied a few days later. On the whole, the PCI preferred evasive answers whenever facing questions concerning its commitment to European defence. The whole issue, as they saw it, was theoretical. It was out of the question that the Warsaw Pact would ever attack, and if NATO attacked the Warsaw Pact, it was of course their duty to defend the Soviet Union.[5] As Amendola put it, no one seriously believed any longer that the Soviet Union constituted a danger to Europe. The PCI attitude towards European unity on the other hand was far more positive from the beginning, certainly more constructive than that of the Gaullists or large sections of the British Labour party. They wanted to restrict the EEC in the early

[4] *Rinascità,* October 12, 1973.

[5] Lombardo Radice, *Encounter,* May 1977; Giancarlo Pajetta, *Corriere della Serra,* May 30, 1976.

days mainly to economic activities, but subsequently they came out in favor of direct elections and the strengthening of European institutions. The overall foreign policy of the PCI was a "phasing out of the blocs" but they did not expect that this was likely to happen in the near future. In the early 1970's the Italian party became the leading critic of certain Soviet practices, its "Marxist" wing with Ingrao as spokesman, for a number of complicated reasons, taking a more emphatic view than the "reformists" under Amendola. But insofar as such criticism was openly voiced, it always concerned "certain abuses," never the basic character of the Soviet regime. In contrast to the Spanish Communists, the Italians never publicly doubted the essentially socialist character of the Soviet regime, nor did they ever criticize Soviet foreign policy which they praised as being in the interests of all mankind. The Italian Communist press followed the Soviet lead in foreign affairs down to small details— such as echoing the condemnation of the Israelis for liberating the hostages at Entebbe. Whatever criticism they voiced concerned the relationship between the Soviet Union and other Communist parties, insisting on a larger measure of autonomy for the latter. If they registered sadness about certain unduly harsh measures taken by the Soviets against dissenters or in the field of cultural policy, they always expressed the hope that such "errors" were bound to be corrected in due time.

In domestic politics their main endeavor was to gain trust and respectability. They had many sympathizers in the media; after 1975 open criticism of Communist policies in Italian newspapers, radio, and television became a rare occurrence. The PCI had not a few members and even more well-wishers in the universities, even in the bureaucracy and the judiciary. An important milestone in its rise to power was reached with the setback suffered by the Christian Democrats in the wholly unnecessary referendum about divorce of May 1974; the regional elections the year after showed that the share of the party had risen to 33 per cent and the general elections the year after confirmed this trend. Yet the party leadership was in no hurry to press its claims to be represented in the government. Their experience in local government had taught them that political responsibility involved difficult problems; goodwill was no guarantee of success. As the country went through a serious economic crisis, the prospect of sharing responsibility for unpopular measures was not particularly inviting, nor was it certain that the Communist party could "deliver" the trade unions insofar as their acceptance of a policy of austerity was concerned. The "historical compromise" meant, in the final analysis, that the Communists intended to come to power and share the spoils, not as the result of revolutionary action, not even in the wake of an electoral victory, but following a *combinazione* in time-honored Italian tradition, an agreement between the party bosses of the Christian Democrats and their own leadership. They hoped that in such an alliance real power would gradually come to rest with their own party, partly because of the greater cohesion of the PCI, partly because of structural changes in the economy and society of the country, which would increase their influence. They were in favor of pluralism, but Luigi Barzini rightly stressed that pluralism was not a synonym for liberty: "But, of course, Berlinguer never mentions the word liberty; he talks of pluralism, which would mean a return to the kind of polity that existed under feudalism where power rested with the barons; and social stability was determined by the equilibrium of power among them. That is pluralism, not liberty, and we can all envisage a modern version of it being installed in Italy via the unions and other corporate organisations. What I want is my liberty guaranteed by the law and lawful institutions, and not by the good will of a Sardinian gentleman (Berlinguer)."[6]

The Italian Communist party acquired in both West and East the reputation of being a more liberal party than all other communist parties. This was certainly true to the extent that the party did not believe in brutal purges as did the PCF (let alone the East European sister parties). Relations inside the party and its attitude towards outsiders, while not lacking passion and, on occasion bitter hostility, were on the whole more civilized than in most other parts of Europe. It is also true that the PCI showed a certain degree of latitude in its cultural policy, and that its intellectual level was higher than that of other communist parties. Within the world communist movement, to repeat once again, it insisted, whenever possible, on its independence and autonomy. It has in some respects shown very Italian features—in its tolerance (and its opportunism), in its desire to be all things to all people—reformist and rev-

[6] George Urban, "Dante, the Italians the PCI." A conversation with Luigi Barzini, *Survey* (Spring 1976), 130.

olutionary, fiercely independent and unswervingly loyal to the Soviet Union, to preach austerity and discipline, and at the same time to foment strikes and the dislocation of the economy. It would be unjust to regard this as mere opportunism and a lack of sincerity; as a mass party the PCI had to accommodate its domestic and foreign strategy to conflicting interests. That the PCI is not a revolutionary party goes without saying, but this is also true for the most orthodox Communist parties in Europe. But all this does not mean that it has become a democratic party, and barring unforseen circumstances it is not likely that it will cut the umbilical cord linking it with the Soviet Union, partly, no doubt, out of the fear that this would cause a split in its own ranks. The PCI is still Leninist, as shown by the lack of inner-party democracy. Some observers had predicted in the 1950's that the PCI would gradually transform itself into a democratic party, but this optimism was not born out by the course of events during the subsequent two decades. The slogan proudly proclaimed by the French Communists certainly applies in equal measure to the PCI—it is not a party like the others.

THE PCF

Communism in post-war France has fared less well than in Italy. In the immediate post-war period the PCF was stronger than the PCI; its share in the elections of 1946 was 28.6%. But it never again had a similar success, and in recent years its share of the poll has slowly decreased. After the end of the war it was for almost three decades the leading force on the left, but after 1973 it was overtaken by a suddenly revived Socialist party. Its membership (350,000–400,000) is bigger, it is far better organized and has much more cohesion than the Socialists, and it is also by far the richer party. But without Socialist help there is little hope that it can break out of its political isolation. The reasons are largely historical; the PCF has been traditionally a working-class party, even though the majority of French workers never joined it. *Ouvrièrisme* has been something of a cult in the PCF which always proudly pointed to the fact that its leaders, from Thorez to Waldeck-Rochet and Marchais, had been manual workers in their youth. While the strong emphasis on its working class character gave the party a secure and faithful base, unlikely to be shaken in its loyalty by events abroad or at home, it has limited its appeal. This is true with regard to the lower middle class, the peasantry, even the intelligentsia. While French intellectuals for the greater part gravitate towards the left, including the extreme left, the number of intellectuals who actually remained in the party was always much smaller than those who had left the PCF. Unlike Italy, the history of the relations between the party and the intellectuals is an unhappy tale of three decades of deviations, purges, mutual recriminations. Nor has the geographical pattern of communist strength substantially changed, despite the process of industrialization. The Nord, the Paris region, Limousin, Languedoc, and Provence–Cote d'Azur have been its traditional strongholds—elsewhere the influence of the party has remained limited.

The internal history of the PCF during the 1960's and the early '70's is of limited interest only in the present context.[7] The party moved into new, streamlined headquarters and at the Twentieth Congress (1972) it was announced that 40% of the delegates (the average age of whom was 33) had joined the party only during the last four years. But if the lower and middle echelons were rejuvenated, the top leadership of the party remained firmly in the hands of men such as Marchais, Plissonier, Kanapa, Laurent, Leroy, and Segui, whose careers had started, and whose political outlook had been formed, in the Stalin era. Waldeck-Rochet who succeeded Thorez in 1964 had cautiously moved towards a more liberal line at home and a more independent stand within the world communist movement. This lasting, roughly speaking, from 1965 to 1968, was so modest in scope as to be noticed only by the experts, and, in any case, remained a mere interlude, for after the Paris "events" and the Soviet invasion of Czechoslovakia in 1968 there was a return to the old orthodoxy. Waldeck-Rochet, who was incapacitated by illness in 1969, was succeeded by George Marchais. Why Marchais was chosen and by whom, has remained something of a puzzle; the Central Committee of the PCF, in any case, did not elect him.

---

[7] The most detailed histories are Jacques Fauvet, *Histoire du Parti Communiste Francaise,* second ed. 2 vols. (Paris, 1977), and R. Tiersky, *French Communism* (New York, 1974). For the more recent developments the following are of interest: A. Barjonet, *Le PCF* (Paris, 1969). A. Kriegel, *Communisme au Miroir Francaise* (Paris, 1974), and Laurens and T. Pfister, *Les Nouveaux Communistes* (Paris, 1973).

The establishment of a united front with the Socialists has been official PCF policy since Thorez's last years. In the presidential elections of 1965 the Communists had voted for Mitterand, and the combined forces of the left had achieved a remarkable success (45%), even if their candidate did not win. In 1969 they had gone it alone, again with relatively good results (21%), but in the final analysis it was no more than another reminder that by their efforts alone they would never escape from the political ghetto. They needed the help of a socialist party which was relatively strong, but not too strong; such a party reappeared under the leadership of François Mitterand in the early 70's. In 1972 a common program between Socialists and Communists was signed; while the *Union de la Gauche* went through a period of considerable stress in 1974/75 when the Communists, feeling threatened by an unexpected increase in Socialist strength, decided to court the Gaullists, there was no break, and the two parties continued to collaborate up to the sudden reversal of the Communist strategy which occurred in the summer of 1977.

Meanwhile, to everyone's surprise, the PCF underwent, almost overnight, a conversion to Eurocommunism. It was sudden, it came late, and it provoked a great deal of incredulity. Whereas in Italy the development towards greater autonomy had been a gradual process accompanied by much debate with its origins back in the 1950's, there was nothing to prepare the outside public for such a startling denouement in France. The PCF had been a most reliable pillar of Soviet policy in Europe, the most ardent advocate of the unity of the camp. True, it had published a short communiqué criticizing the Soviet invasion of Czechoslovakia in 1968, but this had been so grudging and half-hearted as to amount virtually to a justification of the Soviet action. The PCF was, in actual fact, the main opponent of the attempts of the PCI to establish some form of (West European) Communist co-operation; occasionally the French Communists would even outdo their Russian comrades as keepers of Leninist orthodoxy. Jean Kanapa, a leading member of the Politburo complained as late as 1975 that the term "proletarian internationalism" had been dropped in an official resolution adopted by an international Communist Conference, knowing full well what the real meaning of the slogan was, and that it had been deleted precisely for this reason. Yet it was the same Kanapa who only a few months later appeared as one of the main protagonists of both human rights and full independence for his party. This inevitably raised questions of the motive for the conversion of the PCF and whether, and to what extent, it could be taken seriously.

Some resentment against Soviet policy, to be sure, had been smoldering in the ranks of the PCF. This dated back to the early 1960's, and it was rooted in what the French Communists considered as the unnecessarily friendly attitude on the part of the Soviet Union towards de Gaulle. The PCF was even more peeved when such friendship was later extended to Pompidou and Giscard. True, the PCF had also sometimes expressed its appreciation for the "positive aspects" of Gaullism in the field of foreign policy (i.e. its anti-Americanism and its efforts to sabotage European unity) and it had helped to save the regime in 1968. But in their view the Soviet leaders should not have interfered in French domestic affairs in a way that was bound to damage the electoral prospects of the PCF. These quarrels between Paris and Moscow no doubt caused some bad blood, but they did not concern matters of principle.

It was only in 1975 that the French Communists decided to move towards closer collaboration with other West European Communist parties. Their violent opposition to the EEC gradually changed to lukewarm support, or at least tolerance. But they still refused to express any support for Soviet and East European dissidents, and at the time of the struggle for power in Portugal they expressed, unlike the PCI, full support for the rabidly anti-socialist policy followed by the Portuguese Communists under Cunhal. The turning point in the process of their conversion came sometime in the autumn of 1975. In November 1975 Marchais went to Rome and signed a declaration of solidarity with Berlinguer, hailed as historic by the PCF. Having given full support to the Soviet leadership in its preparations for the European Communist conference,it suddenly switched sides and joined the autonomists who argued that such a conference was unnecessary and that, in any case, it should not adopt any binding resolutions.

The next month, a BBC film on Soviet labor camps was shown on French television. When the PCF condemned such "deviations from socialist legality," an angry polemic between *Pravda* and *Humanité* ensued. Relations deteriorated quickly, and in January 1976 Georges Marchais stated that the differences between his party and the Soviet leadership were so deep that any meeting between him and Brezhnev was quite pointless.[8] Soon afterwards at the Twenty-second Congress of the PCF he was to tell the party comrades that the slogan of the dictatorship of the proletariat had been relegated to the dustbin of history. Francis Cohen, a party philosopher, wrote about the necessity for a broader democracy in the USSR, Jean Kanapa even urged democratic socialism—a term bound to provoke great indignation among the old comrades, who had grown up in the Leninist school and to whom such reformist deviations were anathema. The PCF not only fully affirmed its attachment to human rights in general, it also for the first time openly expressed strong support for some Soviet dissidents, such as the mathematician Pliush. In a meeting in Madrid with the leaders of the Italian and Spanish parties the French freely accepted the Euro-Communist label, and upon his return Marchais said that Eurocommunism was not (as some reactionaries argued) a mere farce—it was something serious. But with all this there were fairly narrow limits to Eurocommunist solidarity; when Carrillo was attacked as a renegade by the Soviet press in June 1977 the French, even more than the Italians, were exceedingly reluctant to come to his help, even though they had just signed a solemn declaration with the PCE, promising to respect universal suffrage, political pluralism, and individual freedom.

The sudden switch in the position of the PCF was bound to encounter a great deal of disbelief. It was not only that the party itself had not become democratic in structure: the new "liberal" line was adopted unanimously, without discussion, in the very same manner as the old orthodox line had been introduced at an earlier date. The new policy was somehow out of line with the whole tradition of the PCF; it seemed like a badly fitting suit on a customer who had been persuaded to improve his outward appearance. But the customer still felt ill at ease; it was certainly comforting to know that the PCF had in principle embraced pluralism, but when Marchais mentioned East Germany, Poland, and Bulgaria as examples of pluralist regimes he certainly failed to inspire confidence. True, the leaders of the PCF had accepted the need for some concessions in their dealings with the Socialists, but sub-

[8] Neil McInnes, *Euro-Communism* (Beverley Hills, 1976), pp. 16 ff. Annie Kriegel, *Un Autre Communisme* (Paris, 1977), pp. 49 ff. Heinz Timmermann, *Moskau und der europäische Kommunismus nach der Gipfelkonferenz von Ost-Berlin* (Köln, 1977), pp. 29 ff.

sequent events were again to show how narrowly such compromises were defined. If the PCF has changed, the single most important motive was nationalism. The very nationalism in which their strong anti-American, anti-German, and, indeed, anti-European attitude was rooted also explains their growing resentment against Russian tutelage. Loyal Marxists-Leninists, they were also heirs to a civilization more ancient and superior to that of Eastern Europe. It was bad enough, as they saw it, that there had been so much remote control of the PCF during the first five decades of its existence and there was no good reason that this state of affairs should continue.

Not a few observers of the French political scene mistakenly believed for a while that as far as the PCF was concerned, de-Sovietization equalled democratization. During the election campaign of 1978 it became clear that such optimism was, at best, premature: there is, after all, a time-honored tradition of dictatorship *au couleurs de la France*. The French Communist party remains a non-democratic, monolithic force, more aggressive, less likely to compromise than it had been during the Popular Front period in the 1930's or in the post-war years.

THE PCE

Around 1975 the PCE replaced the PCI as the most outspoken Eurocommunist party, probably to the Italians' relief: "The Spanish say what the Italians think," in the words of one commentator. Prior to Franco's death the leaders of the PCE had been in exile, and even after the legalization of the party, its political importance (as the outcome of the Spanish elections in June 1977 was to show) was not comparable to that of its French or Italian sister parties. If the story of the PCE is nevertheless of considerable interest, it is precisely in view of its avant-garde role among the Eurocommunists.

It was argued in later years that the liberal spirit and the independence shown by the Spanish Communists in the 1970's had its roots in the popular front strategy (the policy of "national reconciliation") first proclaimed by the PCE in 1956. It is true that the declared policy of the PCE during the subsequent years was so moderate, its willingness to enter into alliances with all and any critic of Franco so sweeping, as to raise much criticism on the left.[9] The Communist party, Carrillo declared in 1965, believed less than anyone else in making the Communist revolution in Spain. But such views would not necessarily have brought the leadership of the PCE into serious conflict with the Russians, who at the time were themselves moving towards some form of diplomatic co-existence with the Franco regime. For the deeper roots of the conflict which occurred in the 1970's one has to look to an even earlier period. After their defeat in the Civil War many of the leaders and militants of the PCE went into exile in the Soviet Union. Their experiences in Russia were mostly unfortunate; they certainly did not strengthen their belief in the Soviet version of communism. By the middle sixties the PCE had developed fairly close ties with the Italian Communists, and in 1968 they welcomed the Czech spring with great enthusiasm.[10] Their protest against the Soviet intervention was also among the sharpest. This seems not however to have unduly troubled the Russians: "Yours is only a small party," Suslov allegedly told La Pasionaria. Spanish criticism of Soviet policy continued during the subsequent years; this annoyed the Russians, and since the Spanish party was indeed small and materially dependent on Moscow, an attempt was made to split it. The Garcia-Gomez faction, later joined by Enrique Lister, one of the Civil War heroes, established itself as a rival party; for a while there were two organizations bitterly fighting each other, even two *Mundo Obrero*'s, the party's theoretical mouthpiece. The pro-Soviet group eventually collapsed but not without having caused some damage to the majority faction. These events did not make Carrillo and his friends any more kindly disposed towards Moscow, and this, of course, also helps to explain the particular bitterness of the Spanish criticism of the Soviet Union. So far, the Soviet reaction had been by proxy, but in February 1974 the Soviet leadership directly attacked the Spanish comrades in terms which had not been heard for many years in the world Communist movement. The PCE, it was said, had sided with the declared enemies of the Soviet socialist system by spreading lies about the absence of democracy in the USSR. They were accused of being neutral in the Sino-Soviet dispute and even of trying to impose their

[9] Paul Preston (ed.), *Spain in Crisis* (London, 1976), pp. 139 ff.
[10] G. Hermet, *The Communists in Spain* (London, 1974), pp. 78 ff.

own "European alternative" (the term "Eurocommunism" not having been coined yet) on the other European parties.[11] There was a short-lived reconciliation, but the PCE did not change its basic outlook, nor did it make a secret of its convictions. As Carrillo defiantly declared on the East Berlin conference of June 1976: "For years Moscow was our Rome. We spoke of the Great October Socialist Revolution as if it were our Christmas. That was the period of our infancy; today we have grown up." It is easy to imagine the anger of the men in the Kremlin and the wish to slap down impertinent critics daring to provoke the mighty Soviet Union by comparing the Kremlin with the Vatican, its leaders with Popes and Cardinals, and its "scientific" ideology with a church dogma. The opportunity came a year later. In the first general elections to take place in Spain for more than forty years, the PCE fared unexpectedly badly, polling less than 10% of the vote. This made Carrillo and his party vulnerable to attack, for it showed that his "anti-Soviet" line, far from attracting votes, had actually repelled voters. Even Cunhal in neighboring Portugal had done better. (The argument was not quite convincing, if only because unreconstructed Stalinism was bound to be more attractive in a country at a considerably lower stage of social and political development such as Portugal). But the PCE was now shown to be a small party, and while Moscow had to think twice before frontally assaulting the PCF or PCI, there were no such inhibitions vis-à-vis the Spanish.

While in hiding in Madrid during the months before the elections, Carrillo had worked on a book, *Euro-Comunismo y Estado,* which now became the butt of the Soviet attack.[12] Carrillo in his book had argued "that it is our task to demonstrate that democracy is not the same thing as capitalism as the bourgeois parties claimed." But on the other hand it was also true that socialism did not equal Soviet domination. The Soviet Union was certainly not a capitalist state, but neither was it a workers' democracy; at best it could be regarded as an intermediate phase be-

---

[11] The attack was published in *Partinaya Zhizn,* no. 4 (1974). It was directed against a report made by Manuel Azcarate at a PCE congress five months earlier and was ostensibly directed only against him. But there was every reason to assume that it was directed against the whole PCE leadership. Azcarate's speech was originally published in *Nuestra Bandera,* 4, 1973.

[12] (Barcelona, 1977).

tween a capitalist state and an authentic socialist state.[13] But the transformation of the state had become blocked as the failure of the Khrushchev experiment had demonstrated. The system had not been democratized; on the contrary, it had become a brake on the evolution towards genuine workers' democracy. What is more, it retained degenerative, coercive aspects elsewhere associated only with imperialist states—such as brutally demonstrated in the military occupation of Czechoslovakia. Hence the task of Eurocommunism to demonstrate that the victory of socialist forces in Western Europe would not in the least augment Soviet state power, or mean the extension of the Soviet model of the one-party state: "It will be an independent experience, with a more advanced socialism which will have a positive influence on the democratic evolution of the existing socialist regimes."[14] Therefore it was essential that Communists should remain independent with regard to the Soviet state, some aspects of which were in a certain sense totalitarian.

The Soviet leaders would have put up with the "reformist" and "social-democratic" deviations of Carrillo; they might have accepted the commitment to parliamentary democracy and the playing down of the Leninist doctrine of the vanguard role of the Communist party and the "hegemony of the Proletariat." It is doubtful whether they could have let pass statements such as that the aim of Eurocommunism was not to extend Soviet influence, but to create a multi-polar world in which a European defense system would be independent of both the United States and the Soviet Union. Such equations of United States imperialism with Soviet foreign policy were unseemly to say the least. What they could not possibly accept was that the socialist character of the Soviet Union was called into question and the assertion that it remained a dictatorship "with certain totalitarian features." Thus Carrillo was attacked for his "profound hostility to the Soviet Union," for his conscious anti-Sovietism, for "proposing a program that was bound to strengthen the aggressive NATO alliance."[15] Eurocommunism à la Carrillo, the Soviets argued, was simply anti-Sovietism, a concept of setting the West Euro-

[13] Ibid., p. 209.
[14] Ibid., p. 51.
[15] "Contrary to the Interest of Peace and Socialism in Europe," *New Times*, June 21, 1977.

pean Communist parties apart as a force opposed primarily to the socialist countries. Carrillo, the Soviets argued, had written and spoken about
the Soviet Union and CPSU in terms "which even the most reactionary
writers do not often venture to use."

Carrillo was supported by his own party against the Soviet attacks,
but all the help he received from the French comrades was a single sentence in a *Humanité* editorial (June 24, 1977); the PCI declared that
while they regretted the tenor of the Soviet attack, they did not necessarily agree with all of Carrillo's assertions.[16] The Carrillo case showed
the limits of Eurocommunist solidarity; the big Communist parties
wanted to prevent a split; Carrillo had clearly overstepped the boundary
of what was permissible, and the leader of the PCE subsequently retreated from some of his more exposed positions so as to mend relations
with Moscow.

THE SOVIET UNION AND EUROCOMMUNISM

The Soviet attacks against Carrillo's book were no more than the culmination of a process that had begun several years before. If in the mid-fif-
ties Yugoslavia had been granted the right of ideological and political
autonomy, the Soviet leaders could still argue that Yugoslavia was an
exceptional case, that for historical reasons amends had to be made at
least temporarily for Stalin's tactlessness. Furthermore, Yugoslavia
merely insisted on its own "road to socialism" which in the final analysis
did not radically differ from the other "socialist" countries—it still ad-
hered to the Leninist principle of "democratic centralism," it criticized
Soviet policy mainly insofar as relations between the two countries were
concerned, there was no fundamental critique of Leninism. The case of
China was, of course, different; there had been a real schism, and with
schismatics one did not argue—they were excommunicated.

[16] Some of Carrillo's judgments were "harsh and superficial" Giancarlo Pajetta, the
shadow foreign minister of the PCI, noted (*Der Spiegel*, July 11, 1977), but the Soviet
argumentation had also been "meagre". It had not attempted to reason or argue. In his
view Soviet society was socialist, even though it had its illiberal aspects. But because of
the stormy economic growth of the socialist countries there was every reason to believe
that their institutions would become more democratic.

During the 1950's and '60's most Asian Communist parties drifted away from Moscow without necessarily identifying themselves with the Maoist position. In these circumstances the preservation of the unity of what was left of the Communist camp in Europe and the Americas was all the more important from the Soviet point of view. The Soviet leaders accepted that they could no longer preserve the monolithic character of the Communist bloc, and they realized that the non-ruling Communist parties were exposed to all kinds of temptations, and that there was a need for far-reaching tactical concessions. Even in the Stalin era foreign Communist parties had been given some latitude. But this was a question of maneuvering, of tactics, of approach; there could be no compromise with regard to issues of principles and substance. Thus, the Russians were quite willing to turn a blind eye to certain manifestations of blatant "reformism"; this was, after all, part of the price that had to be paid for détente. They were willing to concede regional co-operation between European Communist parties even though they had misgivings, quite rightly from their point of view, about the possible consequences. Hard pressed, they would refrain from openly opposing the demand for greater autonomy on the part of the ruling parties, provided that these remained loyal to the Soviet Union, acknowledged its leading role in the Communist camp, and abstained from any criticism of Soviet domestic and foreign policy. But they still had a vital interest in the continued existence of the bloc, *their* bloc.

This, in briefest outline, was the Soviet line in the 1960's and 1970's. But meanwhile the trend towards greater independence had gathered momentum as many of the smaller parties split; for example the Finnish, the Greek, the British, and the Danish parties. Sometimes where these splits were quite unconnected with Eurocommunism (as in Finland) the Soviet leaders recognized both parties, and, indeed, tried to bring about a reconciliation between them. Elsewhere, as in Greece, they supported the more orthodox against the "liberal" wing. It has been mentioned that in Spain they had tried unsuccessfully to split the party and in Austria they had helped to depose the "liberal" leadership. But the centrifugal, separatist tendencies asserted themselves in many parties; and from time to time an ingenious compromise formula would be found on the basis of which resolutions could be signed, appeals be issued, and the unity of the camp be proclaimed. But invariably, after a few weeks, it would appear that the various parties gave these resolutions quite different meanings. As the foreign Communists saw it, the Soviet example did indeed offer many lessons, but, not all of them were positive. The Soviet Union had become a superpower, but politically and ideologically its attraction had declined. Outside observers claimed they could detect certain differences in the approach of the Soviet leaders: Brezhnev and his adviser Zaglyadin represented a more conciliatory attitude, whereas Suslov, Ponomaryov, and Zarodov appeared to be hardliners. But these were only minor nuances; inasmuch as the basic principle of Soviet hegemony was concerned there were no differences between them. The Soviet leaders believed, as Dimitrov had said in a famous speech many years ago, that the attitude towards the Soviet Union was still the acid test for every Communist.[17] The Eurocommunists, on the other hand, were firmly convinced that this sort of loyalty test belonged to a bygone period and that the Soviet comrades would have to accept willy-nilly that the world had changed since the days of the Comintern and the Cominform.

Thus an uneasy peace prevailed throughout the seventies in the Communist camp, interrupted by occasional conflicts, polemics, and recriminations. What prevented a final split was the correct realization that both sides would suffer if they were to part ways for good. This *modus vivendi* was unsatisfactory from the point of view of the CPSU, nor was it ideal for the European parties; but, for the time being, there was no other solution in sight.

INTERPRETATIONS OF EUROCOMMUNISM

The Eurocommunist phenomenon has been subject to greatly conflicting interpretations. The idea that it was no more than a giant charade was not shared by many observers. (It was recalled that similar skepticism at the time of the Sino-Soviet split had been altogether erroneous.) World communism was in a state of disarray, but there was no

---

[17] It would have been in questionable taste if such a declaration had come from a Soviet leader and for this reason the invocation of slogans of this kind was traditionally left to the Bulgarians. Cf. T. Shivkoff in *Neues Deutschland*, June 30, 1976; A. Lilof, *Rabotnichesko Delo*, December 16, 1976.

agreement on the implications of this process. Some observers claimed that a profound change had taken place in West (and South) European communism. The more radical proponents of this thesis regarded West European communism in the middle seventies as little more than a movement of urban reform (just as the Chinese Communists had been welcomed in the West in the late 1940's as agrarian reformers). Others were less sanguine in their appraisal of Communist intentions and their commitments to human rights and democratic values. But they too, believed that West European communism was no longer a revolutionary force and that, given certain conditions (such as in Italy), it could be a stabilizing force in a society in a state of advanced disintegration. Practice, as some commentators noted, weighs more heavily than doctrine; if no longer in opposition, if exposed to the realities of politics, Eurocommunism was bound to become even more reformist than it was already. A substantial part of the Communist vote in the West had always been a protest vote; once in power the Communists would lose some of their support and they would, furthermore, be subjected to an acid test: if they could not live up to their promises, they would lose their popularity and suffer electoral defeat. If they reneged on their professed commitment to democratic procedure, they would be overthrown by non-democratic means. True, Communist participation in Western governments would create certain problems for NATO and European defence but these difficulties could well be transient. The PCI after all, did not really want Soviet bases on Italian soil. On the contrary, Eurocommunism (as Mr. Vance, the American Secretary of State, and others had put it) would be more of a problem for the Soviet Union than the West. For, as experience had shown, the Soviet leaders were exceedingly sensitive with regard to the emergence of any Communism different from their own which would put into doubt not just their rigid ideology but the very legitimacy of their rule. In any case (it was argued) there was nothing Western governments could possibly do if the Communists did emerge as the strongest political force in a certain country. Direct interference was *a priori* ruled out, indirect pressure would also be ineffective. If so, a "dialogue" with the Eurocommunists would help to domesticate them, to prepare them for the realities of political power, and perhaps, ultimately, lead to the discovery of some common interests.

The sceptics maintained, on the other hand, that while Communism in Europe had indeed undergone changes, many of these were neither unprecedented nor irrevocable. French Communists, for instance, had been vociferous champions of liberty and national unity at the time of the Popular Front (1935–37) and again at the end of the Second World War (1944–47), but this had by no means prevented a return to Stalinist orthodoxy and cold war intransigence later on. It was quite true that a post-Stalinist generation had grown up and now constituted the bulk of the party cadres. But such rejuvenation of the party cadres was no guarantee of greater freedom. The West European Communist parties had certainly been modernized, but no one could fairly argue that they had become more democratic. Could one safely conclude that a party that was not itself democratic would abide by democratic rules in its relations with others? Those who saw reason for optimism rested their argument on two tacit assumptions, namely that what had happened in the Soviet Union, Eastern Europe, in China, Cambodia, or Cuba was somehow an aberration from the norm ("if only Communism had first prevailed in advanced countries . . ."), and secondly, that, given the democratic traditions and the free institutions of the West, and, above all the new spirit of a young generation, there was little danger that such a process would repeat itself in Europe. But such assumptions were anything but Marxist in inspiration; for a Marxist history is subject to certain rules, and how could it be an accident that communism had prevailed in backward and not economically developed countries? The historical record showed that wherever communism had come to power it had developed into a despotic regime. The trend towards totalitarianism had not been the exception but the rule. Thus, even if one believed in the good intentions of the Eurocommunists, it by no means followed that these intentions were a guarantee for the continued existence of democratic institutions and civil liberties. Perhaps they were sincere, but Lenin too had been sincere (as L. Kolakowski and others pointed out) when, a few months before the revolution of 1917 he predicted in *State and Revolution* that the future Communist society would be free of constraint and oppression, that it would be a participatory democracy, unprecedented in the annals of mankind, and that soon the state would wither away altogether.

The fact that "Communism with a human face" has so far nowhere appeared, is not, of course, conclusive evidence that this can never happen. But the evidence is against it, and the prospects are inauspicious. The main motive force of Eurocommunism in France is nationalism rather than humanism or liberalism, or the ardent desire for freedom. The most one can expect from a party of this kind is a Roumanian-style political regime, more independent perhaps from the Soviet Union but not in essence different. The realities of power sharing and the fear of losing votes may cause a split in Communist ranks. But communist cohesion and discipline is still greater than within other parties, and the likelihood that these will split is also greater. Some Western European Socialist parties include, moreover, substantial groups which subscribe only half-heartedly to the basic tenets of democratic socialism and who advocate close co-operation with the Communists at almost any price.

Some leading political commentators have pointed to the political consequences of popular front rule. All of Europe faces, as Raymond Aron has put it, stagflation—the English disease. Popular front governments would combat unemployment and inflation by measures that are bound to aggravate these evils. Their professed aim is the redistribution of national income; to that end they will further augment the part of the state in the national economy. Investment will decline, new wealth will not be created, the bureaucracy will swell, the productive sector of the economy diminish. Such a state of affairs may continue for a few years, but sooner or later it will lead to a siege economy, something akin to a corporate state, with an uneasy balance of power between unions, employers, and the state. But since all European countries depended on foreign trade, a state of siege economy cannot provide solutions; eventually the country in question will be absorbed in the "socialist world market." This, of course, will not solve economic problems either, as the East European experience had shown. But it will silence criticism, putting an end to the discussions about the advantages and disadvantages of democracy and freedom—and a great many other things besides.[18] Such predictions may be too pessimistic: a popular front government may carry out some sensible reforms and the swelling of the bureaucratic apparatus does not necessarily enhance the electoral prospects of left-wing parties. But even those who take a less pessimistic view of the economic and political consequences of popular front governments can-

---

[18] Raymond Aron, *Plaidoyer pour L'Europe Décadente* (Paris, 1977), p. 482.

not ignore the geopolitical, and political-military implications. If freedom has been preserved in Western Europe since the end of the Second World War, if part of the continent has been relatively immune to Soviet pressure, this was because of the existence of a military balance. But for this fragile balance, even the Communist parties of Italy, France, and Spain would not have been able to express their heretical views. The Eurocommunists took this state of affairs for granted, they had no wish to share the fate of Dubcek. But the inevitable consequence of their policy is to weaken European defense and the American commitment, thus undermining the balance. Berlinguer and Carrillo have stressed on occasion the value of keeping NATO intact a little longer until all military blocs have been removed; Marchais has been bitterly opposed not only to NATO but to all forms of military co-operation in Europe. Such prospects will not alarm those who have persuaded themselves that military power no longer counts in the last quarter of the century; alll others will feel concern.

These, in brief outline, are the main arguments voiced in the debate about Eurocommunism during the second half of the seventies. In many ways it is impossible to generalize about *Eurocommunism* which serves as a label for political movements which differ in some important respects from each other. The motives which caused the PCE to dissociate itself from Moscow are not those that impelled the PCF to stress its "patriotic character." The political context varies from country to country, so does the extent of the heresy. It could be argued, for instance, that there is a chance that the Italian Communists would be sucked into the quagmire, as so many well meaning revolutionaries before them; perhaps their élan would be wasted in the long battles of attrition facing them. There has always been something slightly suspect about Italian revolutionary heroes; as Carlyle told Mazzini—"You talk too much." Admirable in many respects, capable of heroic deeds and self-sacrifice, they have seldom shown an equal measure of perseverance and hard work. Such assumptions are partly based on the civilized and relatively moderate level of political intercourse in Italy on one hand (as far as the major political parties are concerned), but also on the changes that might set in once the PCI becomes a fully fledged pillar of the "system," having to suffer the corrosive impact of intrigues and corruption. But this, in final analysis, is no more than a possibility, and if there is such a chance in Italy, the prospects for a similar development in France are virtually non-existent.[19]

Seen from Moscow, Eurocommunism in 1978 is not a schism but an irritation, albeit, on occasion, a major one. No final break has taken place. Kolakowski has defined the Eurocommunist parties as "slightly heretical and slightly rebellious, yet essentially members of the same Communist fraternity."[20] "Essentially" is surely the key word in this context. The Eurocommunists certainly want to transform the character of their fraternity, they want less discipline and a looser association with limited liability—a non-aligned communism. It is also true that the views of some members of the Eurocommunist group are more radical than those of others. If the Soviet leaders showed considerable nervousness facing such modest demands, it was simply because experience had not taught them how to cope with critics who could not be dealt with by "administrative means"—to use that well-known Soviet euphemism. But the danger of "ideological infection" invoked by some misguided Western observers is minimal. East European countries need no ideological inspiration from outside; they are quite familiar with conditions of life under communism. They are, however, tied to the Soviet Union not by ideological links but by the realities of power. Inside the Soviet Union, Eurocommunist heresy would cause no more than a ripple even if a "Communist regime with a human face" one day emerged somewhere in Western Europe. In view of the specific character of Soviet society, discussed elsewhere in this study, and the absence of a tradition of free institutions, a "liberal" Communist regime would not constitute a serious challenge to the Soviet leadership in the forseeable future.

Eurocommunism, to be sure contains the seeds of a genuine heresy, but not all seeds sprout and grow and not all incipient heresies are pursued to their logical conclusion. Paradoxically, Dimitrov's dictum

[19] Similar mistakes, it will be recalled, had been committed by Western observers appraising Italian fascism in its early days. This is not to deny that Italian fascism differed in essential respects from Nazism, and that it was infinitely more human: the number of political executions during the whole fascist era was minute, and there were not that many political arrests either. Yet the regime was still fascist; nor did the differences prevent Italy from joining Germany in the war.

[20] *Encounter,* August 1977.

about loyalty to the Soviet Union being the decisive test for every Communist remains true in the 1970's. If the Eurocommunist leaders believe or profess to believe, that the Soviet Union constitutes a model of socialism and democracy, a higher form of social and political organization than achieved anywhere else, they are not genuinely independent nor can their commitment to democratic values be relied upon.[21]

And even if they advance to the stage of genuine independence there still remain vexing questions concerning the substance of communist policies. One day, at some considerable risk, their attachment to human freedoms will be tested. Only then will it appear to what extent the character of the European Communist parties has changed; whether, in short, the Communist parties have ceased to be Leninist, aiming at a dictatorship. And it is quite likely that even then there may be no conclusive general answer, for some parties may undergo such a transformation while others may not.

[21] Other recent publications on Eurocommunism include Bernardo Valli, *Gli Eurocomunisti* (Bompiani, 1976); S. Segre, *A chi fa paura l'eurocomunismo* (Guaraldi, 1976); G. Luciani, *Il PCI e il capitalismo* (Longanesi, 1977); Manfred Steinkuehler, *Eurokommunismus im Widerspruch* (Koeln, 1977); Aldo Rizzo, *La Frontiera dell' Eurocomunismo* (Rome, 1977).

5

EUROSOCIALISM

In the 1930's it was more or less taken for granted that Social Democracy had fallen, never to rise again. But the obituaries on its tragic death were premature, for after 1945 social democratic parties everywhere emerged from the ashes, and their political influence was, in fact, greater than at any previous period. During the 1970's, the period under review in the present study, Social Democrats were represented at one time or another in all European governments; sometimes they governed alone, sometimes in co-operation with other parties. When they were not in power they constituted, with one major exception (Italy), the main opposition party.

West Germany was ruled by the Social Democrats (SPD), the senior partner in a coalition government which included the Liberals, from 1969 onwards. In Britain Labour was defeated in 1970, but returned to power four years later. In Austria the Social Democrats formed the government from March 1970 onwards, much of the time based on an absolute majority. In Finland they were represented in most cabinets from 1966. In Denmark they were the governing party except for a short period between December 1973 and January 1975; in Norway they were in power for much of the time from 1971 onwards, and in Sweden they were ousted in October 1976, after ruling the country for several decades, but still remained the biggest party by far. In Belgium, Holland, and Switzerland, even in Eire, they were represented in the government. In Portugal, after the overthrow of the dictatorship, the Socialists emerged as the strongest party. In the first free elections in Spain they came in a close second, and in France the revived PS (Parti Socialiste) constituted the main opposition force. The same is true with regard to Papandreou's "Pasok" since the elections of November 1977. Taking Western Europe as a whole, Social Democracy was the most important political force. Paradoxically the Social Democrats themselves were hardly aware of the fact, partly no doubt because there was not much cohesion and collaboration among the various parties. They did not have that much in common with each other, and the Socialist International was little more (as someone unkindly put it) than a postal address in North West London. Their ideological inspiration differed greatly. The British Labour Party was traditionally Methodist rather than Marxist. Some continental parties were avowedly reformist and pragmatist, others were Marxist in letter but not in practice, such as the Italian PSI. Colonel Khadafi provides ideological inspiration for the Greek "Pasok" party. Yet in many respects they faced problems that were remarkably similar. In most European countries, with the exception only of the least developed, a welfare state came into being after the Second World War, and the question was increasingly asked whether Social Democracy had concluded its historical mission in presiding over the management of such a state or whether this was merely a milestone on the road to a truly radical, socialist transformation of society. A society of this kind was the professed aim of every Marxist, and even Clause Four of the constitution of the British Labour Party said that its aim was "to secure for the workers by hand or by brain the full fruits of their industry and the most equitable distribution thereof that may be possible upon the basis of the common ownership of the means of production, distribution and exchange." This constitution had been drawn up in 1918, and even forty years later great was the consternation when some leaders dared to question it. Eventually it was amended by Aneurin Bevan to mean that the Labour Party's economic and social objectives could be achieved only through an expansion of common ownership substantial enough to give the community power over the commanding heights of the economy. But this formulation too was only of limited help as a guide to policy-making. Experience in post-war Europe had shown that on one hand all governments had acquired tremendous economic power quite irrespective of nationalization, and that on the other hand nationalization was no panacea; the governments which had nationalized least, weathered best the economic storms and, perhaps even more surprisingly, suffered less from strikes and other manifestations of social discontent. It appeared that the issue of nationalization was of only limited interest to the wider public: whether profits or losses were incurred by the state or by a private company was not a matter of vital concern to the average citizen. In theory, nationalized industries belonged to the public, but the public's influence on the conduct of these industries was usually small and frequently non-existent. "Nationalization" was clearly no synonym for "common ownership" or "community power"—real power still rested with the bureaucracy and the state apparatus. Thus among all socialist parties new ideas were mooted about different forms of public ownership, "workers participation," "workers control," "autogestion," or, at the very least, co-determination, *Mitbestimmung*. The Communists revealed less enthusiasm in this respect; experience in Eastern Europe had shown them the advantages of autocratic management over industrial democracy.

The more successful Socialist movements of Western Europe transformed themselves during the post-war period from working class parties into political movements with a wider popular basis. But they still stressed that workers would continue to find their natural place in these parties. The Socialist parties were the champions of social justice and greater equality, advocating equal opportunities for all and the integration of the "marginal" sections of society. This transformation made it necessary to re-examine the traditional aims and the meaning of socialism, a re-examination that had become necessary in any case in view of the technological and scientific revolution which had created problems that could not have been forseen by earlier theorists of socialism. The welfare state could be financed only by a vast increase in public spending. And there was the danger that this increase would outstrip economic growth and that, as a result, investment in industry would decline, thus mortgaging the future. The only realistic course of action open to social democratic governments was to work for slow and steady growth, introducing gradual reforms, supervising profits and prices, and trying to persuade the trade unions that wage claims had to be proportional to the increase in output and productivity. A policy of this kind had a fair chance of succeeding at a time of prosperity, but as a result of the depression of 1973/75 the governing Social Democratic parties of Western Europe found themselves in a most unenviable position: instead of engaging in long-term planning and reform they had to devote almost all of their time and effort to keeping their economies afloat.

Broadly speaking, the social democratic parties of Western Europe faced similar problems, in the field of foreign policy and defence. They all welcomed *detente;* some of them were carried away by the rhetoric of *detente,* forgetting about the realities of political and military power in Europe; others took a more realistic view. Nor did they see eye to eye with regard to co-operation with the Communists. Mitterand and his friends who had to collaborate (or to compete) with a strong Communist party were bound to take a line different from their British and German comrades. In some cases, for example in Sweden and Norway, even big Social Democratic parties depended at times on Communist support, but as the Socialist party was so much stronger this relationship did not involve major concessions. All European socialist parties had to face internal divisions on ideological lines; in view of their democratic character this was only natural, but sometimes these divisions went very deep indeed, threatening or causing splits and paralyzing the party. Some Socialists were ardent Europeans, other parties were divided on this issue, and a few were altogether opposed. In short, if it was difficult to generalize about Euro-Communism, it was no easier to do so about Euro-Socialism.

LABOUR BETWEEN PROTEST AND POWER

With the disappearance of the old reformist-Fabian leadership the British Labour party once led by Attlee and Bevin, by Morrison and Gaitskell swerved to the left; in the trade unions this process was even more marked. The major unions had been headed by moderates such as Deakin, Lawther, and Williamson who worked closely, if not always smoothly, with the party leadership. They were succeeded by more militant leaders such as Frank Cousins and Vic Feather who, in their turn, were replaced by a yet more extreme leadership, some of them Communists, or ex-Communists or in broad sympathy with the far left; a Trotskyite became the head of the party's youth section. By 1977 the radicals of 1967 such as Jack Jones, Hugh Scanlon or Lawrence Daly were considered "centrists," outflanked on the left by more extreme newcomers. True, the realities of politics quite frequently had a sobering effect on the union leaders. Thus Jack Jones, a fiery revolutionary not so long ago, became the chief architect of the social compact and Barbara Castle, another former pillar of the left, permanently ruined her career in an attempt to bring some order into chaotic industrial relations (*"In Place of Strife"* 1969).

These developments greatly limited the freedom of maneuver of Harold Wilson's and Callaghan's government. Yet the strengthening of the radical wing resulted in few if any tangible achievements. The important economic and social changes had been carried out under the previous ("reformist") leadership, the one major measure taken in later years was the re-nationalization of steel. The reason for this failure was twofold. The British trade union movement with its twelve million members was stronger than any other on the continent, but it had neither the ambition nor the ability to provide national leadership: it could break a government but it could not make one.[1] This curious discrepancy between great numerical strength and lack of positive political impact was rooted among other things in the archaic character of trade union structure, the rivalry between unions, the continued existence of craft unions and above all the absence of any effective central leadership in the Trade Union Council. Those with greater industrial muscle achieved excellent wage settlements; the others, the majority, had to settle for the crumbs from the bargaining table. Such practices, even though couched in radical phraseology, had more in common with social Darwinism and the survival of the fittest or, alternatively, with the activities of medieval guilds than with working class solidarity. A consistent socialist policy, to be sure, was made more or less impossible by Britain's dismal economic performance. When the Labour government was defeated in 1970, inflation was already running at an unprecedented 11%; when it returned to power in 1974 the rate was 20%, and it rose to 25% the year after. Throughout the 1950's and '60's Britain had fallen steadily behind the other European countries; whole libraries have been written to establish whether it was the incompetence of British management or the laziness of the workers that was more to blame. Yet in fact British industrial productivity, with some notable exceptions, was not really that low, nor was British management that inefficient, nor was British industry as overmanned, as was widely believed. The

[1] "The T.U.C.'s victory over the Labor government in 1969 . . . contributed to Labor's defeat in the general election of the following year." H. Pelling, *A History of British Trade Unionism* (London, 1976), p. 275. The part of the mineworkers in the overthrow of the Heath government in 1974 was even more obvious.

real problem, as some economists maintained, was that employment in industry had fallen and employment in the service sector had rapidly increased—far more than in any other European country.[2] These would have been difficult years in any case, what made Britain's position even worse was the inability of the governments of the day, Tory and Labour alike, to resist the constant price-wage spiral resulting in slow growth and low investment. When prices increased by 8%, wages rose by 17% and even in 1975, at the height of the recession with inflation running at 25%, average wage increases were 32%. The efforts of the Labour government to reach a social compact were partly successful; the inflation rate was brought down in 1976, but the effects of the recession still continued as shown in the growth of unemployment, which was among the highest in Western Europe.

The severity of the British recession cannot be explained with reference to any single factor. The depression was less acutely felt and more easily overcome in West Germany and Austria, because of the willingness of the German and Austrian unions to curb wage claims which enabled these governments to attain a higher rate of economic growth. British working class militancy, in turn, has been explained against the background of a class ridden society (to use a famous cliché), but it was a sense of class, a matter of life style, the result perhaps of a divisive educational system, rather than differentials in income which were not larger than elsewhere. Other causes have already been mentioned—the archaic structure of the British trade union movement. Such interpretations may be correct as far as they go, but they do not take into account the human factor, shortsightedness, naked egotism, and lack of leadership. Even those aiming at the overthrow of the whole system must have been aware (as the Italian Communists were in a situation not altogether dissimilar) that even a communist Britain would have to compete on the world markets, and that a national economy in ruins was not an ideal starting point for the building of a new society. But for the desperate state of the economy, the strikes about tea breaks and the demarcation disputes among unions would have provided ample material for a satire; they were quite inexplicable to observers from abroad. These

[2] R. Bacon and W. Ellis, *How Britain Went Wrong* (London, 1977). Against the Bacon-Ellis thesis it is argued that but for the growth of the non-marketable sector of the economy there would have been increased unemployment. The debate continues. . . .

antics received wide publicity, but they do not account for the growing militancy and the obstructionism of the 1960's and the 1970's—they were to a large extent the consequence, not the cause, of the British malaise: "What came first was a halving of the rate of growth of industrial output, which has meant that there has been less available to raise living standards. . . . The underlying causes of Britain's troubles must lie elsewhere than in the attempt of the bulk of the working population to increase its living standards at relatively modest rates."[3]

The objective reasons apart, accidents also played a certain role. The leadership of the British trade unions is elected by a tiny percentage of its members. It was an accident that the leaders of the three or four biggest unions retired more or less at the same time and were replaced by extremists.[4] Once these new leaders had taken over, the smaller unions followed suit as they always do.

The Labour party has been from its beginnings an alliance of a variety of groups; some were preoccupied with equality, social reform, and a more democratic society, others were orthodox Marxists, Christian Socialists, vegetarians, pro-labor by instinct rather than on the basis of an elaborate doctrine. This coalition of disparate elements was frequently put to severe tests; it happened, for instance, with the question of Britain's entry into EEC. There was little pro-European enthusiasm from the very beginning; Gaitskell, in a famous speech in 1962, had argued that Britain's entry would mean the end of a thousand years of British history and reduce the country to the status of Texas and California. These arguments were hardly convincing. It is unlikely that de Gaulle would have taken France into the Common Market had there been a real danger that France would become a second Texas. It was argued with greater justification that the short-term economic benefits accruing to Britain from joining would be small; the decisive considerations were long term, and they were political and military as much as economic. The opposition to a closer co-operation with Europe among the "Little Englanders" was instinctive, and while it encompassed sections of the Tory right as well as Labour reformists, the bulwark of the opposi-

[3] Bacon and Ellis, op. cit.

[4] Such accidents are far more frequent than commonly believed. See J. Braunthal, *Geschichte der Internationale*, vol. 3, (Hanover, 1971), p. 85, on the role of accident in the takeover of the Italian trade union movement by the Communists in 1947.

tion were the unions and the Labour left. These radical critics of British institutions became almost overnight the staunchest advocates of a holy war against any "foreign" encroachments on these very institutions and traditions. To forestall a split in the party, Wilson decided on a referendum, unprecedented in British constitutional history, which resulted in a 2 : 1 majority in favor of Britain's entry. But even after that criticism of Europe did not stop in the Labour party, ranging from appeals to leave the EEC to calls to act as a brake from within.

In March 1975 Harold Wilson without any forewarning announced his resignation as prime minister and leader of the parliamentary Labour party. James Callaghan, a former Chancellor of the Exechequer, home secretary, and foreign secretary was elected as his successor. Wilson had been the party leader for the previous thirteen years and prime minister for a longer period than any other British statesman in the twentieth century. He was a superb tactician, a skilled negotiator rather than a leader of force and vision. He was perhaps the only man who could have held the party together in a difficult period; whether the achievement was worth the effort is likely to remain a controversial issue. There was much speculation about the reasons leading to his resignation; he was no doubt tired, having presided over 472 cabinet and 1,000 cabinet's committee meetings and having answered 12,000 parliamentary questions, as he announced in his resignation speech. Yet tiredness was perhaps not the only reason. Wilson claimed that Britain had not become ungovernable (as some foreign critics thought) and that the economy was on the upswing. He maintained in his resignation speech that "we have created a new relationship between government and people to replace the clash and confrontation. . . . This is a far more united and determined people now than for many years. . . ." But as an experienced politician he must have felt in his bones that the main problems that had dogged the Labour party under his leadership had not vanished, that neither party nor people were united. If Churchill had once said that it was not his intention to preside over the dissolution of the British Empire (which in the end he did, after all), Wilson may not have wanted to preside over the disintegration of the Labour party, which seemed a distinct possibility in the middle '70s. The setbacks in by-elections suffered by the party during the year following Wilson's resignation were read as the writing on the wall. The fortunes of the party seemed to improve in 1977. Labour hung on to power through an *ad hoc* alliance with the small Liberal party. But this alliance caused new problems, for as in West Germany, it created dissatisfaction and dissension within the party.

GERMAN SOCIAL DEMOCRACY

The history of the German Social Democratic Party (SPD) during the last decade largely overlaps with the history of the German Federal Republic during that period. The SPD had emerged from the war as Germany's second largest party, with a firm base among the workers; yet it was precisely its class character, and the belief among the other sections of the population that it was the party of the class struggle *par excellence* that made it seemingly impossible for the SPD to attract more than about 30% of the total vote. The Godesberg program of 1959 was an attempt to jettison some of the old ideological ballast; opposed by some left-wing spokesmen, it did in fact little more than take into account the changes that had taken place in political practice in any case. It stated that the SPD was a party of social progress and reform for the whole people, that it was open not only to people who believed in historical materialism, that it was for, not against, national defense. The Godesberg program helped to change the image of the SPD, which continued to make slow but steady progress from election to election. Only in December 1966 did the SPD get its chance to show that it was not just a party of protest and opposition, but a responsible party which could be trusted with the management of affairs of state. After the split in the coalition between the Christian Democrats and the Liberals which had ruled Germany since 1949, the SPD was invited by Chancellor Kiesinger to serve in a "grand Coalition." The SPD passed this test with flying colors. In the 1969 elections it received 42.7% of the poll, and the new government was constituted under its leadership in alliance with the Liberals, who found themselves in broad sympathy with the foreign policy of the SPD—meaning the rapprochement with the Eastern bloc. In the elections of 1972 the SPD did even better, overtaking the CDU for the first time. But during the subsequent four years there were disturbing signs of a loss of momentum and even exhaustion, partly caused by growing internal disunity. In the elections of 1976 the share of the SPD fell, and it was barely able to form a government with the help of the Liberals, who much to the chagrin of the SPD left wing, exacted a heavy price. Willy Brandt, who had been foreign minister from 1966 to 1969 and Chancellor thereafter, resigned in 1974 after an East German spy had been discovered in his entourage. In 1971 Brandt had received the Nobel Peace Prize for his efforts to bring about a reconciliation with the Communist bloc states, and this added more than a little lustre to the prestige of the SPD, both at home and abroad. Helmuth Schmidt, formerly finance minister, succeeded Brandt as chancellor, a more forceful and dynamic politician than Brandt, but despite (or perhaps because of) his pragmatism, less capable of holding the warring factions together, let alone providing leadership. The third important figure in the party top leadership was Herbert Wehner, who had been high up in the Communist hierarchy before the war. He was the great strategist of the party and he had not given up the hope that one day Germany would be reunited.

As the SPD became a genuine people's party its composition changed. If formerly its influence had been restricted to industrial areas and the big cities (since the 1960's almost all major German cities have come under Social Democratic management), after 1966 it succeeded in making headway in other areas, including predominantly Catholic regions and among the middle classes. The part played by middle class intellectuals and semi-intellectuals became notably stronger—both in the "base" and among the leadership of the party. Unlike the British Labour party and the French Socialists the SPD had no desire to nationalize major branches of the economy; such moves would have been highly unpopular because German industry continued to prosper at a time when most other European countries were in the doldrums. On the other hand the party did much to improve social services; West Germany allocated a higher share of its G.N.P. to social services than any other major European country. The SPD also persisted in its policy of giving workers the right of codetermination (*Mitbestimmung*) in the supervisory boards of major enterprises. (In the coal and steel industries there were already an equal number of worker and shareholder representatives, and the system was to be extended.) Its relations with the unions were not free of tension, but the party was certainly not dominated by the unions (as was the British Labour party) nor did the unions fare badly; working class income in Germany was, in fact, among the highest in the world.

Yet despite these achievements, all was not well within the party. After 1971 a process of radicalization set in, a gradual strengthening of the left wing which, while not immediately threatening the leadership of the party, certainly affected its electoral prospects. While most leaders and members saw the SPD as the party of freedom, of radical democracy and of social justice, the left wing did not attribute to these values the same priority. It was not the task of the party, as they saw it, to run a market economy. Under capitalism, they argued, true democracy was, in any case, impossible. The center and the right of the SPD were also in favor of reform, because they thought that by its own momentum the free market mechanism would not guarantee social justice. Nor was it sufficient, as they saw it, if the state encouraged competition, thus averting monopolistic tendencies; the government also had to take a more active part in directing investment. But the left was in favor of reforms that would radically transform the system (*Systemüberwindende Reform*). They were dissatisfied with the performance of the party leadership and claimed, not without justice, that the SPD was not making sufficient advance towards the "long term program" which it had set itself in the early '70's. The party leaders argued with equal justice that the social affairs budget had doubled between 1968 and 1974 and that only at a time of economic growth could the means be found for carrying out even more far-reaching (and costly) reforms. The so-called "double strategy" of the left caused much bad blood: this refers to the activities of the left within the party, coupled with attacks against its leadership in violation of party discipline. Since the electoral appeal of the SPD was mainly based on its image as a democratic party, rather than on a socialist program, the activities of the Juso's (the Young Socialists) were grist to the mill of the Christian Democrats, who argued that the SPD had never quite shed its Marxist orientation.[5] The foreign political orientation of the left was neutralist, and some of its members

[5] According to a public opinion poll carried out by the independent German Institute for Demoscopy in 1973 only 16% of those asked (only 27% of the SPD voters) answered that they would give their vote to a party trying to "introduce socialism" in whatever way this was interpreted.

advocated collaboration with the Communists. Most of the members of the left had belonged to the radical student movement of the 1960's, but in contrast to the extremists they had rejected terrorism and sectarianism, and set out instead on the "long march through the institutions." This they accomplished with some success even though exposure to practical politics (in contrast to university politics) had inevitably a sobering effect on many of them. There was however an important difference between the process of radicalization in Germany and Britain. The influence of the Jusos, overwhelmingly middle class in origins, was restricted to the party apparatus, to universities, schools, adult education and the free professions. They had many more sympathizers among the intelligentsia than among the workers; unlike the position in Britain they had no strong foothold in the unions and thus they lacked a real mass base. Nevertheless, given the importance of intellectuals in modern socialist movements, they became a substantial political factor. The top party leaders, above all Brandt and Wehner, had to spend much of their time and energy pacifying the warring factions, working out compromises, such as the "Orientierungsplan 1973–85," a kind of interim party program, stressing that there was room for diverging views in a democratic movement. At the same time they had to draw a clear line between the SPD and the Communists, a task which, in the words of Herbert Wehner, was a "question of life and death" precisely in the age of detente. It was a labor of Hercules, and it was not made any easier by animosities among the leading figures of the party, rooted in personal antagonism as much as in disputes on doctrine.

SOCIALISM IN FRANCE

Socialism in France reached its nadir with the presidential elections of 1969 when Gaston Deferre, the socialist candidate, the mayor of Marseilles, got a mere 5% of the vote. Seven years later the Socialists had regained their proudly proclaimed position as "the first party of France." The old French Socialist party (SFIO), heir to proud tradition, had suffered grievously in the post-war period. While its program remained strictly Marxist, it pursued policies that were sometimes hardly distinguishable from those of its rivals on the right. Torn by internal dissension, compromised by participating in various ineffectual governments of the Fourth Republic, it lost much of its erstwhile working class support, without gaining the backing of other sections of the population. Like the Radicals it became a party of notables, and with the rise of the Gaullist regime it was reduced to a mere shadow existence. Its membership fell from 350,000 in 1946 to 90,000 in 1959, and it was further weakened when the left split away.

The startling resurgence of socialism in France was to a considerable extent the work of one man, François Mitterand; even close observers of the French political scene called it "inexplicable" at the time. Yet seen in retrospect, the preconditions for a socialist revival certainly existed all along, for there was a considerable reservoir of goodwill for a party of the left. Some of those broadly in sympathy with socialism had drifted to the Communists, others to the center or Gaullism. But there was good reason to believe that the moment a new, more attractive, independent force emerged on the left, it would regain many of these lost votes. Mitterand was perhaps predestined to unify the non-Communist left precisely because he had not been involved in the internal quarrels of the old Socialist party.[6] Born in 1916 he had belonged to a small left-of-center group. By the time de Gaulle took over he had been minister in eleven cabinets, and his political career seemed to be over together with that of other discredited politicians of the unhappy Fourth Republic. Mitterand remained in opposition and as the head of C.I.R., a small, almost insignificant group, the candidate of the anti-Gaullist left. He did well in the presidential election of 1965 and thus became both a national figure and a natural candidate for the leadership of the reunited Socialist party at the Epinay congress in 1971. Better than any other left

[6] The development of the French Socialist party has been documented in great detail. See, for instance, C. Hurtig, *De la SFIO au nouveau parti socialiste 1965–73* (Paris, 1970) and Jean Poperen's *L'unité de la gauche* (Paris, 1975). See also A. Savary's *Pour le nouveau parti socialiste* (Paris, 1970) and P. Joxe and F. Mitterand, *Un socialisme de possible* (Paris, 1971), idem, *La Paille et la grain* (Paris, 1975), as well as the manifesto of the parti, *Changer la vie* (Paris, 1972). The development of the PSU has been related in Guy Nania, *La PSU avant Rocard* (Paris, 1973), E. Depreux, *Servitude et grandeur du PSU* (Paris, 1974), and M. Rocard, *Le PSU* (Paris, 1970), On the history of Mitterand's CIR: P. Ory, G. Delfau, M. Berson, *Les chemins de l'unité* (Paris, 1974) and Claude Estier, *Journal d'un fédéré* (Paris, 1970). A good summary of the arguments for and against the Popular Front on the eve of the elections of 1978 is J. F. Held (ed.) *Si la Gauche l'emportait* (Paris, 1977).

wing leader he understood the importance of mobilizing the *couches nouvelles*, the new social groups which had become of increasing importance in French society. Between 1950 and 1975 the proportion of the population living in the cities rose from fifty to seventy five per cent; once a nation of peasants and small shopkeepers, the great majority of Frenchmen were now wage earners. The program of the old Socialist party (SFIO) combined Marxist rhetorics (paragraph one of its constitution proclaimed the transformation of capitalist society into a collectivist or communist society) with almost excessive pragmatism. The new program of the PS (1972) on the other hand studiously refrained from using outworn slogans. It highlighted the "qualitative change of life" (its official title was *Changer la vie*), and it appealed not only to the old militants, but also to the young generation, to the planners and the technocrats. The new socialist party tried to provide a home for a great many people of very different ideological orientation: Christian Socialists; left-wing Keynesians, old reformists such as Deferre; old "Centrists" (such as Mauroy); Marxists; who, for one reason or another could not identify with the Communist party. This "multiform" character of the P.S. was its great strength, and at the same time its chief source of weakness. For unlike the Communists, the Socialists were neither a monolithic party nor well organized. The P.S. attracted many new supporters but it was not at all certain whether it would be able to keep them in line at a time of crisis and setbacks. Almost single-handed, Mitterand provided the cement unifying the various sections of the party, and he found it not at all easy to restrain its left wing at critical party conventions (Pau 1975, Nantes 1977). The main force on the left was CERES (*Centre d'études de recherches et d'education socialistes*) which was not just a socialist ginger group, as some claimed, but a party within a party with a very distinct political line which on many essential issues was almost indistinguishable from that of the Communists. Headed by several young technocrats among whom Jean Pierre Chevènement and Didier Motchane were the most prominent. Led by these young *enarques* (graduates of the elitist Ecole Nationale d'Administration) the dogmatism of CERES threatened to isolate the party while in opposition, and to create insoluble difficulties when in power through promises that could not possibly be realized. As Mitterand saw it, they

wanted to transform the French into "fifty million Stalins *a petit pied.*" [7]
CERES was the strongest protagonist of the common program with the
Communists originally formulated in 1972.

The Socialists not only strengthened their positions in their traditional bases in the south, the center of France, and the Pas-de-Calais
but also gained new support in the West and improved their standing in
the East. Mitterand argued that the bi-polarisation of French political
life was the result of its economic and social tensions, but it was also the
consequence of an electoral system whose original purpose had been to
keep the Communists out. The Socialists were not unduly worried about
the dangers of close collaboration with the Communists, for they believed that co-operation would benefit them more than the Communists;
that, given the division of Europe into spheres of influence, there was
no danger that France would pass into the Soviet sphere, and that the
Communists would inevitably have to play second fiddle in a Popular
Front government. Some even thought that French Communism had
undergone a profound change and that exposure to the realities and responsibilities of political power would bring about even more far-
reaching changes in the character of the Communist party. The critics
of Mitterand's policy, on the other hand, argued that the Socialist vote
was largely a vote of protest, an expression of discontent, that they
would be able to accomplish little once in power because the cures they
proposed for dealing with the depression would result in a flight of capital and a further decline in investment; and that the further bureaucratization of society was bound to collide with the aspirations of a
basically individualistic nation. The Socialists, on the other hand, maintained that some of the industrial enterprises nationalized after the war
(such as Renault) had performed exceedingly well and that, in any case,
autogestion (self-management) would curb the danger of excessive cen-
tralization. The Socialists had every reason to feel pleased with the new-
found strength of their party, but it remained to be seen whether the re-

[7] J. P. Chevènement, *Les socialistes, les communistes, et les autres* (Paris, 1977). M. Char-
zat, J. P. Chevènement and G. Toutain, *Le CERES, un combat pour le socialisme* (Paris,
1975); P. Guidoni, *Histoire du nouveau parti socialiste* (Paris, 1973); J. P. Chevènement,
Le vieux, la crise, le neuf (Paris, 1974); D. Motchane, *Clès pour le socialisme* (Paris,
1973); J. Mandrin, *Socialisme et Social-Mediocracie* (Paris, 1969).

vival would be a lasting one. The results of the general elections which took place in March 1978 were a bitter disappointment to the Socialist party, and this despite the fact that the PS overtook the Communists for the first time in many years and attracted as many voters as Chirac's Gaullists, But these results fell short of their expectations. It had been assumed that the Socialists, with some 30 per cent of the total vote, would be France's largest party by far, with François Mitterand as the new prime minister.

What had gone wrong? Mitterand charged the Communists with responsibility for the defeat. It is certainly true that the Communists, who were quite obviously unwilling to play second fiddle to the P.S., had sabotaged the chances of the united front during the election campaigns through sudden changes in their line on defense policy, new demands for nationalization, and their attacks against the Socialists. But this was only part of the story: The Socialist party, also rejecting old style "Social democratism," had moved further to the left than most other socialist parties; this might have been a pre-condition for cooperation with the Communists, but it certainly limited the electoral appeal of the party vis-à-vis the moderate elements of the left. There was for the Socialists no easy way out from this dilemma; if they decided to make common cause with the forces supporting Giscard they would be in danger of losing their left wing, whereas closer cooperation with the Communists would antagonize an even wider section of the population. Perhaps the Communists had been so unhelpful because they assumed that the Socialists, unlike their own party would be incapable of keeping their strength in the political wilderness, that at least some Socialist militants would find their way to the ranks of the PCF which would then reemerge as the leading party of the left. Such a possibility did indeed exist, and it remained to be seen what conclusions French socialism would draw from the lessons of the election of 1978, and whether the momentum which had led to its resurgence in the previous years would continue after a setback for which they had not been prepared.

SOCIALISM IN ITALY

The story of socialism in Italy, unlike the story of socialism elsewhere in Europe, was one of steady decline, and of an unending series of splits. There was much talent among the Socialist Party (PSI) leadership when it emerged from the war, and there was also much traditional support. In the elections of 1946 it emerged as Italy's second largest party, just in front of the Communists. Seen in retrospect, the first split which occurred in January 1947 was inevitable. Nenni, the grand old man of the PSI, had reached the conclusion in the years of exile that fascism had come to power only because the working class was not united. Hence his resolve that the PSI had to stick with the Communists through thick and thin even as they went through one of their most sectarian and intransigent phases. For his efforts Nenni received the Stalin prize (which he later returned), and when he finally realized the enormity of his mistake the damage that had been caused to the PSI was beyond repair.

The loss of electoral support was felt only gradually; as late as 1963 Socialists and Social Democrats together polled some 20% of the total. But in the meantime the Social Democrats, led by Saragat who had left the PSI in 1947 in protest against Nenni's policy, had been pushed to the right; they participated in various governments without being able to influence their policy. The PSI, on the other hand, underwent further internal splits, and gradually Nenni lost his hold over his own party. His line was contested by Lombardi, by Lelio Basso, and others; long after Nenni realized that the PSI had been manipulated by the Communists, de Martino, his successor, merrily continued the policy of an "opening" towards the PCI. According to de Martino the main task of the PSI was to reduce "anti-Communist prejudice" among the public. For a short time, from 1966 to 1969, the various socialist factions reunited, but the conflicts on both ideological and personal lines prevented any lasting co-operation and after much bickering the party split yet again.

In 1970 the PSI was divided into five main factions and several smaller ones: Nenni's "autonomists" who favored collaboration with the left wing of the Christian Democrats; De Martino's *Riscosa socialista* who wanted essentially the same thing; the *Manciniani* and the *Bertoldiani* who preferred some form of co-operation with the Communists; and the *Lombardiani* who wanted the same, without any reservation.

The Social Democrats (PSDI), who had lost their electoral base to an even greater extent than the PSI, were split into two factions; on one hand there were the friends of Preti, Ferri, and Tanassi, on the other there was Saragat who had returned to party politics after having served as president of the Republic. Little need be said about the activities of the Socialists during that period. They did not play a major role in the various center-left coalitions. They continued to support these coalitions partly because they wanted to avert a drift to the right, partly because they had a vested interest in a spoils system which gave their members jobs in the administration. But as the general crisis deepened and Socialist lack of unity became even more manifest, their electoral base continued to shrink to a mere 13% for both parties in 1976 and the Socialists ceased to be a serious contender in Italian politics. They precipitated the disastrous elections of 1976, having rejected Socialist participation in the government. But de Martino also opposed the "historical compromise," partly no doubt because it would not have encompassed the Socialists; he was in favor of a "democratic transition to socialism," and asserted that there could be no alliance with the Communists until they dissociated themselves from "socialism" as practiced in Eastern Europe. When B. Craxi was elected secretary general of the PSI in June 1976, even confirmed optimists in its ranks saw few prospects for a radical reversal in the fortunes of the party. There certainly was room for a third force between the Christian Democrats and the Communists, but few believed that, short of a miraculous recovery, the Socialists were still capable of playing this role.

Nenni's policy, in summary, had sapped the strength of the PSI, undermining its ideological and organization base. Once the Socialists had changed course, the party was too deeply divided to function as an effective political force. Objective conditions did not make its task any easier: the PCI was a much more formidable antagonist than the PCF for the French Socialists precisely because a "liberal" policy enabled it to make inroads in what would normally have been socialist territory. On the other hand the Socialists faced the competition of the Christian Democrat left. Preoccupied with their internal quarrels the PSI fell behind in the struggle with these superior forces: as the crisis deepened they missed their historical chance and were relegated to a minor role in the unfolding Italian drama. Their only hope was a decline in Christian

Democratic and Communist influence following their inability to cope with the effects of the crisis, and, based on this assumption, Craxi has provided a greater impetus to the party than his predecessors.

SOCIALISM IN SPAIN

The Spanish Socialist party (PSOE) founded by Pablo Iglesias in the late nineteenth century was for several decades one of the country's leading parties. It passed into oblivion following defeat in the Civil War but had a phenomenal revival after Franco's death emerging as the second largest force (and the single largest party) in the elections of June 1977. During the long years of the dictatorship the "historical" leadership in exile under Rodolfo Llopis became gradually cut off from the few remaining illegal cells inside Spain. Its position was further weakened when in the late 1960's a Socialist party of the Interior (PSI—later PSP) was founded by Tierno Galvan, a well-known Salamanca professor of economics. But the fortunes of the PSOE changed almost overnight when a new generation of young Socialists under Felipe Gonzales, a lawyer from Sevilla, came to the fore and overthrew the "historical leadership." Supported by the German SPD it gained recognition from the Socialist International. While the Galvan faction collaborated with the Communists in the interim period which began even before Franco's death, the rejuvenated PSOE decided to keep out of the various fronts and juntas. They protested against the (temporary) exclusion of the Communists from Spanish politics, but tried at the same time to outflank the PCE from the left with a more radical program. Galvan's group, on the other hand, advocated without notable success a quasi-Marxist "Mediterranean socialism" which betrayed the inspiration (and apparently also the financial support) of some Arab military regimes. The results of the elections were unambiguous: the Galvan faction received a mere 4 per cent whereas the PSOE got 29 per cent, more than twice as much as its leaders had expected. Commenting on the PSOE success, Carrillo, the Spanish Communist leader, wrote that this party became the vehicle for many people who wanted to vote left but who were afraid of voting Communist. In a country traumatized by forty years of the Franco regime, the fact that the King received Gonzales before the election certainly gave the Socialists an aura of respectability. But there were other factors favoring the Socialists. They had in Gonzales, to use that overworked phrase, a charismatic leader. The PSOE, furthermore, had taken great care to reconstitute itself on a federal basis, thus keeping the support of the Basque and Catalan Socialists. Above all, it represented, like Mitterand's refurbished PS, a cocktail that included something for everybody: Orthodox Marxism and liberalism, a strong pro-European attitude coupled with an anti-NATO approach. The PSOE was the only Spanish party that engaged in a modern-style election campaign. The election results conformed with the political patterns of pre–civil war Spain. The PSOE did particularly well in the industrial periphery of the country; Asturia, the Basque region, the Mediterranean coast from Valencia to Murcia; Sevilla, Malaga and Cadiz as well as in Madrid. Since the Democratic Center had its mainstay in the under-developed, agrarian regions which in the years to come are likely to suffer from further depopulation, the future prospects of the Socialists seemed excellent. But such optimism is based on the assumption that the PSOE leadership can contain the ideological differences and political conflicts that are bound to develop inside the party. This will not be an easy task in view of the heterogenous elements which it encompasses and the notoriously fissiparous tradition of Spanish politics.

THE NEW LEFT IN DECLINE

1968 was the year of the students. In Europe, the United States, and Japan the campuses were up in arms. Student unrest played an important part in the defeat of President Johnson, student demonstrations almost resulted in the overthrow of the Gaullist regime which had appeared unassailable. It was not the first time in European history that students had played a major political role, but never before had there been so many students, nor had student unrest affected so many countries. The political activism of the students was as sudden as it was radical, and it received enormous publicity. The belief gained ground that some major earthquake, resulting in irreversible political changes, was about to take place. Yet only ten years later it appeared that the revolutionary upsurge among the students, however fascinating in many respects, had not radically changed European politics; its lasting effects were mainly limited to the universities.[8]

To find the reasons for the decline of the New Left one must go back to the origins of the movement. The year 1968 signalled the appearance of a new generation for whom the Second World War and the cold war were ancient history. Dissatisfied with the progress achieved during the previous two decades, this generation impatiently demanded radical change very much in contrast to the slow, gradual reforms in which their parents had believed. That youth is inclined towards radical politics is a truism; previous generations of students, before and after the First World War, had embraced doctrines of the extreme right. But this option was forclosed after 1945, even though certain elements previously associated with fascism sometimes reappeared under a left-wing cloak; this refers, for instance, to a hardly veiled elitism and the fervent belief in violence. In the United States the Vietnam war was undoubtedly the single most important factor triggering off the new radicalism, but there was also the impact of the counter-culture, the belief in a new life style, and a variety of other motives.

Within less than two decades the number of students in the United States and in Europe had quadrupled; in some cases it had grown even more rapidly. Higher education was no longer the privilege of a chosen few. But the universities were not prepared to absorb an influx of this size. The University of Rome, to provide an extreme example, had been built for ten thousand students, but in the middle 1970's it had to accommodate 165,000. The old universities were quite simply physically incapable of providing an education for such numbers. There was much to be said for opening the gates of the institutions of higher learning, but the preparations for an influx of this magnitude had been quite insufficient. It was no doubt inevitable that there would be a certain decline in intellectual standards, but open admission and/or the preoc-

[8] The literature on the New Left is immense. A bibliography on students and politics by Philip Altbach, published in 1970, even before the great flow of books, pamphlets and articles came under way, ran to 65 pages. An early survey was Tariq Ali (ed.), *The New Revolutionaries* (New York, 1969). An early (critical) attempt to analyze the ideological sources of the left was M. Cranston (ed.), *The New Left* (London 1970). First attempts to interpret the New Left in historical perspective were G. Statera, *Death of an Utopia* (New York, 1975); K. Mehnert, *Jugend im Zeitbruch* (Stuttgart, 1976); and Massimo Teodori, *Storia delle nuove sinistre in Europa, 1956–76* (Bologna, 1976).

cupation with extra-curricular subjects had consequences that hardly any of the reformers had envisaged. Nor had it been taken into account that many graduates would not be able to find work in their field of specialization, and that academic unemployment would lead not just to personal frustration but to a politically explosive situation. The militants of 1968, to be sure, were not primarily concerned with their professional prospects, but these considerations figured quite prominently when there was a new wave of student militancy in the middle seventies.

New Left ideology was a mixture of elements well known to the student of European intellectual history during the inter-war period. Some rediscovered the critical theory of the Frankfurt School, others turned their attention to Korsch and Reich. There was a Rosa Luxemburg and Gramsci revival, and anarchism too attracted its followers. The anti-authorianism of Rudi Dutschke and on a lower level of sophistication of Danny Cohn-Bendit was at least part-anarchist in inspiration. The young militants had nothing but contempt for reformists and "Stalinists" alike; they wanted a revolution that would not result in a new wave of repression. There was one new element in this admixture: the third world cult, the solidarity expressed with sundry national liberation movements. The philosophy of the anti-imperialist struggle, its morally cleansing character, was provided by Guevara, Frantz Fanon, and others. By their very example they had shown that everything was *a priori* possible; their deaths, the supreme sacrifice, made them the saints of a godless age.

This romanticism was bound to end in disappointment. On one hand, even the most militant third world heroes had never argued that the revolutionary strategies and tactics that had been effective in Latin America and Africa were applicable in democratic, highly developed industrial societies. And on the other hand, it appeared all too quickly that once the national liberation movements attained independence they transformed themselves into a new ruling class, and their accomplishments were a far cry from the dreams of yesteryear. Fanon could not have been more mistaken when he predicted that there would no longer be leaders but mass participation, that those who had fought for independence would not tolerate new dictatorships. As a militant of the Algerian revolution later put it, Happy the martyrs, who did not live to see the day. . . .

The anti-authoritarian phase of the New Left revolution did not last long. The students' movement became politically fragmented. Some found a spiritual home in the Communist parties of Western Europe, forgetting all the scorn they had earlier heaped on the "Stalinist bureaucrats." Others turned to Maoism or to Trotskyism; some joined various anarchist groups violent and non-violent, and yet others became involved in one or the other of the countless radical sects which for almost a century had provided a shelter for restless revolutionaries. Some became preoccupied with psychedelics and various exotic cults of the counter culture, and a few opted for terrorism—the Baader-Meinhof group, the Movement of June 2nd, the Red Cells, the British Angry Brigade, various Italian factions. Much has been made of the New Left inspired terrorism, but this was, after all, only one of many species of twentieth century terrorism. It attracted enormous publicity, but it was not new, and its political importance has been greatly exaggerated. I have dealt elsewhere in greater detail with its origins and activities.[9]

Thus the New Left was in a state of disarray only a few years after it had appeared with so much fanfare on the European scene. But it did leave certain traces. Its influence remained strong in Italian, French, and German universities as the revolutionary leaders of 1968 followed their academic careers. Something akin to a new conformism developed; sociologists and political scientists who did not make genuflections to some form of radical politics would have difficulties making their voices heard. This new intellectual climate tended to perpetuate itself; a visitor to a bookshop specializing in politics, history, and economics in many a European city would find mainly Marxist literature, with a strong admixture of ecology, women's liberation, gay and third world studies. There was some irony that Marxism, once a critical theory, had acquired the status of a new ideological orthodoxy—first in the Soviet Union and belatedly in Western Europe. But it was precisely the scholastic and ultimately sterile character of this ideology that was bound to provoke a reaction, first in France, and later, to some extent, in other countries. The new wave originated among participants of the events of May 1968, among students of Althusser, the most orthodox of the interpreters of Marx. The French "new philosophers" realized that

[9] W. Laqueur, *Terrorism* (London and Boston, 1977).

Marxist orthodoxy had been the main reason for their blindness and deafness vis-à-vis the realities of the Soviet system and the Communist parties. Stalin, as they saw it, had been no aberration, but merely the culmination of a process which had begun with Marx: had there ever been a successful revolution that was not totalitarian, and barbaric? And was it not the ultimate betrayal if revolutionary intellectuals ended up, as they almost invariably did, as apologists for such oppression? Such views were anathema not only to orthodox Marxists but to many others on the left, and they accused the "new philosophers," not without justice, of spreading confusion and pessimism. These would reply, with even greater justification, that honest confusion was preferable to a false certainty and an optimism based either on stupidity or, more likely, on a lie.[10]

In Germany the reaction to the new orthodoxy manifested itself albeit in a more narrow framework, in the rediscovery of Eduard Bernstein.[11] The belief in the intellectual poverty of revisionism and reformism had been axiomatic among the New Left, but all they knew about it was secondhand. As some of them studied the old texts they realized, much to their surprise, that they were still relevant, to use one of the fashionable terms of the period; more so perhaps than Lenin's observations about Russian affairs and Rosa Luxemburg's preoccupation with the general strike. If the predictions of the revisionists had not always been born out by subsequent events, this was true, after all, also for orthodox Marxism.

These discoveries made by sections of the New Left raise some interesting questions. The facts about GULAG, the practices of the Communist parties, and the consequences of Leninism which suddenly shocked them so much had been known, after all, for decades. It was not that a great intellectual effort was needed to acquaint oneself with these realities; a new generation of revolutionaries simply had not

[10] The first major contribution to the critique of Marxism from the left was J. M. Benoist, *Marx est mort* (Paris, 1970). But the movement attracted publicity only with the publication of André Glucksmann's *La cuisinière et le mangeur d'homme* (Paris, 1975) his *Les maitres penseurs* (Paris, 1977) B. H. Levy's *La Barbarie à visage humain* (Paris, 1977). Benoist, Levy as well as some other writers of the same school (Nemo, Lardreau) were in their twenties. All had been Stalinists, Trotskyites or Maoists.

[11] See for instance Horst Heimann, *Theorie ohne Praxis* (Frankfurt, 1977); and Thomas Meyer, *Konstruktiver Sozialismus* (Bonn, 1977).

wanted to know about them. For Marxism-Leninism, like other secular religions, had much to offer to those in need of certainties and spiritual comfort. It provided a key to the working of the "system," answer to all the perplexing questions besetting young rebels in a highly unsatisfactory world. It was a doctrine based on the promise of a far more perfect order, and it gave those subscribing to it a sense of purpose which others lacked. Outside the church there was no salvation, only doubts and uncertainties.

This, in briefest outline, was the reason why Marxism-Leninism, despite all the discrepancies between theory and practice, retained a powerful attraction for so many and for so long; why the disenchantment was limited to certain groups of the New Left; and why in some countries, such as Germany, Scandinavia, or Greece, it continued to be the predominant ideology partly, no doubt, in the absence of another cause—with the possible exception of environmentalism.

But it would be quite unfair to deal with the New Left as if it had been a monolithic bloc or to judge it only according to its ideological pronouncements. Its main role was that of a radicalizing force without clear direction in European politics. In its early stages the emphasis was on utopian, anti-authoritarian ideas and an extreme voluntarism ("everything is possible"), but this passed quickly. Once it moved into the orbit of Marxism-Leninism, it entered a field in which hardly a stone had not been turned over by successive generations of Stalinists, Trotskyites, and Maoists. Thus, in retrospect the main achievement of the New Left was the generation of a new mood rather than a new *Weltanschauung;* its cultural impact was markedly greater than its political innovations.

MAOISM AND TROTSKYISM

One of the most curious phenomena of the late 1960's and 1970's was the emergency (or revival) of various Maoist and Trotskyite sects. The Maoist revival was relatively short-lived. The pragmatic character of Chinese foreign policy and also the unfathomable zigzags of Chinese domestic policies dampened the enthusiasm of its supporters in Europe. They had embraced Maoism as an ideology more radical than Soviet communism, sullied by many compromises with Western "monopoly capitalism"—such as, most recently, detente. The search for ever more radical political doctrines has been a regular occurrence in Western political and intellectual history in modern times. Even the most outlandish ideas for curing Europe's ills have found some supporters, and thus it came as no particular surprise that the Chinese (or Albanian or North Korean) model found some admirers and emulators in Western Europe. It was not readily obvious how the villages could possibly "encircle" the cities in countries in which there were hardly any villages left, but these were minor technical details which did not bother true believers. The analyses of sectarian doctrines have a certain charm even if they are of no great political importance. All that matters in the present context is the fact that those who believed in Maoism were not really interested in what actually happened in China or Cambodia, in Albania or North Korea; they needed an ideal and were far happier with their own images of these societies than with the inconvenient realities. The same is true for Trotskyism, only that in this case the great hope was transferred into the future, not to some distant part of the globe. Trotskyite factions had been in existence since the 1930's in various European countries, and they too survived to witness a modest revival in the 1970's. They infiltrated the British Labour Party, helped to trigger off some major strikes in European industries and were publishing monthlies, weeklies, and even daily newspapers in London and Paris.

It is not easy to survey contemporary Trotskyism in view of the fragmentation of the movement. The main groups are the "United Secretariat" based in Paris (Ernest Mandel, Pierre Frank, Livio Maitan, Tariq Ali, and others); the (British) "Workers Revolutionary Party" led by Gerry Healy with branches in some other countries; the unofficial "Fourth International" (Posadistas); and the International Spartacist Tendency (IST). The British "International Socialists" (who changed their name to Socialist Workers Party) also have some allies outside *England,* but, like Pablo, the erst-while leader of the Fourth International, it no longer belongs to mainstream Trotskyism. European Trotskyism is strongest in Britain, France, and Belgium, hardly exists in Italy, and is quite weak in Germany and in Scandinavia.

In some ways the Trotskyites were predestined to benefit from the revolutionary upsurge of the late 1960's. The communist camp was split; even the parties which were not in power had become highly bureaucratic, lacking the radical dynamism that would attract a new generation of young revolutionaries. Above all, the Trotskyites had the great advantage of being unburdened by political responsibility. Their kingdom was not of this world, they did not hold power, they did not have to justify events in Russia (or China or Cuba). They were under no pressure to make concessions to capitalism and imperialism and could always outflank the Communists from the left. Thus the various sections of the Fourth International tried to make the most of that revolutionary situation which after many a false dawn seemed to have arrived at long last. They were in the forefront of the struggle against the war in Vietnam, against colonialism and for other good causes, the first to demonstrate and the last to go home, indefatigable in organizing committees, publishing revolutionary manifestoes and appeals, incessantly calling for revolutionary action. But the Trotskyites suffered from two major handicaps: the constant splits that occurred in their ranks and the intellectual weaknesses and inconsistencies of Trotskyite doctrine. What guidance could Trotskyism offer almost four decades after the master's death? Trotsky had not been a major innovative thinker; his comments on contemporary affairs are of considerable historical interest, but his one doctrinal contribution, the concept of permanent revolution, was of more value as a slogan than as an analytical tool. Up to the end of his life, Trotsky believed in the basically progressive character of the Soviet regime—it was a workers' state, degenerate or deformed perhaps, but basically socialist and progressive, and it had to be defended against outside enemies. For years the Trotskyites believed that it was their duty to enter the Stalinist parties wherever possible in the hope that somehow one day the workers would rise to remove the bureaucracy and restore pristine Marxism-Leninism.

This was the basic perspective of the Trotskyites and it did not substantially change for a long time; their critique of the Soviet system was essentially tactical in character. The Russians were too bureaucratic, not aggressive enough in pursuing the aims of world revolution, but "objectively" the Soviet bureaucracy still served the international expansion of the revolution. In short, the Trotskyite critique of Stalinism was less far-reaching than that of the Euro-Communists of the 1970's.

But Trotskyism too was affected by the winds of change on the political scene. For a while it saw in Maoism a new great hope, and when this hope had failed, Cuba became the closest approximation to that elusive ideal—the non-bureaucratic workers' state. When disenchantment with Castro set in (Castro had denounced Trotskyism in no uncertain terms) the party turned its attention to Malcolm X, Black Power, and various European revolutionary minorities such as the Basques. For a while it even saw in Guinea (under Sekou Toure) the paradigm of the struggle for liberation.

It was a desperate attempt to return to the roots, to unsullied Marxism-Leninism. Even in retrospect it is not easy to find satisfactory explanations for Trotsky's pronouncements that most of the shortcomings in Russia could be explained with reference to Stalin's evil character, that these "negative features" would vanish once Stalin had disappeared and the Soviet Union was no longer isolated. For this was hardly a Marxist argument, and it became, of course, quite untenable after the Second World War.

Trotskyism received a new lease on life partly as the result of the economic recession, partly as a consequence of the fact that the Communist parties in many countries were not able to live down their past. Thus it appeared to some militants of the new generation a more attractive alternative, more radical and apparently also more democratic. But this belief was based on a misunderstanding, for in most respects Trotskyism has remained even more fundamentalist than Soviet communism, less able to adapt itself to the social and political changes in the industrial countries, less capable of exploiting revolutionary situations in the third world. If there was a certain logic and consistency in the Trotskyite critique of capitalist society, its attacks against Soviet communism was disingenuous. It was quite unfair to argue that the Soviet leadership was unwilling to take risks to establish new communist regimes, and the harping on the "bureaucratic deformation" of the Soviet Union was likewise unconvincing, for the same negative features were common to all Communist regimes. "Internal party democracy" was not noticeably more developed among Trotskyite groups than among the Stalinists, nor is there any good reason to assume that a country ruled by Trotskyites would differ essentially from a communist regime.

Some Trotskyite groups, such as the (British) International Socialists deviated from traditional Trotskyite doctrine; in their view state capitalism had prevailed in the Soviet Union. This was certainly a step forward towards a more realistic approach but not a very big one, and in any case it raised a great many thorny questions for a Marxist. For in the modern world all countries have become state capitalist to some extent. What mattered in the last resort was not, of course, the question to whom economic power legally belonged but who wielded effective political power, whether the "toiling masses" could influence in any way the conduct of political and economic affairs. These theoretical inconsistencies might have mattered less but for the fact that the Trotskyite groups, consisted mainly of students and young intellectuals. Groups of this kind could not be satisfied with mere "actionism," they needed at least the semblance of a reasonably persuasive theory to explain the past and a strategy to tackle the future. But Trotskyism could not provide this, and therefore its revival in the 1970's remained narrowly circumscribed. They should have rejoined the communist movement, for as polycentrism spread, a little niche might have been found for them too. But as so often in politics logic did not prevail, the hate and the suspicions of a bygone period still lingered on; sects, as is well known from the annals of history, quite often have a phenomenal staying power. They continue to exist even after the reasons for their existence (and the splits that produced them) have been long forgotten. Sectarians are even less capable than other mortals of jumping over their own shadow: like Tithonus in Greek mythology, Trotskyism seems to have been granted immortality, but not strength and vigor; it can neither live nor die.

THE DILEMMA OF SOCIAL DEMOCRACY

The record of European Social Democracy has been subjected to a merciless critique from both left and right. Measured by absolute standards Social Democracy was, of course, a failure, for it did not build a new Jerusalem in Europe's green and pleasant lands. Measured by the more lenient standards of an imperfect world in which failure is as frequent as success, and in which success is never absolute, the balance sheet is by no means one of unmitigated failure. Social Democratic parties played a decisive part in the social transformation that took place on the continent in the post-war period. If there were major failures, the record of conservative and liberal parties was not more impressive. A revolutionary minority claimed that reformism had failed because capitalism had not been abolished, because inequality still persisted, because the results of the welfare state and a mixed and partly planned economy fell short of expectations. But if the Social Democratic parties did not pursue revolutionary strategies, this merely reflected the views and the wishes of their supporters. The Communist societies in Eastern Europe acted as a deterrent: they had not attained a higher level of prosperity and effectiveness, the differences between the highest and lowest salaries were about as high as in Western Europe, and whatever achievements they had to their credit, had been attained at a price unacceptable to most West Europeans who cherished their traditions of freedom and democracy.

As George Lichtheim has noted, the kind of central planning that vested all control in a political bureaucracy is unlikely to be efficient and certain to be destructive of freedom. "If liberal *laissez-fairists* had no other competition to face, they could save themselves the trouble of trying to prove that capitalism will in due course make everyone rich and happy. People who have once seen a Stalinist or Fascist regime at work will go to great length to avoid having one imposed on them. They will even put up with slumps and unemployment, so long as there is a reasonable chance of getting back to normal. A certain minimal degree of economic planning is after all attainable even under modern corporate capitalism, and the social injustice that goes with the system is preferable to being shot or sent to a labor camp or at best made to queue endlessly for a capricious supply of inferior goods and services. If socialism were to become permanently identified with the kind of life imposed after 1945 on Eastern Europe, few sane people would want it." [12]

Nor is it true, as the extreme left argued, that the popular masses are confused and misled by a mendacious right-wing propaganda, and thus induced to act (and vote) against their own best interests. On the contrary, the intelligentsia and the mass media with their great influence on the prevailing intellectual climate (and indirectly on voting behaviour) gravitate in its majority to the left.

The reasons for the failures of Social Democracy are found else-

[12] G. Lichtheim, *A Short History of Socialism* (London, 1970), pp. 317–18.

where. They are rooted not so much in the mistakes that were committed as in certain dilemmas confronting not just Social Democracy but modern societies in general. In many ways their very success has been their undoing because the steady progress in the standard of living triggered off the frequently invoked "revolution of expectations" (and entitlements), the assumption that such progress would go on forever. On the other hand, stringent government controls and high taxation gradually depress economic growth, result in a lack of drive and the loss of innovation. The prospect of a slow growth economy, of chronic balance of payment deficits and of some unemployment is bound to cause dissatisfaction and even despair. There are no obvious socialist solutions to the new problems. Higher taxation of middle-level incomes antagonizes a sizeable and highly vocal part of the population. "Soaking the super rich" is always a popular slogan, and perhaps an inevitable political strategy in certain conditions. But the money accruing from redistributive taxation, such as an annual wealth tax or a capital gains tax, is by no means sufficient to finance a further expansion of welfare services. At the same time it is bound to have a detrimental influence on capital investment. The trade unions insist on free collective bargaining and maximum wages, but this policy is hardly likely to enhance the chances of maintaining full employment. Some radical economists stress the need for more central planning, yet other radicals emphasize, on the contrary, the need for more popular participation and decentralization. The ecologists oppose the development of risky new sources of energy, and their propaganda has a great deal of support. But again, it is only too obvious what the acceptance of their demands would mean in social and economic costs.

In some countries Social Democratic freedom of maneuver is limited by the presence of strong Communist parties. Collaboration with the Communists, except on a purely tactical level, always involves risks, unless, of course, the Social Democrats are greatly superior to them in strength. For the Communists are doctrinally committed to be the avant-garde of the toiling masses, which implies that an alliance with democratic socialists could be only temporary in character. Western Social Democrats still remember the fate of their comrades in Eastern Europe and the disaster that overtook the Italian Socialists as the result of their collaboration with the Communists. Some argue that these fears are outdated, that the cold war hatchets have been buried, that Western Europe is not Czechoslovakia and that in any case the Communists have changed. This is certainly true to the extent that the Communists no longer believe in an armed coup. But they have not become believers in political democracy nor are their parties democratic in structure. Even left-wing socialists, such as the British "Tribune" group, maintain that "socialism which spurns or neglects to protect freedom of speech, thought or association is no socialism at all."

The main criticism against Social Democracy from the left is, of course, that it has not fulfilled its mission of abolishing capitalism. The historical dispute between revolutionaries and reformists has not been about the ultimate necessity of such change; the bone of contention was whether this should be a revolutionary or a gradual process. The expectations of the revisionists have been justified up to a point; the mixed European economies of the 1970's differ in many ways from the economies of the 1890's. Even the Communists with their new theories of "state monopoly capitalism" admit that much. But it is perfectly true that a mixed economy and even a well-run welfare state is as yet a far cry from a fully fledged socialist society. Social Democracy has retreated from its erstwhile aims because nationalization has lost much of its appeal; too often it resulted at best in some form of a statist technocracy, at worst in a brutal dictatorship. But social changes could also be adduced in explanation of the loss of the socialist impetus: the decline of the number of manual workers and, on the other hand, the emergence of a new middle class, consisting of skilled and white collar workers, civil servants, and employees. The radical left has bitterly attacked the Social Democratic parties for having transformed themselves into "catch all parties," or, to put it more politely, into parties of "mass integration." They are no longer proletarian parties, but then the same is true with regard to the more enlightened European Communist parties.

Many socialist parties accept that state ownership is no longer a shibboleth, and that new and more democratic patterns of participation have to be evolved. At its Frankfurt congress (1951) the Socialist International resolved that "Socialist planning does not presuppose public ownership of all the means of production." The manifesto of the Swedish Social Democrats, one of the most radical parties in Europe, stated that "Social Democracy supports the demand of public control of natural resources and enterprises, to the extent that it is necessary to safeguard important public interests."

The radical left has more sweeping solutions for the dilemmas facing Social Democracy. It agrees that the occupational structure of industrial society is changing, that the intellectual salaried class emerges as a major political factor. But far from accepting the theory of the *embourgeoisement* of large sections of the working class, they point to the "proletarization" of the intelligentsia as a major revolutionary trend. They claim that this "new working class" (Mallet), while non-proletarian in origin and life style, does not oppose the nationalisation of the means of production; on the contrary, it is an enthusiastic ally in the struggle for a more rational social order.

Political developments in France and West Germany such as the emergence of CERES, the Jusos, and similar groups in Sweden, Belgium, and other countries, as well as the phenomenon of student radicalism seemed to justify these assumptions in part. The revival of left-wing radicalism was based more often than not on the intelligentsia, the professionals and technicians rather than the working class. In their perspective the capitalist economy faces not just a cyclical crisis, but structural problems with which it cannot cope. As a result there will be further political radicalization, more and more people will accept that the market economy is bankrupt and that only a radical socialist transformation contains sound hope for the future.

This strategy, not devoid of a certain superficial plausibility, is based on too many doubtful assumptions and conflicting aims to provide a realistic alternative. While subscribing in theory to a new internationalism, be it only to counter the influence of the multi-nationals, the radical left is now strongly nationalist in inspiration, much more so, in fact, than in the 1920's. It is quite obvious that their strategy, if successful, will result in a national siege economy rather than in a "socialist Europe." However laudable *autogestion,* workers' control, and decentralization, these policies are certainly no cure for a recession. Neither the Communists, nor all left-wing Socialists share this enthusiasm for *autogestion;* there is every reason to assume that, if in power, its proponents will have to postpone indefinitely any major experiments in this direction. Above all, it is by no means clear whether an economic recession will in fact strengthen the radical left; past experience has shown that while a depression certainly contributes to polarization, as often as not the radical left is not its main beneficiary. The socialist left tends to misread the mood of European society; there is eagerness for change but there is also fear of radical experiments in an hour of danger.

But the real core of the dilemma of radical socialism is on yet another level. Governments hard hit by inflation, unemployment, and other such misfortunes have to adopt policies bound to antagonize a great many people by either more unemployment or more inflation or more shortages, and adjustment of incomes and social services to productivity, not just for a short interim period but for a long time to come. The more radical the cure, the more opposition it is likely to encounter. In these circumstances there is always the temptation to dispense with the niceties of "formal democracy." The Leninist way out of the dilemma does, of course, always exist and its consequences are known. The tragedy of the socialist left always was that its hour of opportunity arises only in adverse conditions, when it has to choose between the surrender of its radical socialist strategies and its democratic convictions.

So much then about the challenge from the left, but it is by no means the only one facing social democracy at a time of crisis. A recession undermines the belief in the normal functioning of the market system, it increases the faith in a command economy and strong leadership. Social democratic governments are torn between the necessity of increasing production, to stop inflation and provide employment, and between the pressures exerted by powerful trade unions on one hand and their responsibilities towards society as a whole, including underprivileged and defenseless strata. It is a thankless task, and it provides few opportunities of fulfilling its historic mission to make further advances on the road to democratization and social justice.

Thus European socialism is compelled to reexamine its strategy: According to past experience a "radical socialist solution" means state monopoly socialism and, dictatorial rule of a small group through a bureaucracy. It has been argued that such experience is not necessarily a guide for the future, since fully fledged socialism in societies with a firm democratic tradition is likely to be less repressive; only in these countries will it be shown that socialism need not be the enemy of freedom. This may be possible but it remains to be demonstrated.

The dilemma now facing socialism is that as a system of production it will perform no better than a mixed economy and that as a system of distribution it will almost certainly do worse. It can possibly achieve less erratic economic development, provide greater job security, and reduce somewhat income discrepancies. But these will not be revolutionary changes in comparison with the present state of affairs, and they are likely to be accompanied by a slower rise in the standard of living than in recent decades and greater state and bureaucratic interference in the life of the individual. To promise a revolutionary change in the human condition as the result of wholesale nationalization and total central planning is mere demagogy. Such progress towards the socialist ideal can be achieved only through the generation of new values and a new consciousness, a cultural revolution almost without precedent in the annals of mankind, a Herculean task, but the only valid long-term perspective for the future of socialism.

6

EURONATIONALISM

Working under German occupation on his last book and pondering the reasons for the sad state of the world, Johan Huizinga reached the conclusion that the "exaggerated and unjustified tendency to emphasize the national interest" was the curse of this century. This view was echoed by Erich Fromm, who condemned nationalism as "moral insanity," by Schumpeter, who explained it as an atavistic phenomenon attributable to the aggressive mentality peculiar to social groups, and by many others. Atavism or not, nationalism has been quite impervious to denunciations of this, or any other kind.

Europe, which invented nationalism, has suffered more than any other continent from its consequences. The impending demise of nationalism in which nineteenth century liberals believed, and which was also part of Marxist doctrine, did not materialize; on the contrary, it has shown phenomenal staying power. If, after two disastrous world wars, it found its more enthusiastic advocates outside Europe, it remained a major force to reckon with in Europe too. Even in its weakened state, it is sufficiently strong to prevent substantial advance towards a supra-national stage in Europe's political development.

The idea of Europe united on a federal base is as old as nationalism; its origins coincided, in fact, with the rise of nationalism. Mazzini was not only a glowing Italian patriot but also the founder of a "Young Europe" league. No contradiction was seen in 1848 between democracy, nationalism, and internationalism. If the nations of Europe drifted apart during the second half of the nineteenth century, the lessons of the First World War gave fresh impetus to the concept of unity and close co-operation. But this was not to be achieved in a painless way, and some critics had their doubts from the very beginning. Luigi Einaudi, who was to become the first President of the Italian Republic three decades later, wrote in the *Corriere della Sera* in 1918 that a

League of Nations with national sovereignty intact was not even worth discussing. Subsequent events confirmed the fears of the critics: the League of Nations was doomed from the outset; the various Pan-European schemes had not the slightest impact on the course of events. In the 1920's some critics reached the conclusion that the opportunity had been missed, that it was perhaps too late for a European revival and that the result would be a relapse into barbarism (Ortega y Gasset) or a new middle age (Berdyayev).[1]

New momentum was provided by the Second World War; such was the devastation that even desperate cures were considered. By 1945 powerful voices were calling for the United States of Europe which would "as if by a miracle transform the whole scene." In a stirring speech at Zurich University in September 1946 Winston Churchill predicted that if "Europe united in the sharing of its common heritance, there would be no limit to the happiness, to the prosperity and glory which its three or four hundred million people would enjoy. But time was short, unless the breathing space was used it may pass. If we are to form the United States of Europe or whatever name or form it may take we must begin now."

But the breathing space was not used, and Churchill himself was later to say that "we are with them, not of them." Anthony Eden felt it in his bones "that we cannot be members of an European community." The arguments against Europe were more or less the same on the left and on the right. As A. J. P. Taylor wrote on one occasion, "We and the peoples of the Commonwealth belong together. We are one people. I don't see how we can part from them. Politically we share a common heritage with them not with the Europeans. Despite cultural links, we have never belonged politically to Europe, and I see no reason why we should begin now."[2] Mr. Taylor surely exaggerated the extent of the heritage shared with Idi Amin and Ian Smith, but the belief that the Commonwealth constituted an alternative for Britain was as real as the distrust of Europe. At most, it was regarded as an economic marriage of convenience.

[1] Of the enormous literature on the European idea the following should be mentioned, J. B. Duroselle, *L'Idée d'Europe dans l'histoire* (Paris, 1965) and Henri Brugmans, *L'Idée Europeene 1918–66*, second ed. (Bruges, 1966).

[2] *Encounter* (December 1962).

Meanwhile, in 1954, the French parliament killed the project for an European defense force, and the few indefatigable Europeans, such as Robert Schumann, Jean Monnet, and Adenauer, decided to build economic Europe in the hope that this could be one day perhaps the base for political unity. But the crisis of the French Fourth Republic and British reservations prevented the growth of political institutions. France recovered temporarily, there was a second chance, but to de Gaulle with his "certain idea" of what France was and what it should be, the concept of supra-nationalism was bound to appear altogether absurd. He was enough of a realist to accept a Europe of sovereign states and a Common Market, but only within the limited framework of the Six. The more ambitious schemes were undesirable from the French point of view; the only Europe de Gaulle could envisage was one based on French leadership. Periodically, new schemes for a common foreign and defense policy were developed, discussed, and rejected.

The new opportunity to unite Europe arose after de Gaulle's resignation. The Six became the Nine, and at the European summit conference at the Hague (December 1969) it was decided that they should become a monetary and economic union, and that "ways and means towards political unification should be speedily investigated." The secretary generals of the foreign ministries under the chairmanship of M. D'Avignon of Belgium prepared a working paper which was published the year after. In a solemn declaration at the Paris summit meeting (October 1972) it was proclaimed that a European union was to emerge before the end of the decade. Leading West European statesmen went on record with proposals stressing the urgent need for unity, and in September 1973 yet another report to implement it was submitted. It suggested closer co-ordination of foreign policy through four annual meetings of the Europeans. The foreign ministers met more often in fact but the results were meager.

All these suggestions referred to consultation, to method, not to substance, even though in Copenhagen (December 1973) it had been resolved to "expedite the preparations" for the formation of an European Union. The contents of the future European Union were discussed at the Paris summit in 1974. Leo Tindemans, Prime Minister of Belgium, was asked to prepare a report on the subject. He and his collaborators worked for a year and took the advice of about a thousand individuals and hundreds of organizations. Since the advice he received was frequently contradictory, Tindemans sensibly decided not to aim at a consensus, which would at best have resulted in another vague and meaningless blueprint, but to prepare a report presenting his own views on how to attain European unity. He openly criticised the European governments for their lack of political will and noted that this criticism was shared by wide sections of the public which wanted concrete results. If some argued that the time was inappropriate for greater unity because of the depression and because the European idea was in the throes of a crisis, Tindemans maintained that the weakness of Europe was merely a reflection of the impotence of the states, the depression was more likely to be overcome by a common effort, and above all, that a half-finished edifice (such as Europe) was unlikely to weather the storms; it was likely to collapse altogether. In short, the problem was to make progress in order not to lose what had already been achieved.[3]

The Tindemans report was submitted to the public in January 1976. It was discussed at a meeting of the European Council and subsequently shared the fate of all other such reports—it was shelved and forgotten. For the anti-federalists it went much too far insisting, as it did, that without a common defense policy European unity was unthinkable and that there should be a single decision center for foreign policy.

Some had hoped that the oil crisis of 1973, and the disgraceful performance of the European governments would shame them into action. But European solidarity after 1973 was no stronger than before. France, as usual, went her own way; so did Britain and common European political activities were limited to meaningless palavers such as the "Arab-European dialogue" which lingered on for a number of years. There was irritation with the United States and resentment, but this hardly amounted to a common policy. The record was a little more encouraging as far as the preparations for the Helsinki Conference (CSCE) were concerned. The eight co-ordinated their activities in Helsinki and also had discussions during the Cyprus crisis. But Helsinki was in most respects an untypical case. The Europeans did not have to act under pres-

---

[3] On the Tindemans report and its reception, H. Schneider and W. Wessels, *Auf dem Wege zur Europäischen Union* (Bonn, 1977).

sure, it mainly concerned the legal draftsmen and the subject at stake was of no great importance in any case.

Collaboration on Cyprus produced the usual League of Nations style platitudes about the need for peace, justice, good will, and a non-interventionist policy.[4] There was a "policy declaration" on South Africa in 1976 but there was no co-ordination even with regard to such minor practical issues as recognition of the MPLA in Angola: the French again broke ranks. During the Portuguese crisis there were vague policy statements, but any help that was given to the democratic forces came not from the Community but from certain social democratic parties.

All this showed that European foreign policy at the very best remained an inter-governmental process. If there was on occasion common ground between national policies there would be co-operation on an *ad hoc* basis. More frequently there would be non-committal consultantions, and sometimes British and French ministers would not even bother to inform their European colleagues. A common defense policy was even more difficult to achieve. In view of French resistance the EEC could not even discuss these issues and even for the debates a different forum was needed. One such framework was WEU (West European Union) based in London, a leftover from the 1950's, which had the disadvantage of not including Denmark, Norway, and Ireland; another was the Euro-group, comprising the European members of NATO, founded in 1968 over a dinner in Brussels. The European members of NATO had of course a great many common interests: to persuade the Americans not to reduce their presence in Europe, to co-ordinate their own efforts, to standardize equipment, and to engage in co-production. One can hardly exaggerate the importance of strengthening European defense. It would have lessened Europe's dependence on the United States and reduced the European military imbalance and thus the danger of conflict. It would have profoundly changed Europe's place in the world. But this would have been possible only if the countries con-

---

[4] Mr. Carteret-Pendragon advising his young aide to say the usual things in his first League of Nations speech: "Devotion of British Commonwealth of Free Nations to ideals of League, nation of peace lovers, all must cooperate, wonderful work of League, praise of the Secretariat, economy in League expenditure, a word about Woodrow Wilson, and a tribute to the French." "But why a tribute to the French?" asked Donald in surprise. "It's the usual way to finish off a speech here. It does no harm and the French like it." A. G. Macdonnel, *England, Their England* (London, 1935).

cerned had been willing to increase their defense spending commensurate with the Soviet level and if they had agreed on military integration in the same way the Warsaw pact countries did. These were unfortunately unrealistic assumptions.

The state of affairs in the field of energy was equally lamentable. The vulnerability of Western Europe in this respect is well known; as a whole it depends on external sources for more than 60 per cent of its energy requirements. The development of North Sea oil and gas benefitted Britain and Norway, but the dependence as far as Western Europe as a whole is concerned is not limited to oil—coal, natural gas and nuclear fuels have also to be imported. There was no major initiative on the pattern of the early 1950's when the European coal and steel industries had been co-ordinated; the only visible advance was the proliferation of reports. It began with a document on co-ordination of policy in the energy area (1961). In 1962 there was a "memorandum" on the same issue, in 1964 a "Protocol on Energy Problems." In 1966 an "Initial Memorandum" was published—the authors were clearly running out of synonyms for their titles. This was followed by "First Guidelines for a Community Energy Policy," twice brought up to date and complemented by "Guidelines and Priority Actions under the Community Energy Policy" (the Simmonet report) culminating in "Initial Implementation of the 'Guidelines and Priority Actions" and more recently followed by a "New Energy Policy Strategy." The preparation of these reports presumably consumed more energy than was generated by their conclusions and recommendations, which were ignored. A few months before the Yom Kippur War, in May 1973, the Energy Council of the EEC at long last became alarmed by a situation fraught with danger and it discussed ways and means of coping with the impending threat. Both the French and British preferred "national solutions" rather than European co-operation; as a result the inconclusive debates continued, the midnight oil was burned in Brussels but no European energy policy emerged. If there was any European co-operation at all it came through such channels as OECD and the maligned big oil companies.

Progress towards integration, the transference of authority and loyalties to a larger European unit, was agonizingly slow. It was, in fact, non-existent, for in some respects there was retreat, not progress. The Hague summit of 1969 had decided that Economic and Monetary

Union would be achieved by 1980; only five years later this scheme was shelved. The decision to establish an European Monetary Co-operation Fund had a similar fate. The initiatives of the 1950's, which had resulted in the establishment of a European free trade zone, in establishing common industrial and agricultural policies had been more or less successful. The idea of creating a customs union was laudable but there was no good reason to assume that it would lead to political integration. The movement towards a political Europe came to a standstill; elections to a toothless European parliament were no more than a symbolic act without political significance.

The critics of political integration, of whom there were many, argued all along that Europe had achieved as much unity as it wanted and needed. Some claimed that it was most unlikely that an artificial larger unit would be able to solve problems with which the nation-states had been unable to cope, that, on the contrary, supra-nationalism would inevitably create new difficulties that had not existed before. Others claimed that in European politics as in other contexts small was beautiful, and they discovered an early prophet in Leopold Kohr who had written in the 1950's that the small state concept was not only expedient "but of divine plan," for social blessings were concomitants of social size—small size.[5] If the addicts of smallness had gone back a little further in history, they would no doubt have discovered Rousseau who had been firmly convinced that big states were bound to be despotic, and that only in a small state could freedom and equality be realized.

Yet others maintained that a great deal had, after all, been achieved in the past two decades, that European inter-dependence had become a reality, that a war, even a serious political conflict between members of the community had become unthinkable. Was it not true that, even the unification of nation states, such as Germany and Italy, had taken many decades (and a Bismarck, a Cavour, and several wars of unification); was it not unrealistic to expect a quicker advance towards integration between states that had no common language, culture, national consciousness and tradition? Perhaps a pause was needed to consolidate the gains of the 1950's and 1960's; perhaps later on, at some future date, a fresh start could be made. It sounded plausible, and if geography

[5] L. Kohr, *The Breakdown of Nations* (London, 1957), p. 97.

had placed Germany and Norway, Italy and France in Micronesia or Latin America, far away from the military and political pressures of Europe, one could indeed have faced the prospect of a century's delay with greater equanimity.

Progress on the road to political integration was blocked by an inevitable inertia and the vested interests of bureaucracies afraid of losing their power and becoming partly redundant. But these obstacles might have been overcome had it not been for the recrudescence of nationalism. This new nationalism differed greatly from its political and spiritual predecessors. Gone were the days when Lord Curzon had declared that the British empire was, under Providence, the greatest instrument for good that the world had ever seen; even de Gaulle hesitated to repeat Michelet's exalted invocations: "France, when you cease to speak, justice vanishes from the whole surface of the earth." To the extent that nationalism was rooted in economic causes (such as protectionism) it had clearly very much weakened as the result of the ever closer relations between the various nations. Political nationalism, a new secular religion replacing the Christian community of nations, had also weakened. Franz Borkenau shrewdly noted in a study written during the Second World War that Hitler's successes were rooted not so much in his extreme nationalism but in his belief in the decay of nationalism in the rest of Europe, the assumption that nobody, anywhere was any longer prepared to fight for his fatherland.[6] Borkenau was also correct in predicting that whatever happened, Germany would not repeat the attempt of another bid for world power. But he was mistaken in his belief that after the war there would be a greater inclination to oppose "the religion of nationalism." The revival of nationalism was partly the result of Hitler's war; if Napoleon's attempt to dominate Europe had been the main factor in the spread of nineteenth-century nationalism, resistance to Nazi expansion gave nationalism a new lease of life. In a longer perspective it was, of course, true that traditional aggressive nationalism was on the decline in Europe. All European nations emerged very much weakened from the war; caught up between the superpowers, not one of them was any longer in a position to impose its rule on the others. Nationalism based on military strength was a thing of the past, but a

[6] F. Borkenau, *Socialism, National or International* (London, 1942), p. 165.

new nationalism, based on weakness emerged. Neither capable of nor eager for going to war, it was still sufficiently strong to sabotage the attempts to build a new European order. This new nationalism, rooted as much on the left as the right, chose to ignore both the new realities of world power and the lessons of the past. The situation of Western Europe after the Second World War had an uncomfortable resemblance to that of Eastern Europe after the First. It should have been obvious after 1918 to the leaders of the small nations of East and Southeast Europe that hemmed in between two much superior powers, their only chance of preserving their independence was in co-operating with each other. Instead they spent most of their time and energy fighting or intriguing against each other. As a result they were first occupied by Germany and later became firmly embedded in the Soviet sphere of influence.

Gaullism was the most striking manifestation of the new nationalism—frequently imitated, but never with equal style and conviction. It was based on the ideas of Barres, Maurras, and Peguy with the stress on *grandeur,* uniqueness, and France's historical mission. De Gaulle certainly had grown up in the belief that national power and prestige were the overriding factors in French policy. But the power was no longer there, and thus, to restore at least the prestige, French policy had to be based on an European coalition. This could not be, of course, an European federation or supra-national organization. De Gaulle saw himself as the only truly European statesman, all others were *chercheurs de fromages,* they wanted to get on the payroll. Britain had lost its élan, he said, Italy did not exist, Germany was run by big business, the small countries of Europe did not count. Western Europe had to be built, but its physical and moral center was France and unless France assumed its leadership, it would never be organized. De Gaulle's European policy was based on several assumptions, one of which was undoubtedly correct: he was right when comparing Europe to a man who had broken a leg and who could not get accustomed to walking without American crutches. All his other assumptions were quite wrong: the idea that distant America was the main enemy of Europe; the belief that as the result of the reduction of American influence Soviet policy would soften and the Soviet hold over Eastern Europe weaken; the conviction that Europe under French leadership could be the arbiter between the superpowers; the promise that France could give Europe strategic independence.

These ideas were absurd but they appealed to a great many people. De Gaulle "played skillfully on the anti-Americanism of the French mandarinate. He maneuvered intellectual support and silenced opposition on the left by attacking American power, on the right by asserting French power. . . . More often he was forgiven his exaggerations because he had at least expressed legitimate French tendencies. In fact his policies mocked the French people by seeking ends far beyond their means and indeed their hopes. . . ."[7]

After de Gaulle's resignation the policy of *grandeur* and prestige in its more ambitious manifestations was discontinued. But France still remained the chief obstacle to European unity, precisely because some of the sentiments underlying Gaullism, had by no means been the monopoly of a certain party; these sentiments, if not the doctrine, were shared by the Communists and the left-wing socialists. The internationalism of the French left had always been a little suspect; it was an internationalism with Paris as its center, thinking, if not speaking French, *la lutte finale* for the spread of French institutions and French civilization. This applied in particular to the left intelligentsia. A sympathetic observer of the French scene has noted that the last stronghold of old-style French insularity and disregard for other nations was the diehard core of the Left-Bank intelligentsia. Brought up in the belief that French culture alone was complete and universal, they refused to admit that Paris had long ceased to be the cultural center of the world. Their world became a "fortress buffeted from without and partly starved within"; instead of accepting this they "strengthened the barricades and narrowed their front."[8] If de Gaulle had at least accepted the political necessity of closely co-operating with Germany, they turned not only against the "Anglo-Saxons" but also with such vehemence against the *Bundesrepublik* that the proverbial visitor from Mars was bound to reach the conclusion that Hitler was still in power and not the Social Democrats.

Nationalism as a doctrine had never found a fertile ground in Brit-

[7] John Newhouse, *De Gaulle and the Anglo-Saxons* (London, 1970), p. 48.

[8] John Ardagh, *The New France, A Society in Transition, 1945–77* (London, 1977), p. 707.

ain; one would look in vain for an English Maurras or Barres in modern times. They were not necessary because up to the Second World War the feeling of superiority among the upper classes was as self-understood as the patriotic (or imperialist) instinct of the middle class and the instinctive dislike of foreign ways and habits among the working class. In the aftermath of the Second World War much of the world of the Forsythes and Mrs. Miniver had collapsed, but the insularity remained and the inclination to become inward-looking little Englanders grew. Whatever the differences between a Churchill, Eden, or Enoch Powell on one hand and a Gaitskell or Michael Foot on the other, there was the common feeling that the English (as Orwell had put it) were outside European culture—not so much perhaps as the appreciation of "high culture" was concerned but in their national character and their way of life. Englishmen, after all, did have more in common with Americans and Canadians than with Sicilians or even Bavarians. But there was also resentment and envy vis-à-vis continentals who had somehow succeeded in making more progress than Britain in the post-war world. The harping on the links with the Commonwealth at a time when the Commonwealth no longer existed cannot be explained in rational terms; it was rooted, no doubt, in nostalgia. Britain managed to decolonize itself more smoothly than other European nations, but the after-effects were more painful and more lasting; Dean Acheson's harsh words about Britain not finding a new role in the world remained only too true in the sixties and seventies. Again, as in France, the nostalgia was not limited to the Tories; the left found it perhaps even harder to adjust itself to the new realities. There was still the belief that for progressive people of good will all over the globe Britain still was the beacon and the lodestar, the great example and the yardstick according to which true democracy, freedom, and socialism were to be measured. Traditionally, the British left had been even less internationalist in outlook and political orientation than the French. They had never been really interested in ties with socialist parties on the continent and they found it easy to rationalize their instinctive rejection of an Europe allegedly dominated by the monopolies—even when Britain was ruled by the Tories and most of Europe by socialist parties. British anti-Europeanism was less aggressive than was the French, it was perhaps mainly motivated by the wish to be left alone. But there was the same reluctance to make concessions on national sovereignty, to give up or to modify time-honored institutions and habits however outdated and to replace them by doubtful foreign importations which, even if perhaps preferable on the level of abstraction, were thought to be unsuitable for Englishmen. Generalizations about Britain are, of course, about as correct as those concerning other nations. A majority of Englishmen did after all vote for going into Europe. British intellectuals became less insular than they had been before the war, a young generation, more widely travelled, found more in common with foreign ways than their elders. But even among those who had in principle accepted the necessity of moving closer to Europe there was little enthusiasm; it was considered a necessity rather than a great opportunity, involving both an intellectual effort and emotional readjustment. And whenever British interests collided with those of the community there would be no agonizing as to which should be put first.

The attitude of the smaller European nations ranged from the exemplary Europeanism of the Dutch and the Belgians to the chauvinism of the Greeks and Turks (sleeping partners of NATO but not of EEC) almost willing to go to war about the fate of some villages in Cyprus.[9] Germany and Italy, once the most aggressive nations, had experienced in their own recent history the consequences of hypernationalism. But Italy was rudderless and lacked the resources to take a leading role in Europe; Germany had both the resources and relative stability but for obvious reasons was hardly the ideal candidate for leadership on the thorny road to integration. It had been immunized more effectively against the excesses of nationalism running wild than any other European nation. But could one be quite certain that the cure would be complete and lasting; nationalism is an infectious disease, and was it reasonable to assume that the Germans would remain good, selfless, abnegating Europeans in a world of para- and mini-Gaullists? In view of the setbacks suffered by the European idea it was only natural that in Germany too there should appear Germany-Firsters complaining about the constant demands made on them by governments who had no inclination to establish a truly integrated European community. The feeling that more than three decades after Hitler, West Germany was still on

[9] Turkey and Greece together had more men in their armies in 1977 than France and Britain together, and their per capita spending on defence was the highest in NATO Europe— not to deter an outside enemy, needless to say.

probation in the eyes of its neighbors and that the tocsin would be sounded at fairly regular intervals warning against a revival of Nazism, which had allegedly reached alarming proportions, did not strengthen feelings of European solidarity among the Germans either.

The counterpart to the revival of nationalism in Western Europe was the resurgence of separatist movements. These movements appeared in many countries but it was perhaps no accident that they were strongest in Britain and France, i.e. the countries most opposed to political union in Europe, and in Spain which was outside the EEC. European neo-nationalists were struck by a curious form of blindness: de Gaulle would give aid and comfort to the "Quebec libre"; even earlier a distinguished French historian had suggested the establishment in Paris of *"un syndicat des petites nations mécontents."* [10] Surely it must have occurred to de Gaulle that Bretons, Corsicans, and others would argue that if Canada was not a *nation une et indivisible,* the Paris government had no right either to oppose secession. But then nationalists are traditionally blind to the beam in their own eyes.

The phenomenon of unsatisfied (or "regional") nationalism is not, of course, a new one. Given the map of Europe and the distribution of various nationalities the right of self-determination (including secession) is, of course, incompatible with the absolute right of state sovereignty. This had been forseen by Acton who had written in his essay "Nationality" (1862):

> By making the state and the nation commensurate with each other in theory, this principle reduces practically to a subject condition all other nationalities that may be within the boundary. It cannot admit them to an equality with the ruling nation which constitutes the State, because the State would then cease to be national, which would be a contradiction of its existence. According, therefore, to the degree of humanity and civilization in that dominant body which claims all the rights of the community, the inferior races are exterminated, or reduced to servitude, or outlawed, or put in a condition of dependence.

And Acton drew the conclusion that the result would be material and moral ruin.

[10] Charles Seignobos in J. Aulneau et al., *Les Aspirations Autonomistes en Europe* (Paris, 1913).

The peace treaties after the First World War made it clear that no redrawing of the map would make the problem disappear.[11] After the Second World War the issue was partly solved in Eastern Europe by the expulsion of national minorities. But even there, under the firm hand of the dictators, the question of minorities continued to bedevil relations between countries such as Hungary and Rumania or Yugoslavia and Bulgaria. In Western Europe, which had been less afflicted on the whole before the war, old and new nations and nationalities appeared on the political scene, some "historical," others of recent date and doubtful provenance, all pressing their demands, claims, revendications, all complaining about neglect, alienation, oppression, and subjugation on the part of the central state authorities, all insisting on national self-determination, be it as a separate state or at the very least as an autonomous unit.

THE BREAK-UP OF BRITAIN?

Britain's many difficulties in the 1960's and 1970's were compounded by an upsurge of nationalism on her Celtic fringe. Some predicted the imminent break-up of Britain, others believed that far reaching reforms such as devolution would be necessary to save the unity of the country.[12] The conflict was most acute, and its consequences most devastating, in Northern Ireland. The six counties in the Northeast of Ireland had enjoyed almost five decades of relative peace since a partition which no one had wanted but which at the time had been inevitable. According to the constitution of the Free State, Ulster remained *de jure* a part of Eire, but the initiative for reunification eventually came not from Dublin but from the militant Catholics of Belfast. No serious attempt had been made to integrate the Catholics in the political life of Northern Ireland; furthermore, their economic position was certainly worse than that of the Protestant majority.[13] Thus there was a strong temptation to explain the conflict mainly (or exclusively) as yet another manifestation

---

[11] E. Ammende, *Die Nationalitäten in den Staaten Europas* (Wien, 1931).

[12] Tom Nairn, *The Break-up of Britain* (London, 1977).

[13] There is an enormous literature on the Northern Ireland conflict. R. Rose, *Northern Ireland* (London, 1976) provides a good introduction.

of the class struggle. But while socio-economic factors certainly played a role, the conflict was essentially sectarian in character, more so in fact than in the last century when Protestants had been prominent in the leadership of the Irish struggle. In the 1960's religion became the absolute dividing line; the backbone of Protestant militancy also was not "bourgeois" but working class. In theory, the struggle of the IRA was directed against only the British security forces, not their Protestant neighbors; the reality was very different indeed. The Protestants, on the other hand, did not bother to hide their attacks under a cloak of "internationalism."

Modest efforts towards reconciliation had been made under the premiership of Terence O'Neill in the 1960's, but there was no support for a policy of this kind among the Protestants. The armed struggle was sparked off by the civil rights demonstrations in Londonderry and Belfast. Ulster had its "Bloody Friday" and "Bloody Sunday" and many other bloody days. The worst year was 1972 when 467 people were killed; after that date the number of victims decreased but the civil war continued without interruption. The British government reacted by imposing direct rule in March 1972; up to that date Northern Ireland had enjoyed semi-autonomy with its own parliament and government. There were many attempts to mediate between Catholics and Protestants, but such was the hate and distrust between the communities that it proved impossible even to find a common basis for discussion. An independent Northern Ireland would not have been viable even if statehood would have miraculously stopped the civil war. Self-government within the United Kingdom was as unacceptable to the one side as unification with the South to the other. In every civil war sooner or later exhaustion sets in with a lessening in the acts of destruction and violence. But the only political result of the conflict was to inflame national passions even more, and a peaceful solution seemed more remote in 1978 than a decade earlier.

Ulster had been for decades a liability to Britain, and many Englishmen regarded its possible loss at some future date with equanimity. Scotland was a different proposition, and the growth of Scottish nationalism culminating in the demand for independence came as a far greater shock, even though the Scottish nationalists did not resort to violence. Scotland to be sure, had a lower average income than England but not by much (4%), and if there was widespread feeling among the Scots that Scotland was "subsidizing England," it was also true that Scotland had its own church and bank, its own legal and educational system, and representation in London: a Scottish office had been established in the British government as far back as 1885. Many Scotsmen had migrated to the South and their prominent role in business, in the free professions, and above all in British politics is well known.

Modern organized Scottish nationalism developed in the 1920's, but it became an important political force only in the 1960's; concern among the government and the political parties spread after the results of the parliamentary by-elections of 1967/68 had been studied.[14] To a large extent this was a protest vote even if the Scots would deny this. There was little active hostility towards the English, nor was the emphasis of Scottish nationalism on its own specific culture, as in Ulster and Wales. It was far more pragmatic in inspiration and character, based on the conviction that Scottish interests were neglected and mismanaged in Westminster and that consideration of national pride quite apart, an independent Scotland would be far more prosperous, which led hostile critics to dismiss it as mere economic opportunism. Scottish nationalism received additional momentum in the late 1960's as the result of growing bureaucratic intervention from London on one hand, and more decisively yet, the discovery of North Sea oil on the other. The slogan "It's Scotland's oil" had a powerful appeal. With a population of five million and a GNP of some $14 trillion (more than Portugal) as well as the prospect of a substantial income from North Sea oil (and to a lesser extent North Sea gas) the Scottish economy was certainly viable. But the issue of North Sea oil was not, in fact, that clear cut, and it was another example of the problematical character of the demand for self-determination. For there was the problem of the Shetland Islands and Orkney which had a population of 35,000, whose inhabitants had no desire to be part of an independent Scotland. If their wishes were taken into account

[14] The best source for the history of modern Scottish nationalism is H. J. Hanham, *Scottish Nationalism* (London, 1969). More recent events are reviewed in C. Harvie, *Scotland and Nationalism* (London, 1977), and M. Webb, *The Growth of Nationalism in Scotland* (Glasgow, 1977).

during the process of demarcation, two-thirds of the oilfields would remain with England. Scottish nationalists argued, not surprisingly, that the islands were too small to count. . . .

While Scotland is a "historical nation" which became part of Britain only with the Treaty of Union (1707), Wales was in the view of most Englishmen until recently no more than a "geographical expression"—the term Metternich had used with regard to Italy. Furthermore, with the development of industry in the last century there had been a considerable influx of English people into Wales. Only the rural regions remained ethnically homogenous and Welsh speaking. But it was precisely the effects of industrialization together with the rise of non-conformity (mainly methodism), which gave a powerful impulse to the movement of cultural revival. The crusade for education, and above all for the preservation of the language gradually assumed political dimensions. *Plaid Cymru* was founded in the 1920's but as in Scotland, it attained nationwide attention only following some startling by-election results between 1966 and 1968. Westminster responded to local pressure by establishing a Welsh office with its own minister, and the publication of a Green Book (1974) and by accepting bi-lingualism in principle. These concessions were rejected as insufficient by the nationalists who but for some individual acts of sabotage did not however opt for violent action. Welsh nationalists, in contrast to the Scottish, stood for full autonomy, not for an independent state.[15]

The emergence, more or less simultaneously, of nationalist movements in Britain (to which one could add such minor growths as Cornish nationalism) could not have been accidental, and there was a surfeit of explanations. Some pointed to "uneven economic development" and "internal colonialism," social psychologists stressed "relative deprivation," yet others mentioned the decline (and loss) of Empire as the chief reason. But these interpretations were too vague to be of much help. Economic development had been uneven in every country, internal colonialism has accompanied the growth of every nation on earth without necessarily resulting in separatist movements, and even the loss

---

[15] For the background of nationalism in Wales, see K. O. Morgan, *Wales in British Politics 1868–1922*, 2nd ed. (Cardiff, 1971); idem, "Welsh Nationalism" in *Journal of Contemporary History* (January, 1971), and, more recently P. Elton Mayo, *The Roots of Identity* (Plymouth, 1974). See also David Williams, *A History of Modern Wales* (London, 1969).

of Empire, a theory which has much to recommend itself, is hardly convincing with regard to the Irish Catholics, who launched their struggle even before the British empire was founded and whose onslaught was fiercest when imperial power was strongest. Why did Britain face a major challenge at home at the very time that Italy found satisfactory solutions for its minority problems? This question will come up again; it cannot be discussed in isolation from the other "regional" nationalist movements which became an important political factor on the European scene in the 1960's and 1970's.

SEPARATISM IN FRANCE

France is the most centralized country in Europe and it is also the one which in its modern history has had to wage the most destructive war against a national minority—the wars in the Vendée. Some Marxist historians have explained the phenomenon with reference to the specific development of the bourgeoisie in France and the capitalist mode of production, the destruction of local elites, and the systematic discouragement of all local economic initiative. But this hardly accounts for the fact that centralism has been traditionally as strong among the left (from the Jacobins to the Communists) as among the right and, more recently, the technocrats.

Regional nationalists in recent years have been most active in the Bretagne and in Corsica, though there have been other less publicized movements, in Occitanie, among the French Basques and elsewhere. The Bretagne, originally an independent duchy, became part of France in 1532; modern Breton nationalism dates back to the period before the First World War. There was an active separatist movement in the region during the 1930's; some of its members collaborated, and even fought with Germany during the occupation. They were decimated in the postwar purges, and Breton nationalism was discredited. It was only in the 1960's, following a series of peasant demonstrations that it again became a factor of political importance. Yet for almost another decade the belief persisted among prefects and planners alike that insofar as there was a Breton nationalism, it was economic in character. Of the 2.5 million Bretons only a fifth used their native language in daily life, and in the general elections the great majority of the votes went to the major French parties, not to regional groups. The Centralists ignored, as Pierre Fougeyrollas has pointed out, that a *recul de language* does not necessarily imply a decline in national consciousness—as the Irish case has shown and also the Basque. It was also overlooked that less than 40 per cent of the region's electorate participated in the elections. To pacify local grievances, new roads were built and other means of communications developed, agriculture was modernized and new industries created. As a result the economic situation somewhat improved, and emigration, which had been substantial, almost ceased. But these reforms by no means satisfied the Breton nationalists, who accused Gaullism (and its successors) of having attacked the dignity of a noble and proud people, of having tried to transform them into a submissive and prostrate people, searching for charity, given as long as they stayed silent.[16] Breton nationalism is politically divided: SAV (Strollard ar Vro) is broad spectrum nationalist, computing with the UDB (Union Democratique Bretonne) which has moved to the left. Many local Communists split from the PCF and founded their own local party. There has been violence: the *terrorisme souriant* of 1966 with the bombing of government offices, was followed by the destruction of television transmitters in 1974 and other such actions. But most efforts have been directed towards a cultural renaissance; even the most radical Breton nationalists have not asked for an independent state of their own but for political, economic, and cultural autonomy.

The exploits of the Corsican nationalists attracted far more attention during the 1970's than those in Brittany, even though a much smaller group was involved. According to official figures the population of Corsica is about 270,000, out of which less than half are indigenous. According to Corsican nationalists their number is at least twice as much, and it is certainly true that many more Corsicans live in metropolitan France than on the island. Corsica was once ruled by Pisa and Genoa, and enjoyed twenty-two years of independence under Pascal Paoli before it became part of France in 1768, the year before Napoleon was born. The complaints of the nationalists are familiar: that living

[16] M. Philipponeau, *Debout Bretagne* (St. Briene, 1970); see also CELIB, *Une Ambition Nouvelle* (Rennes, 1971); J. P. Le Dantec, *Bretagne* (Paris, 1974); R. Caerlon, *La Revolution Bretonne Permanente* (n.p., 1969); and Elton Mayo, op. cit.

standards are only half those of France and that most goods are more expensive, that they resent the presence of a Foreign Legion garrison, that there is no higher education, that the native language is neglected, that there is virtually no industry and bad transport. The Paris authorities were not altogether unaware of these complaints; efforts were made to develop tourism, which together with agriculture is the most important source of income on the island. But, to add insult to injury, when the economic reforms were carried out in the late 1960's, Corsica became part of the Marseilles economic region, hundreds of miles away, and gained recognition as an independent unit only after energetic protests. As elsewhere, economic reforms were insufficient to placate a small people with a long history, its own language, and, last but not least, a long tradition of violence. The moderate nationalists (ARC) led by Dr. Edmond Simeoni, a lawyer, was gradually radicalized; Simeoni was sent to prison following the siege of a vineyard in 1975 in which some gendarmes were killed. The French threat "to crush separatism without pity" only infuriated the young militants of the FLNC with their time honored slogan of *A liberta o la morte*. There were more than a hundred bombings in 1975 and they threatened to carry the "armed struggle" into metropolitan France. If the ARC merely wanted autonomy, and was willing to leave to Paris the conduct of foreign affairs and defence, the separatists, drawing their inspiration from Castro and Khadafi, insisted on full national independence—a neutralist Corsica.

Corsica provides an excellent illustration of the problematical character of the demand for full independence. Even if the separatists were not actually a minority among a minority, their demands would still be unrealistic. They are directed as much against the Frenchmen and French Algerians, the Sardinians and Moroccans who have settled on the island, as against the central authorities in Paris. Stepping up the "armed struggle" in these conditions could only lead to civil war. The economic development of the island, on the other hand, tourism in particular, can only be achieved through the influx of even more foreigners from the mainland. As a result the share of the Corsicans in the total population is bound to become even smaller. (In 1960 90% of the labor force was native Corsican, by the mid-seventies it was only 30%). The grievances of the Corsicans are real, but separatism offers neither a just nor a realistic solution.

SPAIN

Basque nationalism figured much more prominently in the media during the 1960's and 1970's than Catalan but the latter is the more important. Catalonia, according to the nationalists, counts some eight to nine million inhabitants; but this figure includes not only several hundred thousand Catalans living in France (Roussilon) but also a considerable number of immigrants from various other parts of Spain who do not speak Catalan and have not been assimilated culturally. But with all this, *Catalunya*, economically the most developed part of Spain, is far more secure in the knowledge of its identity than *Euzkadi*, the Basque country. And it is precisely for this reason that, as Arnold Hottinger has noted, Basque nationalism, feeling menaced by Spain and the Spanish language, has developed many more aggressive, loud qualities which have made the newspaper headlines.[17] Basque nationalism in contrast to Catalan has also engaged in unending internal discussions on the essence of its national existence and whether class or nation was more important: secure people usually feel no such need.

The Catalan language and culture were systematically suppressed throughout the eighteenth and nineteenth centuries, and it was only in the 1930's that the Spanish republic was ready to make political concessions to a rising Catalan nationalism. The Catalans had experienced a cultural revival during the last century, and their stormy economic development as well as their close ties with France and Italy made them outward looking, and strengthened their self confidence. Hence the Catalans' belief that patient, constructive work rather than terrorist action would eventually prevail over the repression, which was particularly severe during the early years of Franco's regime. Forced Castilianization, the idea of creating a single Spanish personality, encountered not only passive resistance, but demonstrations, strikes, opposition in the universities and the church. Thus the stage was set after 1960 for a new "explosion of Catalanism." The reaction of the regime was inconsistent, trying to avoid a head-on collision by tolerating certain cultural manifestations. More books appeared in Catalan; there were more broadcasts and television transmissions than before during the declining years of

[17] A. Hottinger, "Spain in Transition," *Washington Papers* 19 (Beverly Hills, 1974), p. 54.

Franco's regime and masses were eventually permitted to be said in the national language. But the political and economic demands were still ignored, and they became the major issue in the negotiations between Barcelona and Madrid as democracy was restored. The Catalans demanded as a very minimum that they should regain the same degree of autonomy they had enjoyed between 1931 and 1939. In the elections of 1977 the local Socialist party (who co-operated with the Spanish socialists—PSOE) emerged as the strongest, not the Communists or the Anarchists as some observers had predicted.[18]

Catalan nationalism, like Scottish and unlike Irish and Basque, is highly pragmatic, not mystical in inspiration. Catalans complain that they pay one-quarter of the taxes, but that only 8 per cent of the highways and 9 per cent of the Spanish railway network is in Catalonia. Like the Scots they claim that they are subsidizing the rest of the country, that Catalonia has been "colonized" by Madrid. This claim has not evoked much sympathy in the rest of Spain, for Catalan industry has developed, inter alia, owing to heavy protectionism, the cost of which has been born by the Spanish consumer. Catalonia, it has been said, is the only metropolis that is trying to secede from her colonies.[19]

But the secessionists are a very small minority among Catalan nationalists; the great majority merely demand political autonomy either on the basis of a Spain federally restructured or a special act granting Catalonia home rule.

The grievances and demands of Basque nationalism are more complex in character. The Basque language is one of Europe's oldest and most mysterious, but a specific Basque nationalism emerged only towards the end of the last century under the sponsorship of the local clergy. Up to the Carlist wars, the Basques had, however, their special regional privileges, the *fueros*. Less than 50% of the ethnic Basques understand the language, and the percentage of speakers is even smaller. The position of the Basque has been further weakened by the massive influx of immigrants, about one million since 1960; according to most estimates at least half of the workers in the Basque provinces are now of

---

[18] Norman L. Jones in P. Preston (ed.), *Spain in Crisis* (London, 1976), p. 251; S. Vilar, *Protagonistas de la España Democratica* (Paris, 1968); V. Alba, *Catalonia* (London, 1965); J. Rossinyol, *Le Problème National Catalan* (Paris, 1974).

[19] Alba, op. cit., 229.

"foreign" origin. If Basque nationalism has been more violent in recent times, this is due in part to the more severe repression under Franco. But there has also been the fear that they would be fighting a losing battle for the preservation of their national identity unless they achieved their aims very soon. As Stanley Payne has noted, "The very shrinkage of the Basque proportion of the population has encouraged a stronger reaction, and the intensity of radical nationalists is perhaps not unrelated to the fact that the clergy have always played such an active role in association with the movement.[20] Vizkaya and Guipuzcoa are among the richest districts in Spain, comparable only to Madrid and Barcelona; for a long time they have also been the stronghold of Basque nationalism. As in Catalonia there have been constant complaints that the Basque subsidize the rest of the country, that the taxes they pay exceed the benefits the region receives from the central government.[21] Like the Catalans, the Basques have been under-represented in the Spanish government, the central bureaucracy, the army and the police. The central authorities have argued on the other hand, not entirely without reason, that there have been few Catalan and Basque candidates from these regions in the first place.

The *Partido Nacionalista Vasco* (PNV) founded in 1894, middle class, middle-of-the-road politically, has been the main force in Basque nationalism. A group of younger militants (*Euzkadi ta Askatasuna,* Euzkadi and Freedom, ETA) split away in 1959 and has been responsible for most of the terrorist acts, beginning with the killing of Manzanas, a high police official in San Sebastian (1968) and including the assassination of Prime Minister Carrero Blanco in December 1973. These and similar operations created a great deal of uproar but their political effect was limited. Nor did ETA's influence grow as a result; in the first free elections, two ETA sympathizers were elected in the Basque region—compared with eight members of the PNV, nine socialists, and seven belonging to Prime Minister Suarez's coalition. Since the late 1960's ETA has suffered from recurrent splits, similar in pattern to, but even more frequent than those among the IRA. ETA 5A drew its inspi-

[20] St. Payne, *Basque Nationalism* (Reno, 1975), p. 250.
[21] J. L. Hollyman, in P. Preston, op. cit., p. 214.

ration from a vaguely Trotskyite orientation (ETA 5A) whereas ETA 6 put its trust in direct "military" action.[22]

Almost immediately after Franco's death greater freedom was given to the use of the Basque language and further reforms were promised. Historical experience has shown that nationalism in Euzkadi, as in Catalonia, gravitates to the left, but not the extreme left. Radical separatist tendencies are limited to small groups of Trotskyites, Maoists and some non-Marxist mini-factions; they regard national independence as a pre-condition for social revolution. But as the economic crisis of the mid-seventies hit Euzkadi, and as terrorist acts discouraged investment in the region, Vizkaya and Guipuzcoa lost their place on top of the Spanish industrial league. It dawned on many Basque nationalists that even if total independence were possible politically, it would by no means assure the economic progress of Euzkadi. A majority of the deputies elected in Euzkadi in the general elections of 1977 combined forces to act as a pressure group, demanding greater autonomy. The green, white, red flag and the tree of Guernica, the symbols of Basque nationalism, returned and with them hope that their basic demands would be fulfilled. Virtually all Spanish parties, except those of the extreme right, were agreed in principle on the need to accede to the legitimate aspirations of the Basque people.[23] That a small minority in Euzkadi would brand any compromise as an act of treason could be safely predicted.

The increasing role of regional nationalism on the European scene over the last decade is unmistakable. In some cases the protagonists and their demands had been in existence for a very long time. This refers, for instance, to Macedonia and Croate nationalism; sometimes such a conflict would endanger the very existence of the national consensus (Walloons and Flammands in Belgium). Elsewhere its consequences would be less grave simply because it concerned only a small minority such as the Jurassiens in Switzerland or the Slovenes in Austria. Some-

---

[22] Ortzi, *Historia de Euzkadi* (Paris, 1975).
[23] "El grito de Euskadi," *Cambio* 16 (September 11, 1977).

times a minority problem would contain the seeds of international conflicts (Macedonia, South Tyrol). In a few cases the emerging regional nationalism could be ascribed to overzealous collectors of oppressed minorities (Sardinia). But the overall picture was not one of uniformly increasing tension: the case of South Tyrol is perhaps the most striking exception. The struggle of the Tyrolians against Italian domination has lasted for almost six decades. Between 1956 and 1963 the radical elements among them again reverted to terrorist tactics. But there was no further escalation. Close collaboration between the Italian and Austrian governments in their search for a solution contributed to a peaceful outcome, as did the willingness of the Italian government to make genuine concessions and the emergence of a new bilingual generation of Tyrolians to which the old forms of *Volkstumskampf* appealed no more. Tyrolians had long complained about the threat of Italian immigration, but relations with the new immigrants were not that disharmonious, and, in any case, immigration ceased in the 1960's; some of the newcomers left again, mainly no doubt, for economic reasons.[24] But there is no denying that more often than not the trend was towards the aggravation of national conflicts, a phenomenon which also manifested itself in the growing tension between the local population and the new immigrants (or "guest workers") in Germany, France, Britain, and some other European countries.

What were the causes? It was not that the objective situation of national minorities had suddenly deteriorated; there had always been some inequality, some political frustration and cultural alienation. But the perception became more acute as the central state power became weaker. A strong centralist government could almost always contain minority problems, as the example of the Soviet Union, a country ethnically far less homogenuous than any European nation, has shown. Bureaucratic interference from the center was resented in the Soviet Union as in Western Europe, but despite some grumbling it was accepted, because any active resistance would have had unpleasant consequences. Such defiance in the West was far less risky, hence the growing belief that the national groups would attain their objectives through

[24] S. Magnago, *30 Jahre Pariser Vertrag* (Bozen, 1976); H. Sehn (ed.), *Die Behauptung Tirols* (Innsbruck, 1973); C. Pan, *Südtirol als Volkliches Problem* (Wien, 1971); A. E. Alcock, *The History of the South Tyrol Question* (London, 1971).

determined pressure.[25] Since right-wing parties were traditionally centralist, and since liberal and left wing movements gave, at best hesitant support to the "ethnics," the minorities established or rebuilt their own regional parties.

The rediscovery of the "ethnics" coincided with the civil rights movement in the United States and the emergence of the New Left in Europe, and it was influenced by them to a certain degree. There emerged a curious mixture of real grievances and economic opportunism, of genuine political frustration and the ambitions of local politicians, of a sincere feeling of "being different" and a questionable nostalgia and sentimentalism. To a considerable extent a revulsion against certain aspects of modernity was involved, and there was also the mistaken belief that capitalism was in the final analysis to blame for all these evils. In actual fact, it should have been clear that in a post-capitalist society, less chaotic and more centrally administered, national groups fighting for self-determination would face the same, if not greater, difficulties.

Quite frequently the "search for roots" had reactionary undertones beneath a "progressive" facade. This refers to the inevitable myth-making and falsification of history, the belief that individuals could show their human dignity only in the framework of a national group, the orientation towards the past rather than the future, the emphasis on divisive rather than unifying factors. The whole concept of "forbidden nations" was based on the doubtful proposition that nations, like Greek gods, enjoy eternal life (and youth), that each has a specific mission to fulfill, and that mankind is the better for the presence of these divisions. But history has shown that nations and nationalities have come and gone and that their loss of identity has by no means always been an unmitigated disaster. On the level of abstract reasoning every national group has, of course, an *a priori* right of self-determination. But this right is not, and can never be, absolute because it usually clashes with the aspirations of other national groups and because, furthermore, it gives the right to any group, however small, to have its own state. This process, if unchecked, would lead, needless to say, not to total freedom but to total anarchy.

[25] See S. Salvi, *Le nazione proibiti* (Florence, 1973); the special issue of *Temps Modernes,* August–September 1973, and the periodical *Europa ethnica,* Vienna.

Given the complexity of the contemporary world neither the desires of all individuals nor of all groups can be fulfilled and it is the task of politics to accommodate conflicting aspirations with a minimum of friction. This has been achieved more successfully in West Germany and Italy than in Britain, France, and Spain by setting up regional assemblies and governments with a fairly large degree of authority in economic planning and local affairs in general, including education. In West Germany even the radio and television services are organized on a regional basis. In Italy, five "regions of special status" were established (Sicily, Sardinia, Valle d'Aosta, Trentino-Alto Adige, Friuli-Venezia Giulia) with special administrative functions.[26] It is not certain whether devolution on these lines would work in Britain, France, and Spain because the magnitude of minority problems are on a different scale in these countries. But there is little doubt that solutions for the problems of the small national groups could be found with greater ease in a united Europe; in its absence the difficulties are likely to be aggravated.

The increasing demands of the minorities, the Gaullism of the small groups, are, to repeat once again, the other side of the coin of European neo-nationalism, and it highlights the negative, fissiparous character of nationalism in its most recent transfiguration. This takes us back to our starting point: the national movement of the first half of the nineteenth century was democratic and liberal in character, though it included even then the seeds of intolerance and aggression. According to its ideologies it was no more than the expression of the democratic will and the individuality, without which neither liberty nor equality were possible. This nationalism did not preclude international co-operation, for a nation which, as Mazzini once wrote, claimed independence for itself could not but recognize the same right in other nations. Nationality, according to Mazzini, was synonymous with peace, brotherhood, and co-operation between nations for the moral and spiritual elevation of all mankind. His inspiration was Dante and Machiavelli. As nationalism turned into an end in itself and became official state ideology towards the late nineteenth century, it became all too often aggressively hyper-patriotic in character, with the emphasis on the

[26] For a general survey of West European regional policies, see James Cornford (ed.), *The Failure of the State* (London, 1975).

overriding importance of the national interest and the denial of the legitimate rights of other. This was the age of nationalism of the patriotic march music, of chauvinistic speech-making and history writing, of militarism and imperialism, of anti-semitism and various other anti movements culminating in the concept of the absolute sovereignty of the state in the fascist era.

The most recent upsurge of nationalism is again different in character. It is no longer an all-embracing, integral, political philosophy; relegated to a modest place in the new balance of power, even the major nations of Europe can no longer nurture dreams of aggression and domination. Old style jingoism and anti-semitism have become unfashionable, and even national power in the traditional sense is no longer a realistic aim, be it only because the maintenance of big armies has become so costly. National honor and solidarity and the *pro patria mori* have been replaced by a free-floating resentment and vexation and above all by the fear of the unknown. European nationalism in decay has become less dangerous inasmuch as it no longer constitutes a threat to world peace. Yet even in its state of weakness it remains a factor of some political importance. It is backward looking in anger or complacency. It can no longer aim at territorial aggrandizement, let alone the building of empires, but the narrowness remains and the new nationalism is still sufficiently strong to prevent any real advance towards integration and unity beyond the stage of economic co-operation. There are certain striking parallels with reactionary movements in the nineteenth century and with fascism in the twentiety. These movements were usually based on classes and groups of people that had lost privileges, power and wealth. Fearful of even worse setbacks, they turned against the modern world and looked for salvation to past ages. They became enemies of change, because change, as they saw it, could only be for the worse. The landed gentry, which had lost its preeminent position in the state, the middle class which lost its property through inflation, the artisans, displaced by modern industry, the small traders ruined by department stores and supermarkets, found a new political abode in these retrogressive movements. Their political coloring varied, quite often it expressed itself in a populism which, as history has shown, can with equal ease turn right or left. But there was never any doubt about the identity of the enemy—the sinister international forces (and the traitors at home supporting them) which are responsible for the world's and the nations' misfortunes. Such populism is bound to be nationalistic in Europe as in the rest of the world, and if world trade, and the international division of labor had not developed beyond the point of no return, it would, no doubt, have opted for autarky.

What is true for declining classes also applies to once powerful nation-states passing through the painful process of adjusting themselves to a changed world. It is more painful for those who emerged as victors from the Second World War than for those who suffered total defeat; the greater the past glory, the more difficult the process of adjustment; hence the particular psychological problems facing Britain and France. Even relative economic prosperity could compensate even at the best of times only in part for the loss of political power and the feeling of insecurity.

The challenge facing Europe in the post-war period is not the wholesale dismantling of the nation-state but simply the surrender of certain sovereign rights, which have become anachronistic. The economic case for European unity was, and is, overwhelming:

> It is obvious that a large economic unit must be more powerful than its small constituents, but it is also true that its economic efficiency can be far greater than just the sum of its parts. It creates an economic environment conducive to large scale production, industrial concentration and the movement without hindrance of capital, labor, raw materials and goods. Specializations can take place in those localities most favorable to them, and resources can be used in the most productive manner without artificial restrictions.[27]

The case for an European defense and foreign policy is equally obvious, and while European integration is no panacea, it is certain that at least some of the domestic difficulties, such as the revendications of national minorities, insoluble within the framework of the nation state, could be settled in an European framework.

The historical justification of sovereignty and state power was in the maintenance of the social fabric, in the defense of society against

[27] G. Parker, *The Logic of Unity: A Geography of the European Economic Community* (London, 1975), p. 5.

anarchy. To the extent that it proves incapable of coping with this task the sovereign state has to look for supra-national arrangements so as not to lose its *raison d'être* altogether. The fanatical insistence on sovereignty and the exclusive preoccupation with the national interest have become irreconcilable with the solution of the political problems of the modern world.[28] But the power of the dead hand of the past should never be under-rated and, like so many anachronisms, nationalism obstinately persists. Largely instinctive, it is impervious to rational argument, it will be shaken neither by refutation nor denunciation. Doomed in the larger historical perspective, it is still strong enough to fight major rearguard actions, causing a great deal of destruction in the process.[29] Major political changes, experience shows, do not usually take place as the result of friendly persuasion, they are caused either by great convulsions or are imposed by force. The Second World War could have been a shock of this kind, but its effect was not lasting, as subsequent events have shown. The integration of Europe is inevitable, but it may take a very long time, and it has become increasingly clear that the learning process will involve further grave shocks and disasters, unless, of course, unity will be imposed from the outside.

[28] A. Cobban, *National Self-Determination* (London, 1945), p. 71.

[29] Such criticism of European neo-nationalism, needless to say, is not based on the belief that the abolition of national identities is either possible or desirable, and that national heritage and consciousness should be discarded. I agree with Hugh Seton Watson that it is foolish as well as arrogant to despise nations formed by long historical processes; with their own speech, culture, beliefs and institutions they are in any case virtually indestructible. (H. Seton Watson, *Nations and States* [London, 1977], pp. 13, 482). The criticism is directed against the unwillingness and inability of European neo-nationalism to rise beyond the insistence on absolute state sovereignty and to move towards closer cooperation.

7

DETENTE IN EUROPE

Europe had been the main battleground of the cold war, and in Europe the idea of detente released a tide of optimism. In the first flush of excitement there was a strong tendency to forget that detente meant different things to different people. It took several years and a great deal of disenchantment for more realistic counsels to prevail.

The moves towards detente began soon after Stalin's death; but the "spirit of Geneva" was short-lived and the decade that followed witnessed tensions and confrontations in various parts of the world. The second flowering of detente began in the late sixties when President Johnson proclaimed his policy of "bridge building" with the Soviet Union and when negotiations on arms control showed a measure of agreement. This process was interrupted, but not for long, by the Soviet invasion of Czechoslovakia and the proclamation of the Brezhnev doctrine. Under Nixon the foundations were laid for "leading the world out of the lowlands of constant war, and onto the high plateau of lasting peace" as the president announced in his report to Congress in June 1972. With the ten formal agreements of 1972, military and non-military, as well as the five declarations of cooperative intent, U.S.-Soviet relations moved "from confrontation to negotiation." The first SALT agreement of 1971 was the cornerstone of the co-existence declaration of May 1972 and it led to the accord on avoiding war, signed in June 1973.

Thus a new relationship was established between the two superpowers. Nixon and Kissinger detected in Brezhnev a willingness to cooperate in establishing a structure of peace, a new international system in which the participants would "operate with a consciousness of stability and permanence." As Mr. Brezhnev told a group of American businessmen during his visit to Washington in June 1973: "We have certainly been prisoners of those old trends, and to this day we have not been able fully to break those fetters." In the general mood of goodwill it seemed tactless to ask to what extent American and Soviet concepts of detente coincided, whether for the Soviet leaders, as for the Americans, detente was a concept implying "generations of peace" (another of the catch phrases of this *annus mirabilis*), stabilizing not just the arms race but the international order in general. Even the famous grain deal was held up at first as an example of mutually advantageous relations. Not to seek "unilateral advantages at the expense of the other" as stated in the "Basic Principles" of May 1972, was an admirable sentiment, but what did it mean in practice? Nixon and Kissinger may have had few illusions on this score. The ideological differences would of course persist and so would the ultimate aims of the other side. No one could reasonably expect the Soviet leaders to give up their basic beliefs overnight. But was there not at least a good chance that detente would develop a momentum of its own, that the development of common interests would eventually diminish the intensity and rigidity of Soviet doctrine? Was it not likely, in other words, that if this state of affairs lasted long enough, the Soviet Union, too, would become a status quo power—if indeed it had not become one already?

What marked the essential difference between the international constellation in 1971/2 and on previous occasions, was above all, the advent of nuclear-strategic parity between the U.S. and the U.S.S.R., the Sino-Soviet conflict, and the willingness of the Russian leaders, to engage in practical talks about mutually beneficial cooperation. Whatever the reasons which had induced the Soviet leaders to decide on a new peace plan at their Twenty-fourth Party Congress in March 1971, it was thought in Western capitals that this was clearly an opportunity not to be missed. What if the Soviet leaders regarded peaceful co-existence only as a tactical phase in their ultimate strategy of expanding their power? Was it not possible that a lengthy period of peaceful co-existence and collaboration would trigger off irreversible changes in the Soviet system—not, of course, in a year or two, but in a perspective of several decades? Was it not true that the Soviet leadership had become largely bureaucratized, guided by *Realpolitik*, expediency, and enlightened self-interest, and could not American leaders influence Soviet policy by strengthening the hands of the Soviet pragmatists against their doctrinaire rivals? Was not the age of the superpowers drawing to an end, and with it the rigidity of military bipolarity which had over-shadowed more than two decades of post-war history; was not the emergence of a new "pentagonal balance" (of which Europe was thought to be one of the pillars) making for new and dynamic rela-tionships in a world in which power no longer translated automatically into influence, and in which smaller nations had an unprecedented scope for autonomous action? And even if it were only a maneuver, even if it did entail risks, was it not a worthwhile endeavour in view of the great issues at stake?

The more sanguine Western proponents of detente believed that the Soviet leadership had decided on a basic shift in its foreign policy and that it would be foolish and self-defeating not to accept the out-stretched hand. The cold war had been the result of misunderstanding, suspicion and distrust, and, to a considerable extent the fault of West-ern statesmen who aggravated the struggle by "ideologizing" what was, after all, an old-fashioned conflict between great powers. The reduction of strategic arms and force levels was not enough to dissolve the sources of distrust. Only by political agreements, by a psychological readjust-ment, by a halt in propaganda warfare, by no longer viewing the other side as an enemy but as a partner in the great common task facing mankind in the years to come, could a gradual erosion of hostile atti-tudes come about. This, in turn, would require keeping criticism of the other side to the very minimum and becoming better acquainted with each other through cultural exchanges. As Brezhnev had said, "To live at peace, we must trust each other, we must know each other better." Such a policy, it was fairly widely believed at the time, would eventually lead to a convergence of the two systems and thus to lasting peace.

Such views were by no means voiced only by Senators Fulbright and McGovern; they were widely echoed in editorials and speeches on the left as well as on the right, among leading businessmen and trade unionists and even in the policy statements of the governments of the day. Official Western policy was based on certain correct assumptions, namely that the Soviet Union was indeed interested in certain specific agreements with the United States and the other Western countries. These included strategic arms limitations, the prevention of major mili-tary conflicts, "businesslike contacts," meaning credits and greater access to Western technology. On the other hand it was not appreciated that the Soviet leadership had not the faintest interest in "bridge building," that the "intensification of the ideological struggle during detente" demanded by Moscow was not just a philosophical exercise, and thus an irrelevancy, but a crucial political issue. For ideology provided legitimacy to the Soviet regime; "ideological struggle" was a synonym for political conflict. As the Soviet leaders saw it, this struggle was not only justified but was a moral imperative. For as the Soviet Union stood for progress and mankind's highest ideals, attacking the reactionary West did not harm detente; on the contrary it enhanced its prospects. On the other hand, any Western critique of the Soviet system was *a priori* reactionary, a threat to detente, it poisoned the atmosphere, it was by definition slander, vilification, and subversion. For if the Soviet regime was superior, any criticism was by definition an attack against detente, against peace and progress.

The failure to recognize this among the more ardent Western advocates of detente was bound to lead to a misreading of Soviet intentions and thus, eventually to disappointment. Those in the West who took a less sanguine view were in fact much closer to the Soviet interpretation of detente. To provide but one example: one of the more moderate Soviet commentators wrote in 1973 that peaceful co-existence did not put an end to the class struggle in the internal arena, did not "abolish the political and ideological struggle, nor the economic competition between the two systems."[1] These conclusions were virtually identical with those reached by a British observer, who said that the Soviet Union remained basically hostile to the United States, that she would like to see a weakening of America's power and influence all over the world, and primarily in her military support for the West: "Moscow would like to see America's alliances disintegrate, and her resolution and determination to aid her friends fade and disappear."[2]

Such warnings were not however very popular at the time, and in retrospect it is easy to see why. Following the end of the Vietnam war and two decades of confrontation in Europe there was an ardent desire for real peace and for dismantling the ruinously expensive military and

---

[1] Osipov, *Izvestia* (Feb. 17, 1973).

[2] Malcolm Macintosh, "Moscow's view of the balance of power," *The World Today* (March 1973).

political apparatus inherited from a bygone period. There was a willingness to make unilateral concessions—military, political, and economic—to demonstrate goodwill. But an excess of goodwill was not without dangers. In this particular case it tended to undermine the foundations of detente. Nixon and Kissinger as well as the West European leaders knew, of course, that Western military strength was a precondition of detente. Western weakness was unlikely to produce a spirit of conciliation and concession, even temporarily, on the part of the Russians. But many Western observers and policy makers, including some who should have known better, found it difficult to reconcile this simple truth with the rhetoric of detente. If, as they had been told, confrontation was over, there was obviously no need to continue massive (and ruinous) defense spending. Thus in the United States as well as in Western Europe, defense budgets were cut, while in Eastern Europe they were increased; the trend was unmistakable and it was bound to produce a reaction sooner or later.

This was only one of several dilemmas engendered by detente facing Western governments. Trade relations between the two blocs grew, but Soviet and East European indebtedness increased at an even faster rate. A good case could be made for the promotion of trade, it was less certain whether economic aid should be given to a system which stressed all along that it wanted to prove its superiority over the West, rather than to the more needy countries. Strategic arms control talks made progress, but only at a snail's pace; there was no advance at all in the talks aiming at balanced force reductions.

While these vistas of lasting peace, friendly relations and close cooperations prevailed in the West, the Soviet Union continued its military build-up, caught up and in some respects overtook the West. Through the good offices of the Cubans, the Soviet Union engaged in wars by proxy in Africa; the outbreak of the war in the Middle East in 1973 had shown that the process of consultation did not work too well either. Cultural contacts were restricted to a bare, inoffensive and ineffective minimum; the human rights policy of the Soviet Union remained what it had always been.

As a result, in the West, the high hopes of 1971/2 faded and there were second thoughts about the nature of detente. There was general agreement that efforts should be made to curb the arms race and that there should be some form of crisis management, so that a conflict would not get out of hand. A few inveterate optimists continued to claim that political conflicts were always based on misunderstandings, and that if reasonable people with a minimum of good will would only sit long enough around a table, and listen to each other's arguments, all the misunderstandings with the Russians could be cleared up. But such claims were no longer widely accepted. The very term "detente" became discredited. In March 1976 President Ford announced that he no longer intended to use it because it had been subject to so many misleading interpretations. The preoccupation with human rights during the early months of President Carter's administration further irritated the Soviet leadership, and the fact that Washington subsequently muted its criticism did not at once placate the Soviet leaders.

Seen in retrospect, it was not altogether fair to blame the Soviet Union for the cooling-off in West-East relations which set in after 1973. If Western spokesmen had competed in the rhetoric of detente, spreading hopes that could not possibly be fulfilled, Soviet leaders had never made a secret of their long-term intentions and perspectives. As they saw it, detente, though not without certain risks, was well suited to achieve their aims. Historically, Soviet foreign policy has always made more progress in periods of relative calm than during the "cold war" and its predecessors in the 1920's and 1930's. They had learned the lesson of the Aesopian fable of the sun and the wind who had a bet about getting a man's cloak off. The more the wind tried to do it by huffing and puffing, the tighter the man clasped the cloak around him; then the sun smiled, and the man took his cloak off.[3] The mistake of Western leaders, in short, was not that they accepted detente, but that they were willing to play according to the rules suggested by the Russians.

Illusions about detente in Europe were somewhat less widespread than in the United States. But there were also marked fluctuations in the European mood; for a while, the same speeches and articles about "structures" and "generations of peace" fired the imagination (and dulled the critical sense) of men and women of goodwill in London and Paris, in Bonn and Rome. Such attitudes, it ought to be noted in passing, were a constant source of bewilderment to the Chinese, who failed

---

[3] Sir William Hayter, in G. Urban, *Detente* (London, 1976), p. 27.

to understand how reasonably sane people could display such naiveté. But the honeymoon was short-lived. By 1974 detente had already lost much of its momentum, and the earlier illusions had given way to a more sober assessment. It was now widely (though not yet universally) realized that certain vital interests were indeed shared by West and East. But it was also accepted that in other respects the conflict would continue, not as the result of regrettable misunderstandings, but because Soviet political aims were, to put it cautiously, not identical with those of the West.

Detente in Europe meant, above all, German *Ostpolitik* and its course followed a pattern roughly similar to the ups and downs in U.S.-Soviet relations. There were no diplomatic relations between the German Federal Republic and its East European neighbors (except the Soviet Union) for twenty years after the end of the war. For the Soviet bloc, West Germany was a "revanchist and militarist" force, a danger to world peace, and periodic Soviet threats to Berlin created a dangerous situation in the heart of Europe. There had been earlier efforts by West German leaders to remedy this state of affairs, but to no purpose. Bonn was unwilling to recognize the DDR and thus to renounce the concept of German unity, as expressed in the Hallstein doctrine, according to which Bonn, and Bonn alone, represented the whole of Germany. This policy narrowly limited West German freedom of political maneuver, and it was only in 1966 under the "Grand Coalition" that a new initiative was undertaken to achieve a "positive solution." In 1967 diplomatic relations were established with Rumania and Yugoslavia, and this, despite the fact that these countries of course, also recognized the DDR. But Rumania and Yugoslavia were special cases and it soon appeared that without an overall agreement with the Soviet Union there would be no further progress towards normalization of relations with the other East European countries. Thus, after protracted negotiations between Egon Bahr and Gromyko, something akin to a non-aggression pact was concluded in Moscow in August 1970. It ruled out the use and the threat of force (*Gewaltverzicht*) and confirmed the inviolability of all European frontiers—including the Oder-Neisse line. It also prepared the ground for treaties between Bonn, East Germany, Poland, and Czechoslovakia, the representation of both German states in the United Nations, and the further development of West German-Soviet relations.

Meanwhile Willy Brandt had twice met Stoph, the East German prime minister, in Erfurt (March 1970) and Kassel (May 1970); but their discussions only made it too clear that the gulf between the two German states was still unbridgeable. West German advocates of *Ostpolitik* expressed the hope that the relations between the two German states could be normalized through a policy of "small steps," and that change would come through gradual rapprochement (*Wandel durch Annaeherung*). But Ulbricht, whose authority was at the time still unquestioned in East Berlin, wanted neither change nor rapprochment. For him German unity was ruled out, West Germany was a hostile, capitalist NATO state with limited sovereignty. Exploratory talks between Egon Bahr and Michael Kohl, representing the DDR, continued throughout 1970 without any manifest achievements. The main bone of contention was the four power status of Berlin on which the West Germans insisted; this proposition was unacceptable to the other side. But the international constellation favoured the West Germans. Ulbricht's obstinate stand made it difficult for the Soviet leadership to promote detente with the major partner in the Atlantic alliance. In May 1971, Ulbricht suddenly resigned (or, more likely, was forced to resign) and soon after the Soviet Union made it known that it was willing to accept in principle four power sovereignty over the access routes to Berlin. With this breakthrough the stage was set for several treaties culminating in the Four Power treaty on Berlin (September 1971), a traffic agreement between West and East Germany (May 1972), and lastly the Basic Treaty (signed in December 1972, ratified in June 1973). These agreements regulated most outstanding questions between the two German states and provided for the establishment of "permanent diplomatic missions" in Bonn and East Berlin. This was less than the full diplomatic recognition on which the East Germans had previously insisted, and a little more in line with the West German position that there was one German nation, and that the two Germanies could not therefore be foreign countries to each other.

Even earlier, on the occasion of Brandt's visit to Warsaw, a treaty with Poland had been concluded, again confirming the Oder-Neisse line. Diplomatic relations were established and in a subsequent treaty (1975) the Poles agreed to permit the emigration of 125,000 Polish citizens of German origin, and the Germans committed themselves to providing substantial economic help to Poland. Lastly, in December 1973, a treaty with Czechoslovakia was concluded, in which West Germany declared that the Munich *Diktat* of 1938 was null and void.

Brandt's *Ostpolitik*, for which he received the Nobel Peace Prize, was generally welcomed in Western capitals and it certainly strengthened West Germany's position in the world. Brandt established cordial relations with Brezhnev during his visits to the Soviet Union, and cruder attacks against German revanchism in the Soviet and East European media ceased. Trade between the two sides substantially increased. Within three years of the traffic agreement 27 million West German and West Berlin citizens visited East Germany; the numbers of visitors in the other direction was admittedly much smaller. The Christian Democrats had opposed the treaty mainly because it had given legal sanction to the division of Germany. They argued that if North and South Koreans were to agree on the existence of a Korean nation, why should it be impossible to insist on a similar formula for Germany? The Social Democrats and the Liberals shared this sentiment, yet it had become clear to them that, but for a concession on this point, there would have been no progress at all.

It was certainly true that the basic East German attitudes had not changed. Even if Ulbricht had gone, his successors pursued no less firmly the policy of *Abgrenzung,* of jealously insisting on all the issues that divided the two Germanies. Normalization of relations was one thing, but the "development of good-neighborly relations" pledged in the Basic Treaty was never taken seriously in East Berlin. After a short interval, the East German media resumed their attacks against the *Bundesrepublik,* East German citizens trying to escape to the West were still shot, there was frequent interference with traffic to Berlin, and the attempts to nibble away at Berlin's status also continued. Even the increase in trade with the East Bloc nations was not that impressive; it was no more than about one-fifth of Germany's trade with the Benelux countries. Furthermore, much of this trade had to be financed by substantial credits, since East European imports from West Germany grew more rapidly than their exports.

Measured against early expectations, the achievements of Brandt's *Ostpolitik* were modest. It soon appeared that there were narrow limits to normalization; relations between the two German states were still bad, and after 1974 the pace of *Ostpolitik* slowed down and in some respects the situation actually deteriorated. The treaties had not been a "trap" as some had claimed, nor had they caused any estrangement between West Germany and her Western allies as some had feared. Normalization had been an inevitable, overdue political decision. On the other hand it quickly emerged that it had been illusory to hope that normalization would lead to positive changes in East German policies at home and abroad.

Ostpolitik then was one of the pillars of detente in Europe; the European Security Conference was the other. This idea had its origins in suggestions made by Molotov, the then Soviet foreign minister, at the Berlin Four Power conference in 1954 aiming at a system of collective security. The purpose, at the time, was the neutralization of Germany and the withdrawal of all foreign troops from its territory. The Soviet leaders were not however ready to concede the establishment of a German government on the basis of free elections in the whole of Germany, for reasons that need hardly be spelled out. In the years that followed West Germany joined NATO, the Sino-Soviet split occurred as well as a great many other changes in world politics. The idea of a security conference was still mooted from time to time but with decreasing frequency and without marked enthusiasm by Soviet spokesmen. It was revived in March 1969 when the Warsaw pact countries at their Budapest meeting issued a new appeal to convoke a Conference on Security and Cooperation in Europe (CSCE). There was one major new element in this venture; previously Soviet policy had made no secret of its intention to bring about the dissolution of NATO. By 1969 it was accepted in Moscow that NATO would not soon disappear, and that Soviet strategy would have to be modified accordingly. No mention was made of the dissolution of NATO in the Budapest appeal or subsequent manifestoes: and another impediment on the road to the conference was removed when Soviet representatives declared, January 1970, that they no longer opposed the participation of the United States and Canada. After lengthy medium level preparatory talks, there were further talks on a higher level in 1972; the foreign ministers removed the last obstacles in July 1973 and the conference eventually took place in Helsinki in July 1975. The CSCE Final Act was signed on August 1, 1975. While Brezhnev in his comments on the conference stressed that he saw it as a major political fact marking the "close of an era," President Ford said that he regarded CSCE not as a surrogate peace conference, but as part of a process, "a challenge, not a conclusion."

The expectations attached to CSCE varied from country to country. There were no exaggerated hopes in the West; the general inclination was to cooperate with the Russians if only because it would not have been wise to leave to the Russians the initiative of promoting causes so desirable and lofty as peace and security. There was some apprehension that the Soviet Union would merely use the conference to gain formal recognition for their conquests after the Second World War. But there were no excessive fears with regard to the practical results that could be expected from a meeting that resembled more a jamboree than a businesslike conference. Eventually, representatives from thirty-five countries attended, including Malta and Cyprus; Albania boycotted it.

Soviet attitudes towards CSCE underwent a marked change as the date of the meeting drew closer. CSCE had been originally conceived in Moscow with the intention of gradually bringing about a new European security system in which the Soviet Union would play an increasingly important role. But as the preparations continued it became clear that the results were bound to be far more modest. Furthermore, the Soviet Union had to accept "Basket Three" (cooperation in humanitarian and other fields) which, though a political, not a legal commitment, was clearly unwelcome from the Soviet point of view. While Soviet enthusiasm waned somewhat, the idea of a security conference found eager proponents in Yugoslavia and Rumania, and also in Finland and Sweden. These countries had a special interest in a document affirming equality, territorial integrity, and the principle of non-intervention in internal affairs.

The Helsinki Final Act can be briefly summarized as follows. The Declaration of Principles (Basket One) includes ten principles. The signatories pledged to respect each other's sovereign equality and right to freedom and political independence; to refrain from the threat or use of force; to regard as inviolable the frontiers of all European states; to respect the territorial integrity of all states; to settle peacefully all disputes, to refrain from intervention in the internal and external affairs of other states; to respect human rights and fundamental freedoms, including the freedom of thought, conscience, religion and belief; to respect the equal rights of peoples and their right to self-determination; to develop cooperation with one another; to fulfil in good faith obligations under international law. In addition there was a document on confidence building measures including prior notification of major military maneuvers exceeding a total of 25,000 troops, discretionary notification of smaller maneuvers and exchange of observers to attend the maneuvers.

Basket Two produced six main documents dealing with economic cooperation. The subjects included commercial exchanges; industrial cooperation and projects of common interest such as energy and the development of road networks; cooperation in the fields of science and technology; trade and industrial cooperation including harmonization of standards; environment, including control of air and water pollution, protection of marine environment, and so on; and lastly some other areas such as transport, development of tourism, economic and social aspects of migrant labour.

Basket Three consists of four documents listing a wide range of human contacts, including regular meetings on the basis of family ties; reunification of families, marriage between citizens of different states, travel for personal and professional reasons, improvement of conditions for tourism on an individual or collective basis; meetings among young people; and sports. Secondly, the participants affirmed their wish to facilitate freer and wider information of all kinds—oral, printed, filmed, and broadcast—and to improve the working conditions for journalists. The third and fourth documents covered language tuition and teaching methods. In a special document the participants expressed their wish to deepen and improve their relations with other states in the Mediterranean area and to promote security and stability in the region.

The final document was a compromise between the Soviet wish to establish a permanent political organ (and thus to institutionalize gradually an all-European security system without the United States and Canada) and the Western demand not to establish a permanent machinery but to review from time to time the implementation of the Helsinki resolutions with a view to furthering the process of detente in the future. It was agreed to hold the first such review meetings in Belgrade in 1977.

Helsinki was a product of detente rhetoric and also its zenith. Seldom in history were so many righteous intentions pledged outside a place of public worship. The real importance of CSCE was that the meeting took place in an atmosphere that was at least superficially cordial and that there was so much talk about peace, mutual trust, cooperation, respect of independence, freedom and human rights even if for some of the participants this was no more than a ritual without much practical significance. While the conference by itself was certainly not "confidence building," it could still be argued that even a climate of hypocrisy is preferable to an atmosphere of confrontation and open conflict. No one expected a sudden dramatic change in European politics as a result of Helsinki; the sentiments expressed in the Final Act could after all also be found in the United Nations Charter and similar such documents, and the practical suggestions were not unprecedented either. But there is no harm in reaffirming assurances of peaceful behaviour and probity; such rhetorical exercises may have reverberations even if there is no intention of abiding by them. To this extent the Helsinki Conference was, of course, a positive phenomenon.

Those who had assumed that Helsinki would be more than a forum of speech-making on the desirability of the avoidance of war were disappointed by the aftermath of the conference. The Soviet Union and its allies continued to claim that the imperialist [sic] countries had had to swallow detente only because of the "political, economic and above all the military might of the Soviet Union."[4] The Warsaw bloc forces in Central and Northern Europe were further strengthened. West-East trade somewhat increased after 1975, but this process had started well before Helsinki. (Soviet exports to the EEC countries actually decreased from 6.1% to 5.2%; Comecon exports increased slightly from 4.1% to 4.5%.) The "confidence building measures" envisaged in Helsinki had been exceedingly modest in scope but even so, little use was made of them. The Warsaw pact countries invited Western military observers only on a few occasions, and accepted Western invitations even more rarely. There was no noticeable progress in information exchanges. Soviet and East European books and newspapers were as before freely sold in the West, but the Soviet Union imported only a token number of Western newspapers and even some Western Communist organs were censored as belonging to the category of "hostile propaganda," Western

[4] Erich Honecker, *ADN* (March 17, 1977).

correspondents were expelled from Moscow and East Berlin or not permitted to visit Prague in the first place. The jamming of some Western radio stations continued, while any criticism of East European broadcasts in Western languages was indignantly rejected. Tourism and exhibitions continued more or less on the previous level. There was an International Book Fair in Moscow in September 1977 but certain books were removed, though some Western publishers had engaged in preventive self-censorship. ("We want books to serve the cause of peace and progress" commented *Sovietskaya Kultura*). *Literaturnaya Gazetta* made it known in July 1976 that more than 500 books by Western writers were annually translated in the Soviet Union—many more than the number of Soviet works translated in the West. But this referred partly to classics of Western literature; the contemporary Western writers chosen for translation were carefully selected in accordance with the political message of their works. True, there were exceptions, but then there had been such exceptions even in Stalin's days when Mrs. Marple and M. Hercule Poirot, not known for their interest in dialectical materialism, had made their appearance on the Soviet literary scene. The "general line," in short, had not changed. As *Izvestia* wrote (September 4, 1975), the Final Act does not involve an obligation to "fling open the door for anti-Soviet subversive propaganda." This ruled out non-Communist Western political literature, and also most historical, economic, philosophical, psychological, and sociological studies. Western entertainment, was, within limits, acceptable but any serious intellectual dialogue was not.[5] Such practices caused no major shock in the West; few Western observers had expected that the Soviet leaders would expose their citizens to non-Communist ideological influences. But there was one issue which deeply disturbed many people in the West—the question of human rights. Dissent in the Soviet Union was not a new phenomenon. The persecution of Pasternak, the prison sentence meted out to the poet Josef Brodski, and the arrest of other unpolitical writers in the 1950s had been noted in the West. Subsequently the protest movement spread among members of the in-

[5] At a meeting between Soviet and American publishers in November 1977 in Washington the former "made several specific proposals for publishing ventures including books relating to the 1980 Moscow Olympic Games and books of Russian and American fairy tales," *Washington Post* (Nov. 16, 1977).

telligentsia; Bukowski, Ginsberg, Pavel Litvinov, Yuri Daniel, Siniavski, Galanskov, and many others were arrested; some received lengthy prison terms, others were exiled. The mathematician A. S. Essenin-Volpin was one of the many who were given "psychiatric treatment"; Solzhenitsyn and Sakharov were saved from arrest only by their world fame. Such practices were not new; they had been used in Tsarist Russia and they were perfected under Stalin. Before 1953 the dissenters would undoubtedly have been shot; it could be argued that there had been some progress towards more humane methods in the Soviet Union.

But even if the writers and the other intellectuals were not executed, they were still effectively silenced, and as the new wave of Soviet repression coincided with a campaign for human rights in the West, Western reaction was far stronger than in the past. Western protests had no official blessing except during the early months of President Carter's administration. West European governments were, in fact, acutely embarrassed by the American initiative and accused President Carter of naiveté—or worse. It was not that Callaghan, Giscard d'Estaing, or Schmidt did not care about human rights; the Western governments had, after all, insisted on "Basket Three" in the Helsinki conference. But they were against linking human rights with other political issues; they suspected that the Russians would react angrily; they claimed that quiet diplomacy could achieve far more substantial results, and that speaking out boldly would only cause greater repression. Above all, these sources maintained that undue emphasis on human rights would adversely affect arms control negotiations, the overriding concern for the survival of the human race.

These were threadbare arguments reflecting the mood of appeasement prevailing in some Western circles, official and unofficial. There was no danger that a strong emphasis on human rights would provoke a "new ice age" (as one commentator put it) or unleash "international ideological warfare on a global scale" as another put it at the time. For the Soviet Union had made it clear that such warfare was a categorical imperative, detente or no detente. It was even less to be feared that arms control talks would be affected. If Brezhnev did not hesitate to receive Marchais or Berlinguer there was no compelling reason why Western presidents or prime ministers should refuse to see leading Soviet dissenters or send them messages. Yet this is precisely what happened in the capitals of the West, and such weakness in defending the cause of freedom was bound to spread confusion and demoralization. There was no reason to fear that greater repression would ensue in the Soviet Union as the result of Western protests. As Professor Sakharov has written, "Resolute and ever-growing pressure by public and official bodies of the West—up to the highest—the defence of principles and of specific people can only bring positive results."

Moral considerations quite apart, it should have been clear that the struggle for human rights is not just a lofty and impractical endeavour, divorced from the harsh realities of world affairs, but itself a kind of *Realpolitik* with a direct bearing on international security. Governments which systematically disregard the rights of their own people are not likely to respect the rights of other nations. Secretary of State Marshall had noted this in a famous speech in 1948, and in the three decades since, the dilemma had become even more acute. For it is perfectly obvious that unless the declarations about peaceful coexistence between countries with different political, social, and cultural systems are translated into the language of reality, insurmountable difficulties are bound to arise, and have in fact arisen in West-East relations. For genuine detente, as Brezhnev correctly pointed out, cannot exist without mutual trust. This refers above all to arms control. It is obvious that meaningful agreements on strategic and conventional arms have to be based on effective means of inspection. With technological advance, the so-called "national means of verification" are no longer sufficient. Thus there are no effective means of inspection, and they do not exist precisely because of the absence of democratic checks and balances in the Soviet Union and the other Warsaw Pact countries and the unwillingness of their leaders to open up their countries to foreign inspection and free, unlimited travel. If there were an agreement and if American or West European leaders cheated, the facts would soon be revealed by the media; in communist countries such violations would of course, not be made public. Thus, the prospects for genuine progress in arms control are not good unless and until the Soviet system becomes more open and democratic. The movement towards the protection of human rights far from being a hindrance is an essential part of this process. The same applies, *mutatis mutandis,* to trade with the Soviet bloc which is largely based on credits and loans, which are also a form of trust. It was quite untrue that, as Soviet spokesmen argued, the human rights campaign aimed at changing the Soviet social system; the question whether Soviet factories and farms should be nationalized or not is obviously not for outsiders to decide. But it is perfectly true that the campaign aimed at changing the political system, or, to be precise, at making the Soviet leaders live up to their own constitution. Seen in this light the human rights campaign is of threefold importance—a moral, humanitarian imperative, and an effective weapon in the "ideological war" which the Soviet Union wishes to intensify during detente; but above all, it is the only known tool for developing a climate of understanding, which is the pre-condition for any lasting agreement. The world faces two alternatives, again to quote Sakharov, "Either the gradual convergence of the two super powers accompanied by democratization inside the Soviet Union, or increased confrontation with a growing danger of thermo-nuclear war." Sakharov subsequently envisaged a third possibility: "The capitulation of the democratic principle in the face of blackmail, deceit and violence." These were harsh, grating words, bound not only to anger the Soviet leaders but also to irritate Western diplomats trained to refrain from controversial and polemical statements in their dealings with the Soviet Union. It is the assignment of Western diplomats not to provoke the Russians, to look for the issues of common interest between West and East rather than the divisive issues. It is not their task to "rock the boat" and to pick quarrels. It may be unfair to compare them with the Halifaxes, the George Bonnets, the Neville Hendersons of the 1930's. But when all allowances have been made it is still true that there is always a strong tendency towards capitulationism among Western diplomats in their dealing with dictatorships, and the Soviets have traditionally made the most of it.

Following the Helsinki conference, human rights groups came into existence in Moscow, Kiev, Prague, Bucharest, as well as in the Georgian, Armenian, and Lithuanian Soviet Republics, and there were some stirrings even in East Germany, hitherto the most faithful of satellites. These groups made it quite clear that they had no intention of changing the existing order; the Czech "Charter 77" denied *expressis verbis* any intention to engage in political opposition. They simply wanted to monitor the observation of the spirit of the CSCE documents, and to draw attention to and document violations and suggest remedies.

But such seemingly innocuous activities were an intolerable provocation as far as the Communist authorities were concerned, for it meant, of course, taking seriously the pledges of freedom of speech, assembly, and all the other freedoms. A systematic campaign to suppress the human rights groups was launched in 1976 and reached its climax in 1977. The Soviet and East European human rights campaigners were accused of fabrications defaming the Soviet state and anti-Soviet (or Czech or East German) agitation and propaganda, or even treason; foreign currency, pornographic photographs, and on occasion even a few weapons were planted on them so that they could be charged with criminal offences. Among the milder forms of harassment used against them were periods of house arrest, repeated summonses for interrogation, searches, threatening letters, cutting off telephones, dismissals from their jobs, victimization of their children and relations. Since Soviet and East European authorities were aware that arrests and prison sentences would invite only more publicity and protest in the West, and since by 1976/7 these repressions were denounced from time to time even by Western Communist parties, it was decided that in many cases it would be more advantageous to deprive dissidents of their citizenship rather than to arrest them. The East Germans specialized in exiling some of their leading intellectuals (Biermann, Rainer Kunze, Sarah Kirsch, and many others); the Soviet Union and Czechoslovakia too, preferred this practice on the whole to prison terms and "psychiatric treatment." By mid-1977 the human rights monitoring groups in the Eastern bloc had been effectively suppressed, though individuals would still protest from time to time against the systematic infringement of human rights. Such complaints, however, would be dismissed by the authorities as baseless anti-Soviet propaganda and it was argued that Western concern for the fate of the Eastern bloc human rights campaigners was in violation of the Helsinki treaty ("interference in the internal affairs of other countries"). Furthermore, it could always be claimed that the British had beaten up some members of the Provisional IRA and that the American government violated the rights of millions of citizens who had a right to work but were unemployed.

The effects of CSCE were symbolical; if forty copies of the London *Times* or *Le Monde* were sent to Moscow for public sale, they were sold to foreign tourists rather than Soviet citizens; if Eastern bloc trade statistics became a little more detailed, this was the result of the pressure of Western trading partners rather than a consequence of Helsinki. "Sensitive" information such as data on foreign debt, debt service, or foreign reserves was still not published. Yet the general feeling in Western capitals immediately after Helsinki was one of satisfaction even among those who had followed the negotiations with misgivings. It is certainly true that the worst fears had not materialized, for Western efforts were more or less coordinated on this occasion and there were no undesirable changes in the Final Act. On the other hand, the Soviet Union and her allies exposed themselves to criticism and even a little pressure by accepting, however reluctantly, Basket Three. But the Soviet leaders felt confident that they could handle the critics at home, such as the Orlovs and Sharanskis who took Basket Three seriously. They probably anticipated that Western governments would needle them from time to time with reference to non-compliance. But they were reasonably sure that the West would be unwilling to use this as an effective political weapon against them, putting the Soviet Union on the ideological defensive. Thus, in the final analysis, the Helsinki talks resulted in a draw; they gave no major political advantage to either side. Nor did they promote the cause of peace and security in Europe.[6]

THE SOVIET UNION

A review of Helsinki and its aftermath inevitably turns into a discussion of Soviet policy. The Soviety Union is both a world power and the strongest European power. Throughout Europe, Soviet policies have

[6] There is a vast literature on CSCE, MBFR and European security in general, but these books, of necessity, deal only with certain aspects and phases. What follows is no more than a representative sample: T. W. Stanley and D. M. Whitt, *Detente Diplomacy* (Cambridge, 1970); Josef Korbel, *Detente in Europe* (Princeton, 1972); Gerhard Wettig, *Europaeische Sicherheit* (Düsseldorf, 1972); K. Kaiser and K. M. Kreis, *Sicherheitspolitik vor neuen Aufgaben* (Frankfurt, 1977); L. Ruehl, *Machtpolitik und Friedensstrategie* (Hamburg, 1974); G. Urban (ed.), *Detente* (London, 1976); N. Brown, *European Security 1972-1980* (London, 1972); R. J. Vincent, *Military Power and political influence* (London, 1975) (Adelphi Paper 81).

For the results of the Helsinki conference, J. Delbrueck et al., *Gruenbuch zu den Folgewirkungen der KSZE* (Koeln, 1977).

been a matter of paramount concern, Soviet intentions a topic of speculation and dispute since the end of the Second World War. West European foreign and defense policy can be analyzed only with constant reference to events in the other half of the divided continent.

The changes that have taken place in the Soviet Union since Stalin's days are a matter of historical record, and this is true not only with regard to the economic progress that has been achieved. The Khrushchev cult and subsequently the Brezhnev cult have not been remotely comparable to the adulation of Josef Stalin. There have been no bloody purges for many years. The few courageous dissenters have been harrassed and imprisoned but not one of them seems to have been shot. Power is no longer wielded by one man; the Soviet Union is ruled today by the 21 members and alternate members of the Politburo, the 11 secretaries of the Central Committee (6 of whom also belong to the Politburo) and the 426 members and alternate members of the Central Committee. The Committee is convened only rarely, only because its members are dispersed all over the Soviet Union. Within the Politburo there was in the mid-seventies an inner group constituted of the four senior members—Brezhnev, Suslov, Kirilenko and Kosygin—all of them aged over seventy.

There has been a great deal of continuity since the Khrushchev era, only five Politburo members have lost their positions for political reasons in more than a decade. Below the supreme leadership there are the district and regional party secretaries, the central and the local party and state apparatuses, altogether a bureaucracy, consisting of some three million cadres. But all orders emanate from the center; the vision of freedom of speech at least within the party, periodically invoked since Stalin's death, is still a chimera. If Khrushchev made a modest effort to decentralize, to give some more autonomy to local representatives of the party, this process was reversed and de-Stalinization in this respect as in others ended with Khrushchev. The party secretaries rule a population which is largely apolitical. The observation made by foreign visitors of Tsarist Russia that the Russian government has always treated the people as minors, not fully competent to look after their own affairs, is as true now as it was at the turn of the century. Appeals for mass participation, to be sure, are issued almost without interruption; but these are always combined with calls for iron discipline and the need to strengthen the state and the party; mass participation, in short, in order to demonstrate conformity. A few observers of the Soviet scene have drawn encouragement from the fact that some local issues such as the number of hospital beds or of kindergartens to be provided are decided locally, sometimes even following a discussion and that, in any case, the supreme leadership is not omnipotent in so far as totally arbitrary or unrealistic schemes cannot be imposed on the population. This is quite true, but it was also true in the past. The central party leadership cannot be bothered with coping with all minor issues, and even Stalin was not all-powerful, for after all, the shortcomings of human nature (and sometimes of nature, *tout court*) put a limit on the realization of decrees issued from the Center. There was always some debate in the Soviet Union, ranging from abortion to linguistics, but never on issues of political significance. The monopoly of political power, the character of the institutions, the instruments of propaganda and control have not been essentially affected; they have been streamlined in many ways but not liberalized. The Soviet Union is no longer ruled by one man, but by several representing an administrative class monopolizing power. (No women are found in the supreme party leadership.)[7] If challenged these men will admit in moments of candor (as their revolutionary predecessor did) that Russia was created by the autocratic rule of a centralized bureaucracy, which saved her from dismemberment and political annihilation, and ultimately made her a great power. As far as they are concerned any basic change in this respect is altogether unthinkable in

[7] Whether the leadership and their retainers constitute a new class or a stratum or a commanding social layer or an elite has been discussed *ad nauseam*. According to official Soviet ideology, a class that does not own the means of production is no class; it simply administers the political and economic system on behalf of the Soviet people. But class has been defined by Marx and the Marxists in many different conflicting ways, usually with the stress on the relationship of the members of a group to the means of production. Legal ownership is important in a bourgeois society; in a dictatorship it is not of decisive significance. With equal justice it could be argued (and is argued) that a society in which the means of production are not in private hands is by definition socialist. But even Marxists no longer accept such manifestly absurd assumptions; public ownership is meaningless unless the public has the right to express its views as to how its property should be used. It can be left to Trotskyites or Maoists to decide whether such a society is "state capitalist" or "degenerate worker's state" or "fascist," or yet something else. All that matters is that the elite has a monopoly of political power, is not subject to public control, and has no intention of making itself redundant.

the foreseeable future because it would result in economic breakdown and political anarchy.

The idea that modernization is bound to bring about a diffusion of power, that in an increasingly complex society experts ("the intelligentsia") will play an important role, or that ultimately the managers will take over has been disproved by events so far. But is it not possible that, as some argue, pressure from below will eventually result in far-reaching changes in the Soviet system? This refers above all to the unsatisfactory economic situation and the aspirations of the national minorities. Measured by official promises, Soviet economic performance has certainly been less than brilliant; according the the party program of 1961 per capita production in the Soviet Union was to overtake the United States by 1970. In actual fact Soviet per capita G.N.P. is still on the South European level. Seven years after the promised date there has been a relative decline in the production of consumer goods. Furthermore, the Soviety economy faced considerable difficulties in its endeavour to increase productivity and capital formation. The years of stormy progress were over, the Soviet economy has aged, or to put it more elegantly—matured. Soviet economic development was less violently shaken by cyclical ups and downs than the non-communist nations. There is no unemployment (except the hidden one which is not that extensive), and the mineral wealth of the country makes it less vulnerable to crises in the years to come than most other industrialized countries.[8] On the other hand, it will have to extend considerable help to its less fortunate allies and satellites. The Soviet regime provides its citizens with a living standard which is still low by Western standards, even though it offers more security. The real problem facing the Soviet leadership in this respect is not an acute crisis but the fact that human beings are notoriously ungrateful, that unfulfilled promises have given additional impetus to rising expectations, that even the most accomplished propaganda cannot make up for a working day that should

[8] A comparison of the Soviet growth rate with that of the other six leading industrial nations shows that in 1971 the Soviet Union ranged third (after Japan and France), in 1972 it was seventh, and last, in 1973 and 1974 it was second, in 1975 it led the field—but this was a year of general crisis and Soviet growth (two per cent) was not impressive either. In 1976 and 1977 Soviet rates of growth were about average in comparison with other industrialized countires.

have become much shorter, for living space that should have become far more ample, and for consumer goods which should be in far greater supply. Popular dissatisfaction may well bring about some economic reforms at a future date; such reforms were vaguely discussed in the late fifties and early sixties but have been shelved since. It is not at all clear however, in what way economic reform would essentially affect the monopoly of political power.

The problem of the nationalities with their manifold claims and aspirations was and continues to be in many ways more threatening. According to the last Soviet census, Russians constituted 53.4 per cent of the population of the USSR; there is some reason to assume that this figure was slightly exaggerated in the first place, if only because of the difficulty of finding a valid, universally applicable criterion for defining "nationality." For this reason and because population growth is considerably higher among Turkish peoples of the Soviet Union than among the Slavs (the former have increased by fifty per cent since 1960, the latter only by about fifteen per cent) it is no longer certain whether the Russians actually constitute the majority in the Soviet Union. There would be little reason to worry if it were true that the peoples of the Soviet Union, as officially maintained, were coexisting and collaborating with each other in a spirit of friendship and solidarity unprecedented in the history of mankind, thus creating a new and higher type of national community. But, in fact, there are many indications that the global trend towards nationalism has reinforced latent tensions in the Soviet Union. Soviet nationality policy under Stalin was one of undisguised, forced, often brutal Russification; this has been modified since his death. But since the early 1960's warnings against bourgeois nationalism among the non-Russian peoples were again voiced at frequent intervals, even though it is not easy to understand how such nationalism could possibly exist among peoples who have no bourgeoisie now, nor, for the greater part, had one in the past. In some Russian circles, on the other hand, there emerged within the last decade something akin to a cult of the Russian past such as the village tradition, Russian folk customs and art. Even if mainly cultural in character and strictly unofficial in inspiration, this trend too shows that there has been a revival of nationalism, however inchoate, and so far without any clear political aspirations.

The main problem is not just that the non-Russian peoples are forced to accept the Russian language and all that goes with it; there is a strong resistance against this. The gradual emergence of Russian as a *lingua franca* is a natural process, and it is certainly not true that the non-Russian peoples have been culturally neglected. Higher education has, in fact, spread more quickly among them than in the Russian Republic. But experience in Ireland and in other parts of the globe has shown that linguistic assimilation by no means makes for political solidarity; on the contrary, the emergency of highly educated local cadres creates new tensions as it reinforces the pressure for the de-Russification of the local party and state apparatus. Russia, in any case, was never really a melting pot, and the political limits of cultural assimilation are now clearly discernible.

Soviet nationality problems were on the whole handled with considerable expediency. There seems to be an awareness of the potentially explosive character of these issues. National problems are hardly ever discussed in public, the need for tact and consideration is always stressed. The policy with regard to Soviet Jews and Germans has been to increase the number of exit visas and at the same time to arrest the militants among them. (The number of visas issued to Soviet Jews decreased after 1975, for reasons that cannot be discussed in this context.) Radical purges of leading cadres have been more frequent in the non-Russian republics than in Moscow, but on the other hand, by way of compensation, there has been a deliberate effort to co-opt more non-Russians into the Politburo (including the secretary generals of the party of Kazakhstan, an Azerbaidjan, Uzbekistan, Balt, and, of course, some leaders of Ukranian origin). The Russian leaders probably have no illusions that there will be a truly integrated Soviet nation in the foreseeable future. Conflicts are inevitable, and present policy is to defuse them by establishing close collaboration with the leadership of the non-Russian nationalities. Hence the attempt to create an identity of material and political interests with these leaders and to make them feel that they have no future outside the wider framework of the Soviet Union. In the given circumstances this may be the only possible policy but there is no guarantee of success. While the Russian Republic has grown richer over the last two decades, most of the non-Russian peoples, being less industrialized, have grown relatively poorer. While non-Russian leaders are treated with respect in Moscow, it is also true that none of them even remotely plays a role in the party leadership comparable to that of a Stalin, a Beria, or even a Mikoyan. The same seems to be true for the army supreme command and the state security organs. Nor is it certain to what extent the collaborating elites in the national republics can be politically relied upon in Moscow; their own ambitions quite apart, they have to represent, at least to some degree, the claims of their fellow nationals, if they are not to lose their credibility at home. This is not at all easy to accomplish, for at a time when even the smallest national groups in Asia and Africa have attained national independence, with a seat in the United Nations and diplomatic recognition, Uzbeks and Georgians, Azerbaidjans and Kazakhs want at the very least to be masters in their own house. The syndrome is a familiar one, and since the Soviet Union is the last surviving multi-national empire, it is potentially quite vulnerable. Some concessions will eventually have to be made, and they could have a political momentum of far greater significance than economic reforms. Hence the enormous sensitivity shown by Soviet leaders to separatist propaganda from outside.

All this is not to imply that the days of the Soviet multi-national empire are numbered; for in the light of historical experience empires disintegrate only if their rulers lose their self-confidence and their nerve. There are no signs that this is the case in the Kremlin. Nor is there a united front of the non-Russians, as there was, at least for a little while, in 1917. On the contrary, the claims of some of the non-Russians groups collide with the interests of others which opens a great many possibilities for a policy of *divide and impera* as practised by the Tsarist regime. It is fairly safe to predict that the centrifugal trends will increase and that a new Soviet leadership will have at the very least to devote far more attention to nationality policy.

The challenge represented by sections of the intelligentsia is almost insignificant by comparison; they can be contained without undue difficulty. Once upon a time the Russian intelligentsia was a revolutionary force, but it ought to be recalled that what made it unique—the loyalty to great ideas, the willingness to fight and sacrifice—was always confined to a small number of people. For every Belinsky, Herzen, and Chernichevski there were a hundred others whose attitudes ranged from giving platonic support to the critics of the regime to blatant conformist. It is true that "public opinion" (i.e. the intelligentsia) in its majority turned decisively against the Tsarist government towards the end of the century. Equally there are very few members of the intelligentsia now who are not critical of at least some aspects of the regime, be it only as the result of the erosion of the incentives they receive. But the Soviet regime can live with this kind of passive opposition, critical mumblings and anti-establishment jokes. Threats and promises will keep the intelligentsia in line. With the exception of some individuals of exceptional courage, the record of the Soviet intelligentsia has not been much better than that of intellectuals under other dictatorships. It has, of course, in fairness always to be remembered that intellectual resistance under Tsarism was far less risky.

Some Soviet intellectuals joined the ruling group and became *na-chalniki,* bosses of one sort or another; these were usually neither the best nor the brightest, and they made their career paying fulsome praise to the historical mission of the party and its giant achievements. The great majority, while paying lip service to the official slogans, tried not to get too involved in politics. Talented young people of integrity tend not to choose a political career. Among the young members of the intelligentsia, official ideology is treated with scepticism, even open cynicism. But sceptics and cynics lacking firm beliefs and values, will not, as a rule, choose the road of open defiance with all the danger involved. They will not risk their careers but opt for the "private sphere" and will invest their energies in the field of their professional specialization. They may follow politics closely, at home and abroad, and be better informed than the average Western intellectual, but they will be passive onlookers, only too aware of their impotence. Most of them complain about the stifling cultural atmosphere. There is no reason to doubt that Soviet thinkers, writers, or artists are at least as gifted as their Western counterparts, yet it is difficult to think of major Soviet artistic achievements, plays or movies, of philosophical, economic, sociological, or historical studies of lasting value to have come out of Russia for a long time. The general tiredness if felt in the cultural sphere perhaps most acutely; even the late fifties were an exciting period in comparison with the 1970's; once there were at least hopes of a thaw, in the seventies there was mainly boredom or withdrawal into the "private sphere."

Twenty years ago it was widely believed among Soviet experts in the West that the Soviet Union could not possibly stand still; it would either be transformed or degenerate. Yet there was a third possibility, and the years since have shown that economic development on the domestic scene coupled with political, social, and cultural stagnation is equally possible and that it may, in fact, go on for a long time.

The general stagnation reflects itself in the prevailing ideological confusion. It has been noted that among the population at large, including the overwhelming majority of members of the Communist party, there is little interest in theoretical issues. But ideology cannot simply be written off—it provides, after all, the legitimation for the present political system, for the dominant role of the party. Classical Marxist-Leninst doctrine had very little to say about the future Communist society, and what it did predict (in Lenin's *State and Revolution*, for instance) has been embarrassingly unrealistic. There is no ideological guidance in the works of the founding fathers on the future development of Soviety society or on the role of the Soviet Union among the other Communist states. It is still the custom to stress the importance of historical materialism and the vital importance of the socialist mode of production. But if there is any truth in what Engels wrote about the jump from the realm of necessity to the realm of freedom, subjective ("idealistic") factors should in fact be of increasing importance. For according to all the predictions, under communism man should have become master of his own destiny, no longer subject to blind, anonymous forces as in past socio-economic systems. Hence the need for a new philosophical approach, or at the very least, for a new "creative" use of Marxism-Leninism. Soviet society faces many problems ranging from the relationship between the individual and the collective (the question of individual freedom) to the future of the family, of education, the problem of remuneration for work. This applies to the setting not only of economic but also of social targets, to integrating new scientific insights into the official state philosophy. In principle, Soviet leaders, including Stalin, have always opposed "dogmatism," yet in practice they have shied away from even modest attempts at innovation. The official philosophers have devoted most of their energy to criticizing bourgeois, "revisionist," and Maoist doctrines rather than thinking about the future of their own system. Thus the Soviet Union, to all intents and purposes, today lacks an ideological compass suitable for orientation in the present period, let alone for future planning and development. Non-communist societies or old-style dictatorships may be able to exist without an official philosophy; the Soviet Union vitally needs it for reasons that need hardly be elaborated. Individual problems may be solved in a pragmatic way, but there is a limit beyond which pragmatism becomes an *ersatz* philosophy, and this, of course, is not acceptable either to the Soviet leadership.

A conservative policy at home, does not however imply non-interventionism abroad. Historical experience from the French revolution to Cuba shows that it is precisely in the post-revolutionary phase that expansion takes place. While Brezhnev and his colleagues showed caution, they tried persistently and not unskilfully to build up Soviet military strength and expand their political sphere of influence. By and large they have shown more initiative abroad than at home. The idea that the Soviet leaders have no wish to see Communists in power in still more countries, because this, according to past experience, will only cause tension and conflict, is based on a misunderstanding of Soviet psychology and policy. The Soviet Union is still the leader of the communist camp (or what remains of it); if it became a *status quo* power, if it were not to press for the victory of communism on a global scale it would lose its legitimacy as the leader of the communist world. The Soviet Union is a superpower, but not by virtue of its economic performance or by the irresistable attraction of its official ideology. It is mainly through its military strength that it has acheived superpower status, and it is through military strength that it will maintain and reinforce it. No Soviet leader is ignorant of this fact; no one will be able to disregard it in the foreseeable future. And he also knows that, in order to justify the economic shortcomings and the political dictatorship, Soviet citizens have to be persuaded even at a time of detente that powerful enemies still threaten the socialist achievements and that the utmost vigilance and iron discipline are needed as much now as in the past. Stagnation at home reinforces the need for an active, "dynamic" foreign policy.

There has been a great deal of speculation in the West about the policy of a future generation of Soviet leaders—the successors of the Brezhnevs, Suslovs, and Kosygins. But will it matter all that much what leader or group of leaders emerge? It could be of importance if the struggle for power results in a one-man dictatorship. A new Stalin, even a new Khrushchev, would certainly make a difference; no one can say in what way, for nothing is known about his personality. In the Soviet system only the leader who has already reached the center of the stage can show any individuality, but in order to reach the center of the stage he must suppress his personality. One-man rule however seems an unlikely prospect except perhaps in an acute national or international emergency. The trauma of the Stalinist era (and to a far lesser extent, of Khrushchev's rule) has taught the upper bureaucratic crust the obvious lesson that their tenure, indeed their physical survival, cannot be assured in conditions of totally arbitrary rule; hence the necessity for a balance of power at the very top.

The generation of leaders who will come to the fore will be only moderately well-informed about the outside world. This is not to say that they will be "Russia firsters." The fact that the Soviet Union is a superpower has a logic and a momentum of its own, and Soviet leaders are drawn into foreign affairs as irresistibly as American presidents. There is bound to be continuity. They will strengthen the Soviet military potential; making the most of Western weaknesses without causing a breakdown in detente, they will secure and expand the Soviet sphere of influence. They are likely to be more dynamic, partly because younger people are usually more enterprising than their elders, but also because in contrast to their predecessors, they have as yet to prove their competence and legitimacy as the heirs of Lenin and Stalin, as the leaders of the Communist camp. No major changes can be expected on the domestic front, for the present system with all its great defects is still workable, and it certainly guarantees the interests of the stratum the party leaders represent; far-reaching experimentation, it is feared, could only have dangerous consequences. Only a grave internal crisis or major challenge from outside could provide a spur to radical reform; at present there is no such need.

The stagnation of political and social systems is not a new phenomenon in history, sometimes it has lasted for centuries. Prolonged stagnation had admittedly become rarer in an age of rapid technological and economic change. Our experience with the capacity for change of totalitarian regimes is limited, but the evidence so far suggests that a country can make economic and technological progress while retaining a totalitarian power structure. Such structures do not wither away even after the revolution has run its course, and the political system which it has created cannot be maintained without strict control from above.[9]

Some of the destabilizing factors threatening the Soviet political regime have been mentioned, but there are others pointing in the opposite direction. The growing complexity (and vulnerability) of modern societies reinforces the trend towards strict controls and the concentration of power in the hands of a small elite. If there is discontent in the Soviet Union there is also a substantial section of the population, counting perhaps millions, which has a vested interest in the maintenance of the regime. It will oppose any change out of the fear, quite rightly perceived, that such changes would adversely affect its status and privileges. This refers not only to those in the key positions of party and state, the economy, the army and the state security organs, but also to the lesser secretaries, officers, instructors, and bureaucrats. Given the fact that the tools of coercion and propaganda are monopolized in their hands and that they have become far more effective than ever before in history, their number is quite sufficient to maintain law and order—and, of course, their own rule. Military defeat (such as happened in Germany or Italy) or a disaster of similar magnitude could bring about the downfall of a totalitarian regime. But the nuclear age seems to have ruled out global war, and changes in the system can reasonably be expected to come only from within. On rare occasions in hisotry, dictators and ruling groups have lost their hold, sometimes without an apparently objec-

[9] Some observers have maintained for a number of years that the Soviet political system is no longer totalitarian but that, as a result of social and economic changes, it has lost its revolutionary dynamism, large-scale terror is no longer necessary, and the regime is more open to pressure from below. The ruling party still monopolizes political power, but its function has changed; to impose its rule it need no longer apply extreme (totalitarian) methods, and more flexible (authoritarian) ones are more effective. Such interpretations are not altogether new; some of the earliest attempts to explain totalitarianism (by Hans Kelsen, for instance) were based on the assumption that it was simply an extreme form of dictatorship and étatism (statism), the difference between totalitarianism and an authoritarian regime being the degree of power concentrated and applied. Consequently, there is no qualitative difference between them. This approach has certain merits, especially with regard to countries such as Poland. But it creates new difficulties inasmuch as the authoritarian label can be quite misleading. A term applied to the Soviet and Chinese regime on one hand, and to countries such as Afghanistan, Morocco, or Iraq on the other, is not of much help on the theoretical level and does not provide political guidance.

tive reason; there have been sudden or gradual changes of heart; some have mellowed because they grew older, in other cases generational conflict has been the agent of change. But such prospects are not very likely for the time being in a regime in which the dictatorship has been deeply institutionalized, and which can reproduce itself—biologically, if not ideologically.

The defects of the Soviet regime would be more glaring, the present leadership would find it much more difficult to defend its record, if Western societies were better able to cope with their own difficulties. This is true for the economic as well as the political situation; it refers to the general drift, the weakness of leadership, the lack of purpose, the emergence of separatist movements in many Western countries. Soviet leadership may be mediocre but its achievements have to be measured not by absolute standards but by comparison with the present leadership of the Western world. Since Western weakness also extends to the defense of its own freedom and since it is coupled with deep-seated confusions about the character of the Soviet system (ranging from delusions about its impending downfall to fantasies about its democratization and liberalization); Soviet leaders need not be unduly worried about the Western danger. Lastly, there is the possibility of a split in the Politburo following a dispute on political or personal lines. If one of the parties to the conflict (or both) appealed for support not just to the Central Committee, if the tug-of-war spilled over into the middle echelons of the Communist party and perhaps even to its lower ranks, this could conceivably result in the institutionalization of factions in the party and the open airing of political disputes as happened in the 1920's. Such a development would be a giant step forward compared to the present monolithic set-up. Events in Hungary in 1956 and in Czechoslovakia in 1968 have shown that, though movement towards freedom in the Communist block might originate in Warsaw, Prague, or Budapest, it can only succeed if it coincides with a parallel development in Moscow. The existence of conflicts in the Soviet leadership can be taken for granted, but the prospects for a lasting split resulting in the dispersal of political power are at present unlikely; for the interests linking Soviet leaders are still much stronger than the issues that may divide them. Even if there were a stalemate in the party leadership this could invite a coup by a military leader, or by a group of army and police officials. The odds against democratization in the Soviet Union seem to be overwhelming at the present time.

Optimistic Western predictions in this respect have rested on the assumption that modernization will inevitably lead to a democratic revival in the Soviet Union. It is still quite widely believed in the West, and not only by Marxists, that dictatorship somehow disappears once it becomes "objectively" superfluous, an obstacle to progress. But experience so far has shown that while economic development may lead to *embourgeoisement* (within limits), and the erosion of ideology, it does not lead, by its own momentum, to a free society. Marxists still refuse to accept that while their theory may be of use to explain bourgeois revolutions, it is of no help if applied to the Soviet Union or other communist regimes. In a communist society a new elite (or vanguard class) is the holder of all political power. That this new elite claims to act on behalf of the working class is of no great relevance; it was one of the central parts of Marx's argument that by abolishing all classes the working class would not only emancipate itself, but abolish class rule altogether and make society self-governing. Since dictatorship continues in the Soviet Union, it must be taken that either class rule has not been abolished or a new ruling class has simply replaced the old one; alternatively, it must be accepted that political oppression is a phenomenon quite independent of the existence of social classes.

The Soviet regime is without precedent, not because the revolution from above has accomplished its aims, but because for the first time in history its political results have been successfully "frozen." Historical experience is therefore of limited help in assessing the future of the system. True, there are enormous differences between the situation now and in 1950, just as Russia in 1925 was a freer country than twenty years later. There have been periods of senseless slaughter, and others in which a bare minimum of violence was used. But the decisive lesson is that all these changes have taken place within clearly defined parameters, all scheduled to keep the regime in power with little coercion if possible, with brutal means if necessary. All political and social regimes are subject to change, and the Soviet Union is no exception. But if one day there is to be a movement towards freedom in that country, it will be triggered off by forces and take place in circumstances that cannot be forseen today.[10]

EASTERN EUROPE

The 1970's were, on the whole, uneventful years in Eastern Europe as well as in the Soviet Union. The only major changes in leadership were the resignation of Walter Ulbricht, of which mention has already been made, and of Wladislaw Gomulka, following the strikes and riots in Poland in December 1970. Edward Gierek, who succeeded Gomulka, faced a similar crisis in June 1976 when the Polish government tried to introduce substantial price increases affecting essential commodities. It was forced to retreat temporarily, at any rate, and Gierek, in contrast to Gomulka, managed to ride the storm.

Economic progress in Eastern Europe was quite remarkable in the years up to 1974. But after that date the effects of the world-wide recession caused a substantial slowdown, partly as the result of higher raw material prices, partly as the consequence of higher defense spending (about 10.6 per cent annually between 1970 and 1976) but above all as the result of serious imbalances that had developed—consumer expectations that could not be met and import requirements that outran export capabilities. Bulgaria's hard currency indebtedness to the West was four times its annual exports, and it was almost as high in Poland. A study of the U.S. Congressional Joint Economic Committee published in 1977, predicted that without help, debts to the West were likely to become unmanageable by 1980 and that drastic cutbacks in economic growth would ensue.

This process has affected all Eastern European countries. Hungary and Poland pursued a relatively liberal line, the former because there was little open domestic opposition, the latter because, on the contrary,

[10] There have been painstaking studies of the Soviet economy (*Soviet Economy in a New Perspective,* Joint Economic Committee of the U.S. Congress [Washington, 1976]) but nothing even remotely on a similar scale on Soviet domestic and foreign policy in the 1970's. The most comprehensive effort is *The Soviet Empire: Expansion and Detente,* (Critical Choices for Americans, vol. 9 [Lexington, 1976]). Some relevant articles published in the periodical literature are listed in D. K. Simes, *Detente and Conflict: Soviet Foreign Policy 1972–77.* Washington Papers, no. 44 (Beverly Hills, 1977).

criticism of the government was almost universal. East Germany and Czechoslovakia used tough measures of control and repression. Yugoslavia and Rumania continued to the best of their limited ability to pursue an independent line, trying not to antagonize the Soviet leadership more than necessary; there were ups and downs in their relationship with Moscow as there had been in previous years. There was apprehension in Western capitals that Yugoslavia would enter a period of acute crisis after Tito's disappearance from the political scene. In 1977 Albania turned against China, its only ally; it could not be said for certain whether ideological reasons were involved, or whether China had simply lost interest in that small outpost of Stalinism in Europe. Eastern Europe, to summarize, was faced with major problems and a perspective of even greater tensions ahead. The fate of the region no doubt continued to worry the Soviet leadership, but there was no reason for acute concern, for its hold over the Warsaw pact countries was secure. Though the Brezhnev doctrine was no longer invoked, everybody took it for granted that it was still in force. Eastern Europe belongs to the Soviet sphere of influence. The presence of the Soviet armed forces is a sufficient guarantee.

THE MILITARY IMBALANCE

Of all the problems affecting West-East relations the question of European security has been the most important since the end of the Second World War, and it became even more acute in the 1970's. There have been considerable differences of opinion in the West about both the extent of the Soviet and East European military build-up and its meaning. Up to 1975 it had been generally assumed, on the basis of CIA estimates, that the Soviet Union spent some 6 to 8 per cent of its G.N.P. on its armed forces, but following some more thorough investigations it was announced in 1975 that this had been an underestimate by no less than 50 per cent.[11] By comparison the United States allocated some 6.6 per cent of its G.N.P. to defence between 1970 and 1975, and the NATO allies in Europe only 3.7 per cent. It emerged furthermore that

[11] A. Marshall, in *Survival* (March 1976); W. T. Lee in *Airforce Magazine* (March 1976).

military spending in Eastern Europe, mainly on mechanization and modernization, grew in the 1970's at an even quicker rate than in the Soviet Union. The net result was a slow but steady improvement of the Warsaw bloc military capability while the position of NATO deteriorated; since there had been an imbalance between the two sides from the very beginning this became a matter of growing concern. The arguments against "alarmism" adduced by some Western observers are briefly as follows. It is no longer maintained, as in the past, that the West has always over-estimated Soviet and East European strategic and conventional military capability, that the "military-industrial complex," be it for reasons of profit or self-aggrandizement, has constantly engaged in worst case analysis to obtain greater defense allocations so causing a rearmament spiral, an "action-reaction chain." The facts and figures about Soviet bloc armament that emerged in the middle of 1970 can no longer be explained in the light of these assumptions. Albert Wohlstetter, in a pioneering study, has demonstrated that while there was in the early 1960's a Western over-estimate of Soviet ICBMs (the famous "missile gap"), Soviet strategic deployment has been systematically underestimated ever since.[12] The arguments of the "anti-alarmists" concern not so much facts and figures but their interpretation. Thus it is argued that the Warsaw pact G.N.P. is smaller than that of the NATO countries, and that their economies are less efficient; hence they need to spend more on defense than the West without necessarily achieving greater results. It is maintained, furthermore, than even if the Western forces are numerically inferior, they have the edge in quality, and that recent technological developments, such as precision-guided ammunition (PGM), favor defense rather than attack. Insofar as overall Soviet aims are concerned, it is said that these are purely defensive, that Western analysts tend to forget that the Soviet Union faces potential enemies in the East as well as the West, that the Russians have always been great believers in figures, and that the trauma caused by the German invasion of 1941 has strengthened their resolve never again to neglect their military power—but always for defensive purposes.

These arguments are open to increasing doubt. The Soviet and Warsaw pact forces in Europe are, after all, much bigger than those

[12] Reprinted in *Defending America* (New York, 1977).

deployed on the Chinese border. If the Russians had suffered a shock in 1941, so had Britain, France, and even the United States in the Second World War. And even if one concedes, for argument's sake, that Soviet intentions are at present purely defensive—an assumption that is doubtful in view of the concentration of arms systems of an offensive character—there is no guarantee that these intentions may not change at some future date. Nor is it any longer true that the West has a "monumental qualitative lead"; it has qualitative superiority in some respects, there is rough equality in others, and it is inferior in some fields. NATO weapons, in contrast to those used by the Warsaw pact, are not standardized and interchangeable, to mention but one other major Western weakness.

The fact that there is an imbalance of forces has no longer been open to legitimate doubt for years. An American study prepared in 1976 reached the conclusion that Warsaw pact air-ground forces in northern and central Europe outnumbered NATO in nearly every category. The Soviet side, it was claimed, could quickly achieve the classic ratio of 3 : 1 superiority in ground combat forces that many military men cite as a prerequisite for successful offensive operations.[13] It is true that a comparison of divisions is misleading because NATO divisions are bigger than those of the Warsaw pact. In terms of manpower, 940,000 Warsaw pact troops in 1977 faced 635,000 NATO troops. But this figure also conveys a somewhat misleading picture, for the logistic tail-to-combat ratio is different or, in non-professional language, the Warsaw pact forces have more combat soldiers, whereas a much higher ratio of NATO troops is engaged in logistics. (Of 190,000 U.S. troops in U.S.

---

[13] *U.S./Soviet Military Balance.* The Library of Congress (Washington 1976), p. 9. An official American study prepared in 1977 reached the conclusion that the Warsaw pact had only a 2 : 1 superiority but mentioned a "distinct tactical advantage" due to the Warsaw Pact's ability to mass combat power on major attack routes. (New York *Times,* January 6, 1978.) Growing American unease about the situation in Europe was given official expression in the annual statement to Congress by the Secretary of Defense (February 2, 1978). Dr. Harold Brown, not known as a "hawk" given to alarmist outbursts, said on this occasion that he was "seriously concerned" about the increasingly precarious balance between the Warsaw Pact forces and NATO. Substantial increases in U.S. capability to reinforce NATO in Europe were announced on that occasion. The prospects for agreement on the limitation on conventional forces in Europe would have been infinitely better, had such readiness to match the Soviet military build up been manifested earlier—yet another proof that the road to lost opportunities in West-East relations is paved by good intentions.

Army Europe only 75,000 are in combat divisions.) The Warsaw pact forces have 19,000 main battle tanks in North and Central Europe, compared with 7,000 NATO tanks. NATO has 2,700 field medium and heavy guns, mortars and rocket launches as compared with 5,600 of the other side. This discrepancy is striking but what matters even more is the fundamental strategic asymmetry between the essentially defensive nature of the Western alliance and the Warsaw pact forces presenting the "classic profile of mobile striking-forces designed to carry out swift offensives on a continental scale."[14]

This leaves the airforces of the two sides, a field in which NATO has traditionally outclassed the Warsaw Pact, even though the latter had numerical superiority in almost every category.

	NATO	WARSAW PACT
Light bombers	185	225
Fighter/ground attack	1250	1375
Interceptors	375	2050
Reconnaissance	275	550[15]

But it is precisely in this field that Warsaw bloc modernization has made most progress both through the introduction of new types of aircraft and more sophisticated electronic equipment. If there is still a gap by 1977, it has narrowed rapidly; in this field as in most others, technology can hardly ever entirely offset numerical advantages.

No mention has been made of the comparative naval strength of the two sides. Here, too, endless discussions about numbers and their meaning have taken place. Numbers can be twisted to meet a multitude of requirements. One of the most authoritative Western sources has reached the conclusion that "so far as strength of the fleet is concerned, it has become apparent that the Soviet Navy has reached a plateau of numbers. . . . However, the armament of the new ships and the introduction of carrier-borne aircraft has suggested an extended outlook beyond that of pure defense."[16]

What then is the significance of the Warsaw Pact build up? Noting

[14] E. N. Luttwak, in *Defending America*, op. cit., p. 176.

[15] *The Military Balance*, 1976/7, IISS (London, 1977), p. 102.

[16] John Moore, *Jane's Fighting Ships 1976/7* (London, 1976) quoted in *Seapower* (September 1976).

that the number of Soviet divisions in Europe had increased from twenty-six to thirty-one during the last ten years, whereas U.S. forces were reduced by one third, the *1977/8 Military Balance* nevertheless reached the conclusion that the overall balance is still such as to make military aggression unattractive. "The defences are of such sizes and quality that any attempts to breach them would require major attack. The consequences for an attacker would be incalculable, and the risks, including that of nuclear escalation, must impose caution."[17] Other experts have taken a less optimistic view. Robert Close, a Belgian general, and former director of studies at the NATO defense college in Rome, wrote in 1976 that the disparity of forces is such that the Warsaw pact could put thirty-nine divisions into the front line in a first offensive wave within forty-eight hours; a second wave augmented by major Czech forces could be in action in six days. NATO's defense forces, on the other hand, consist of twenty-two divisions, and it would take much longer to reinforce them. Other Western study groups have also reached the conclusion that since the Soviet Union has at least reached nuclear parity with the U.S., its advantage in conventional strength creates a new situation in Europe which makes a new NATO strategic concept imperative. Lastly it is argued that Soviet military doctrine differs in essential respects from Western thinking as it does not share the belief that numbers of strategic weapons do not matter once a certain limit has been attained and that the Soviet Union is as vulnerable to a countervalue attack as the United States. Evidence to this effect has been adduced from Soviet sources. "There is profound erroneousness and harm in the disorienting claims of bourgeois ideologists that there will be no victor in a thermonuclear world war."[18] Hence the conclusion that a Soviet attack can not be ruled out despite the risks involved.

Fears of a Soviet attack are considered far-fetched by most Western experts. But there is no question that the Western consensus on Soviet intentions has shifted. There is a general feeling that the NATO conventional force posture has become less credible and that while a major conflict in Western Europe is still unlikely, a "crumbling of NATO

[17] Ibid., p. 109. The same figures for force levels had appeared in the *Military Balance* for 1971/2, p. 80.
[18] N. V. Karabanov, quoted in R. Pipes, "Why the Soviet Union Thinks it Could Fight and Win a Nuclear War," *Commentary* (July 1977).

strength might tempt the USSR to apply greater pressure on Western Europe, that this could lead to miscalculation and some risk of conflict."[19] For whatever way one looked at the Warsaw pact build-up in Europe, it can no longer be explained with references to legitimate defense interests. If, on the other hand, an attack also seems no more than a distant possibility at present, the purpose of a build-up involving the allocation of resources the Soviet leaders could ill afford to waste, seems inexplicable in purely military terms. As a recent authoritative American study has noted, "With each passing year it has become more difficult to explain the continuing momentum in the Soviet defence buildup."[20] But these difficulties exist only as long as the political motives behind the build-up are ignored. Soviet leaders do not share the belief widespread in the West that in the nuclear age military power can no longer be translated into political influence.

Edward Luttwak has pointed to the different functions fulfilled by NATO and the Warsaw pact. While NATO forces were (and are) deployed for purely military—and purely negative—defensive purposes,

> The first mission of the Soviet forces is to secure the unwilling obedience of the peoples of Eastern Europe; the second is to project military power into Western Europe, in order to obtain a degree of political leverage which neither their provincial culture, nor their unattractive society, nor their primitive economy can secure for them; and it is only their third mission to defend the Soviet Union in the exceedingly remote possibility that a NATO military threat might materialize.[21]

The implications of the Warsaw Pact military build-up were only gradually and reluctantly accepted in Western Europe. This was a painful process; democratic governments, and a fortiori public opinion in democratic societies, are willing to go to almost any length to deny the existence of threats to their security unless and until there is a clear and present danger to their very survival. Mr. Chamberlain's appeasement

[19] H. Owen and C. L. Schultz (eds.), Setting National Priorities: The Next Ten Years (Washington, 1976), pp. 27, 67.
[20] B. M. Blachman et al., The Soviet Military Buildup and U.S. Defense Spending (The Brookings Institution, Washington, 1977), p. 54.
[21] Luttwak, op. cit., p. 185.

policy in the 1930's was not the exception but the rule. The instinctive inclination of democratic governments is always to placate, and to give into blackmail. Some justification for a policy of this kind can always be found. Germany, after all, had not been given a fair deal at Versailles in 1919, and the Sudeten Germans had overwhelmingly opted against Czechoslovakia and for Germany. The arguments used in the 1970's were different in kind: it was said that the situation had greatly improved since Stalin's days, and that it was the main endeavor of the Soviet leaders to work for a better life for their people. If there were doves as well as hawks in the Kremlin was in not wiser if Western governments behaved in such a way as to strengthen the position of the former? West Europeans could think of a great many reasons why they should not match the Warsaw pact military effort; Frenchmen and Italians would believe; or pretend to believe, that they were not immediately threatened in case of war; in Britain it would be argued that defense cuts were perfectly legitimate, since Britain had been spending a little more on a per capita basis than its European neighbors even though in real terms it was spending less. The logic was curious, for the defense efforts of a country should be commensurate with that of its potential adversaries because it is unlikely to fight its friends. But it is vain to look for logical consistency behind arguments that rest not so much on rational analysis as on a deep-seated desire for peace. Cuts in defense spending were explained in some West European countries with reference to the economic situation, the need to provide better social services, and a dozen other good reasons. But once all the reasons had been adduced, it is still true that the gross national product of Western Europe is considerably greater than that of Eastern Europe including the Soviet Union and that as a result of neglecting their defenses they have maneuvered themselves into a potentially dangerous position. At the very least they have perpetuated their dependence on the United States.

Initial West European reaction to the Eastern bloc military build-up was to ignore it—but this was difficult once the imbalance became too marked. Subsequently, it seemed a good idea to intensify the search for an agreement on disarmament. The history of the "Mutual and Balanced Force Reduction Talks" goes back to a resolution adopted by the NATO foreign ministers at their meeting in Reykjavik in June 1968.

This declaration was reiterated at a meeting in Rome (May 1970) and the same month Mr. Brezhnev, in a speech at Tiflis, expressed interest in the proposals. Yet another three years were to pass before representatives from nineteen countries first met in Vienna on January 31, 1973. The reasons for the delay on the part of the Warsaw Pact were obvious. During the early 1970's there was strong pressure in the United States for substantial, unilateral troop withdrawals from Europe (such as the Mansfield Amendment) and there were similar domestic pressures in most European countries. In these circumstances there was little inducement for the Soviet leaders to make any concessions, and they became more interested only after it appeared that there would be no unilateral Western withdrawal. The MBFR (mutual and balanced force reductions) talks continued for years with various summer and winter recesses, but there was no agreement even on token reductions. The negotiators faced many difficult problems. They had to agree about the area in which forces were to be reduced, about the nature of the forces and the equipment to be affected. There was the question of data; as in the SALT talks, negotiations proceeded on the basis of figures provided by the West. These figures were always contested by the Warsaw Pact representatives who did not however furnish detailed figures of their own.[22] NATO representatives faced a double disadvantage. On one hand there was the Warsaw Pact superiority in troops, tanks, artillery, and other equipment. But there was also an in-built geopolitical imbalance. A Soviet division withdrawn from a demarcation line to be agreed upon would be moved some 650 km, whereas an American division would have to retreat 5000 km. The geographical imbalance could not be changed, but its existence reinforced the insistence of the NATO representatives on balanced force reductions. The Warsaw Pact, on the other hand, rejected the notion that there should be a common ceiling. If the Warsaw Pact forces were stronger, this was so for historical reasons that were not to be questioned. As the Warsaw Pact build-up continued, and as the East European forces gained in mobility, it was no longer certain whether even an asymmetrical force reduction (such as

[22] After three years of talks they provided a few figures, according to which they had only a few thousand more troops than NATO; but there was no detailed breakdown, and since they opposed verification, there was no certainty that the figures were correct.

suggested by the West) unless very substantial, would make a major contribution to European security.

Thus, albeit reluctantly, most European NATO countries reached the conclusion that they could not afford to cut their defense spending any further, and some of them, notably France, West Germany, Belgium, and the Netherlands, decided to reverse the trend.[23] Britain and Denmark on the other hand, continued to reduce their armed forces, even maintaining that the cuts would not affect their military strength. Little need be said about the validity of these arguments, since it is not even certain that they were meant to be taken seriously.

An interim balance sheet of detente in Europe shows that the "dramatic transformation" of the world and European scene that had been predicted in 1971 certainly has not materialized. The general atmosphere of West-East relations improved at first, only to deteriorate subsequently. Nevertheless there is reason to believe that detente is likely to continue for the time being, albeit in a lower key. A Soviet military attack is still improbable, nor does it seem likely that an attempt will be make by the Soviet Union in the next few years to impose political control on Europe through direct threats of force. Nevertheless, if present trends continue, there is the possibility that the balance of power in Europe could change, with the Soviet Union emerging as the dominant power on the continent. The political consequences of such a change have been widely discussed in recent years, so has the issue of Finlandization to which we have to turn next.

[23] It is, of course, much too early to state with any degree of certainty when this turning point occurred. Most NATO nations reduced defense spending between 1964 and 1974 until their quantitative inferiority reached dangerous proportions and their qualitative superiority also began to deteriorate. During 1974 and 1976 the NATO authorities made some modest efforts to redress the balance, but the neglect of a whole decade could not be repaired in such short a time. Furthermore, a consensus on the major measures to be taken was still lacking on the highest political level; a first step in this direction was the London summit in 1977 which decided to improve the efficiency of NATO and to increase by 3% (in real terms) annual defense spending. The NATO Long Term Defense Program of May 1977 decided on high priority measures in ten critical fields. The results that have been achieved since are reviewed in detail in J. Galen, "Restoring the NATO–Warsaw Pact Balance," *Armed Forces Journal* (September 1978).

8

FINLANDIZATION

The history of Finland since the Second World War is not only of considerable intrinsic interest, but also of significance for all of Europe, as the debate on "Finlandization" has shown. But Finland has largely remained *terra incognita;* there has been no systematic press coverage from Helsinki, and the existing scholarly literature in languages other than Finnish is not extensive. It is also not altogether reliable, because the self-censorship practiced inside Finland has infected Western publications on Finland. The reasons underlying this are not altogether dishonorable. To report the whole truth about Finland is to give offense to the Finns, who have to maneuver in a very delicate situation. To describe the predicament of the Finns is not to make it any easier. In the circumstances, many Western friends of Finland have shown great circumspection and restraint in their writings—not to put it more strongly.

All this is quite admirable, but it has resulted in belittling the dilemma constantly facing Finland. It has created a distorted image of Finland as an independent country enjoying the best of both worlds, and it has injected an element of unreality into the debate on Finlandization which has now preoccupied Europeans for more than a decade.

Finland, which gained independence in 1917, was attacked by the Soviet Union in 1939 and defeated after a stubborn resistance. It had to cede part of its territory. To regain what it had lost, Finland joined Germany in the war in June 1941; in 1944 it made a separate peace treaty with the Soviet Union and turned against the German army. Stalin could have incorporated Finland in 1944/5 but he preferred not to do so; there may have been good reasons for this magnanimity—the war, after all, had not yet ended, and the annexation of Finland at this date would have precipitated a conflict with the West. In all probability there was not just one reason but several; strategically Finland was less important than other territories annexed by the Russians. The Russians had a healthy respect for the Finns who had fought stubbornly for their freedom for a long time and who would have been more difficult to digest than the Latvians and the Estonians, for instance. Nor is it unthinkable that Stalin wanted to keep Finland as a showcase for Russia's basically benevolent intentions towards the rest of the world. Be that as it may, Finland did not become a Soviet republic, but a price had to be paid, and continues to be paid to this very day. The price to be paid can be summarized, very briefly, as follows:

1 Finland is a neutral country, but not vis-à-vis the Soviet Union towards which it has special obligations. It must not oppose any major Soviet foreign political initiative nor enter any commitments without Soviet approval, and it is expected to give active support to some aspects of Soviet foreign policy.

2 Finland is permitted to have an army, but only within the limits set by the Soviet Union.

3 The Soviet Union does not interfere in Finland's internal affairs. But only political parties approved by the Soviet Union can participate in the government, and the same applies *a fortiori* to the president and prime minister. There is no censorship, but the Finns are expected to exert self-censorship. Communist participation in the government is desirable, but it is not a *conditio sine qua non*. On the other hand, Finnish statesmen are expected to make frequent declarations stressing the friendly, mutually beneficient relations with the Soviet Union.

4 Finland is expected to have close commercial relations with the Communist bloc, but in this respect there are no hard and fast rules, and pressure has been more sporadic than in other fields—perhaps in view of Finland's limited importance as a trading partner and Comecon's limited capacity to supply consumer goods.

5 To deny the existence of Finlandization is an essential part of the price.

The issue of neutrality has been endlessly discussed but it is perhaps the least important aspect of the Finnish predicament. According to the first two articles of the Soviet-Finnish Treaty of 1948 and subsequent agreements, Finland made certain, definitive commitments, such as holding military consultations with the Soviet Union, which are not compatible with neutrality however liberally interpreted. It is true that Finnish Spokesmen (such as Max Jakobson) have argued that the treaty does not commit Finland to anything beyond the defense of her own territory. Unfortunately, this interpretation has not been accepted by the Russians. Mr. Jakobson's book was bitterly attacked in the Soviet press, and given the facts of political and military power, it is, of course, the Soviet interpretation that counts. Mr. Jakobson, it will be recalled, was a candidate for the post of Secretary General of the U.N. some years ago. The Soviet Union vetoed his appointment; that Mr. Jakobson is of Jewish origin probably did not help in this context. But the decisive consideration was no doubt that he was not thought to be politically sufficiently "safe," he was suspected of taking neutrality seriously. Seen in this light, President Kekkonen's frequent claims that "all Great Powers have explicitly recognized Finnish neutrality" are either a statement of intent, not of fact, or are based on an interpretation of neutrality which radically differs from the one generally accepted. Insofar as the Soviet Union is concerned, Finland, to repeat once again, is not a neutral country; it is in a special category, belonging to neither the so-called socialist countries nor the real neutrals. President Kekkonen is frequently praised in Soviet publications for having explained to his countrymen that they would suffer if they insisted on the "formalist-legalistic interpretation" of neutrality.[1] On the other hand, it should be noted that President Kekkonen and other Finnish spokesmen have emphasized Finnish neutrality—as they interpret it—on every possible occasion, and on a few opportunities, such as at the Helsinki Conference, they have managed to smuggle references to Finland's neutrality into international accords signed by the Russians.

Neutrality is a very complicated problem in international law; it can be discussed endlessly and without much profit. The issue of independence, on the other hand, is, of course, infinitely more important; it is of immediate practical relevance to the political, social, and cultural life of the Finnish people. Compared with Russia's East European satellites, Finland is independent and free. It has many political parties (ten), and many (too many) elections. Its institutions are democratic, its constitution is scrupulously observed. There are no arbitrary arrests; in fact, no one ever has been sent to prison for political reasons. Finns can freely

---

[1] Thus said V. V. Pokhlebkin the author of the most substantial Soviet study of Soviet-Finnish relations *SSSR-Finlandia* (Moscow, 1975), p. 392.

travel abroad; the larger part of its economy is not nationalized. Most of its trade is with its Scandinavian neighbors and the West. There is a vigorous cultural life and Soviet influence in this respect is certainly not overwhelming. Foreign books and newspapers are freely available. Finland, in short, enjoys the same freedoms which are the share of the Western nations.

But there is another side of the picture, less visible but always present. These are the consequences of the Kekkonen line according to which Finland's survival is assured only if Soviet confidence in Finnish policy is maintained. Indeed the maintenance of this confidence has been Finland's policy for the last two decades. Thus, to provide but a few examples, when the United Nations voted for the withdrawal of Soviet troops from Hungary after the Soviet invasion in 1956, the Finnish government did not join the majority but insisted that it was up to the governments of the Soviet Union and Hungary to reach an agreement. When President Kekkonen visited Prague one year after the Soviet invasion of 1968, he admonished his hosts to behave in such a way as not to give rise to conflicts, and Foreign Minister Leskinen, speaking in 1971, said that the handling of the Czechoslovak crisis by the Warsaw Pact and by NATO was a "triumph of European understanding." Some triumph, some understanding! If Soviet confidence could be gained at the price of foreign political concessions, the price might be bearable: it would be understandable, in any case, in view of Finland's geographical position. But according to the Kekkonen line, it is also imperative that Finnish political leaders, the parties, the media and individual citizens behave "responsibly"; unless they do so, they endanger the very survival of the country. To act responsibly means to refrain from doing anything the Russians may not like. It involves not only self-censorship but also the need to anticipate Soviet wishes so that tension and open conflict are avoided. Self-censorship, as a Finnish observer has pointed out, is a generally accepted part of Finnish life but "it has remained an unpleasant subject which is touched upon as little as possible."[2] It is, according

[2] Carl-Gustaf Lilius, "Self-Censorship in Finland," *Index on Censorship* (Spring 1975). Lilius's article was published in 1975. Since then there have been more and more voices, most of them belonging to the mainstream of Finnish politics warning, albeit in cautious and measured terms, against certain "unhealthy" tendencies in Finnish politics. Thus the well-known publicist Skyttä compared contemporary Finland to the second Reich of Wil-

to this source, a sign of fear, a hide-out: Finns try to hide themselves from the Soviet Union, trying to forget that the Soviet Union exists: "Lack of knowledge of the Soviet Union exists to an amazing extent in Finland. The Russian language is among the least studied in Finnish schools." And "behaving responsibly" means lastly to accept a Soviet veto, if self-censorship breaks down. The existence of a Soviet veto is denied quite brazenly in the face of the truth by the proponents of the Kekkonen line. Their arguments are curious: "If this were so, Finland's position in Europe would have weakened, not improved, she would not have hosted the Conference on Security and Cooperation."[3] But there were quite a few Soviet vetoes during the last two decades, and if there have not been many in recent years, it is precisely because of the Finnish governments' willingness to refrain from any action that could have possibly caused one. The most blatant cases of Soviet intervention were in 1958, the so-called "winter frost crisis," when the Soviet Union demanded the resignation of the Social Democratic Fagerholm government, and the "crises of the notes" in 1961, when the Soviet Union threatened to invoke the 1948 treaty unless Kekkonen was re-elected president. Seen in retrospect, Kekkonen's compliance with Soviet wishes in 1958 was quite unnecessary as there was no direct Russian threat. At the same time it legitimized Soviet interference in Finnish domestic affairs, as distinct from intervention in its foreign and defense policy. There have been other interventions since concerning, for instance, Finland's ties with the European Common Market, but they have been less dramatic because by then certain rules of the game had been established, some of which have already been noted. A Finnish

helm II and Bismarck; Professor Ilkka Heiskanen wrote that Finland had become "autocratic," and a colleague, Professor Merikoski, reached the conclusion that Finland was a non-democracy. The editor of the Swedish *Expressen,* Bo Strömstedt, wrote that Finns are "subjects, not citizens"; another Swedish correspondent said at a seminar in Hanko about press ethics that a strange fear was spreading in Finland and that anxiety and prostration vis-à-vis the Soviets were very much in evidence; yet another Finnish professor, Osmo Jussila, said at a conference in Jyväskylä that Finland was on its way to a kind of monarchy. These and many other critical comments showed both growing concern (even if there would be a united front against critics from outside) and that there still was infinitely more freedom of press in Finland than even in the most liberal Communist regime, even though some of the critics were taken to task by the authorities for "fouling their own nest" or "trying to harm their country."

[3] Erkki Maentakanen, in *Yearbook of Finnish Foreign Policy* (1974), p. 34.

president or prime minister or member of the cabinet has to be democratically elected, but he has also to be "approved" by the Soviet embassy in Helsinki or the appropriate institution in Moscow. Parties and personalities who have not been approved may be represented in the parliament, but they must not be in any position of influence and decision making. Thus, the Finnish Social Democrats—the biggest party in the country—became eligible for serving in the government only after its old leadership had resigned and the younger leaders had recanted and wholeheartedly embraced the Kekkonen line. It is quite true that the Finnish Social Democrats "were not compelled" to change their line, as an American writer on Finland has written; with equal justice it could be argued that no one is compelled to suffer pain or deprivation, after all one can always commit suicide. Despite the self censorship exerted by Finnish political leaders and the media, Soviet complaints about Finish transgressions continued almost without interruption. These complaints are reinforced by warnings on the part of Kekkonen and his supporters, such as Kalevi Sorsa, the leader of the Social Democratic Party; Karjalainen, when he was foreign minister, at one stage even threatened the Finnish broadcasting service. Some Finnish newspapers have suggested that such pressure was compatible neither with the principles of democracy nor neutrality. But Soviet blame has been mixed with praise for those Finnish leaders who have supported Soviet foreign policy initiatives, such as the appeal for the neutralization of Norway, which, if successful, would clearly be against Finland's best interests. As a Finnish parliamentarian once said off the record, if Sweden and Norway were reduced to Finland's present status, Finland would soon become another Poland.

Typical of the official policy of "confidence building" were President Kekkonen's frequent speeches and statements published in Russian and English every few years. Their tenor is that Soviet-Finnish relations are excellent and are getting better all the time. Upon receipt of the Lenin prize, Kekkonen praised Lenin for his great role in granting Finland independence; at the time of the Communist youth festival in Helsinki he expressed admiration for the enthusiasm with which the Finnish national anthem was sung. On another occasion he claimed that the anxiety of the Russians was real "because I have read in the history of Russia that she has been attacked fourteen times in the last 150 years and that Minsk, the capital of White Russia, has been in enemy hands 101 times." This is sheer fantasy, but on the whole Kekkonen, who is not a Marxist, not even a man of the left, cleverly combines lavish praise for the Soviet Union with stressing Finnish national traditions. There have been exceptions when he tried quite needlessly to outdo his friends and protectors; thus, after Allende's defeat he quoted Lenin to the effect that it was absurd to think that the transition to socialism could be affected by peaceful means. (According to the official Soviet line, Allende was overthrown, inter alia, as the result of the extremism of his ultra-revolutionary supporters who antagonized sections of the population.) The declarations of Finnish Social Democrat leaders have been even more abject, and they have tried to persuade the Social Democratic parties of Western Europe to maintain close, direct relations with the Communist parties of Eastern Europe.

It has been argued that statements of this kind should not really be taken too seriously. What does it matter if Mr. Kekkonen gets his Russian history wrong, or if he makes statements about Chile, or even if Finland suggests that Norway should leave NATO—everyone knows that it won't happen anyway. If *Paris vaut une messe*—so does Helsinki. If certain declarations made to preserve Finland's freedom are untrue and aesthetically displeasing, they have after all been effective. The protagonists of the Kekkonen line argue that no one would have benefitted if, as the result of acting and talking according to their conscience, Finns had lost their freedom. Having convinced the Russians that the present Finnish leadership can be trusted, Finland has received a special dispensation to be an associate member of EFTA (European Free Trade Association) and to sign an agreement with the EEC. (Finland's participation in a Scandinavian customs union, Nordek, on the other hand, was vetoed by the Russians.) Kekkonen's policy of bringing the Finnish Communists into the government did not have fatal consequences; on the contrary, the Communist party split, and the more liberal wing denounced the Soviet invasion of Czechoslovakia in no uncertain terms—very much in contrast to the Finnish government. And when a Soviet ambassador too blatantly supported the Stalinist faction of the Communist party, he was withdrawn following Finnish representations made in Moscow. If strong Soviet pressure was exerted to give it the contract to electrify Finland's railways, the Finns made so many stipulations and conditions that it is not certain who got the better of the bargain in the end. If the Finns had to pay the highest price in the world for their (Soviet) oil, they did not have to pay in hard currency.

One could mention other instances showing that the Finns have been quite adept in handling the Russians.[4] But they have been able to do so only because there was a balance of power in the world and in Europe, and in any case, they have given the Russians a power of veto in their internal affairs and this is bound to have a demoralizing effect in the long run. Some observers have stressed that with all its apparent achievements, the Kekkonen line has undermined Finnish willingness to resist Soviet encroachments on their sovereignty. For even if only half of the wonderful things about the Soviet political and social system contained in the speeches of Kekkonen, Sorsa, Karjalainen, et al. were true, it will be difficult to explain to a young generation of Finns why they should still keep their distance and not become part of the Soviet Union, that "great federation of free peoples," as their Karelian brothers have already done.

The effects of Finlandization on the Finnish Social Democrats are quite unmistakable. They attended, to provide just one illustration, the celebrations of the sixtieth anniversary of the November Revolution in Moscow, the only Western non-Communist party to do so. Since, on the other hand, quite a few Communist parties were not invited to attend, the Soviet leaders obviously consider Finnish Social Democracy closer to them in orientation than some parties in their own camp. Most Finnish political parties have undergone a process of *Gleichschaltung* for which there are, of course, well-known historical precedents. They have

---

[4] A western writer on Finnish affairs has pointed to the publication of a study inside Finland on "Conflicts in Finnish-Soviet Relations" (*Acta Universitatis Tamperensis Scr. A vol. 47* [*Tampere, 1972*]) as an indication of the relaxed intellectual climate. But even a cursory reading of this study shows that it is not really subversive, be it only because it is written in American political science jargon. ("Responsiveness according to the definition given by Karl W. Deutsch . . .", "According to Russett, responsiveness can be divided . . . ," etc.) Towards the end of his study the author reaches the unstartling conclusion that if one accepts the definition of dependence as used by Esko Antola (who defines dependence "by the degree in which the selection of action alternatives by one actor restricts the available action alternatives for another actor") it "becomes apparent that the degree of dependence in Soviet-Finnish relations, mainly [*sic*] on the Finnish part is quite high. . . ." One would have reached the conclusion, one suspects, on the basis of any definition of dependence.

to follow the Kekkonen line not only in foreign affairs (which would be justifiable within limits) but also in domestic policies as well. As a conservative politician (Ilkka Kanerva of the Coalition Party) put it: Is it not quite senseless to criticize the Finnish Communists while we strive to intensify our cooperation with the Soviet Union the experiences of which have been unquestionably favorable? Such a point of view shows consistency—but this is exactly what Finlandization is all about. For the time being the process of *Gleichschaltung* has not been pushed to its logical conclusion, and this again is one of the main pecularities of Finlandization in contrast to the People's democracies." Finnish *sisu* (roughly translated as "guts") have been frequently praised by outside observers, but the constant repetiton of a basically fraudulent official ideology is bound to have an effect, even though Kekkonen clearly believes that nationalism is in the long run a stronger force than communism. Again to quote C. G. Lilius; "In the prevailing atmosphere it becomes easy for hypocrisy and apathy to spread, with the pretence that everything is as it should be. And a mentality of this kind entails a measure of corruption, detrimental to the spirit of national self-assertion."

Throughout history small countries have had to accommodate their policy to meet the wishes, the interests, and the whims of their more powerful neighbors and, seen in this light, the Finnish case is, of course, by no means unique. The attitude of small nations has traditionally ranged from taking care not to provoke the great power in their proximity to paying tribute or Danegeld and appeasing it in every possible way. Great powers on the other hand, have interfered in the domestic affairs of their small neighbors; they have picked as rulers their chosen candidates and ostracized those whom they did not trust.

The foreign policy of the Roman Empire was largely based on the existence of client states and there were elaborate rules to control these semi-independent countries. The rulers of eastern client states (to quote Edward Luttwak) did not actually have to *see* Roman legions marching towards their cities in order to respond to Rome's commands, for they could imagine what the consequences of disobedience would be.[5] Some-

[5] Edward N. Luttwak, *The Grand Strategy of the Roman Empire* (Baltimore, 1976), p. 32. The management of the client states under the republic has been described in detail in

times Roman remote control would be straightforward, more often there would be a screen of false independence, or to be precise, the client states would be left to manage their internal affairs as they saw fit, provided they accepted Roman foreign political and military hegemony. Throughout the Middle Ages and in modern history there have been countless protectorates and semi-protectorates, ranging from fully fledged satellites to almost independent countries.

Nor is self-censorship an unprecedented phenomenon. It had to be practised, for instance, in the countries defeated by Napoleon. When the London *Times* savagely attacked Louis Napoleon in 1851, the British Government of the day asked the editors for restraint so as not to endanger peace. But the editors disagreed; it was the duty of diplomats to behave correctly, whereas journalists had to state facts and express opinions without fear or favor to inform the public. Sterling principles, but it was easier to stick to them in Britain in 1851 than in Switzerland or Sweden after the outbreak of the Second World War. Once again newspapers were called upon by the authorities to behave "responsibly" in terms virtually identical with those used in recent years by Mr. Kekkonen. Thus the Swedish Prime Minister, Mr. Erlander, attacking certain anti-Nazi Swedish newspapers in October 1939 said, "The Swedish people will not tolerate that individuals will compromise confidence in our neutrality." Or, a year later, Mr. Guenther, the Swedish Foreign Minister, "Nothing inspires me with greater fear for the future than the position taken by the Swedish press with regard to the change in the balance of power in Europe. . . ." The warnings did not deter a few Swedish newspapers from denouncing Hitler's New Order, and when the tide of the war had turned, the minority became an overwhelming majority. Despite the warnings to behave "responsibly," at least some Swedish and Swiss newspapers were quite outspoken on foreign affairs even during the darkest hours of the Second World War.

There are certain new ingredients in the Finnish dilemma. One is the impact of ideology, another the existence of a Communist party. During the nineteenth century when Finland and Poland were part of the Russian empire, the Tsar did not really expect his Finnish and

P. C. Sands, *The Client Princes of the Roman Empire under the Republic* (Cambridge, 1908), and E. Badian, *Foreign Clientelae* (Oxford, 1958).

Polish subjects to praise him in fulsome terms for his wise and benevolent rule—it was sufficient if they obeyed him, *Oderint dum metuant*[6] (Let them hate us as long as they fear us). In our age appearances and pretence have to be kept up; thus Soviet-Finnish relations are not only "rooted in friendship" but "based on the principles of equality."

It is not that small powers are now necessarily more at the mercy of their powerful neighbors than in the past. Cuba has defied the United States for a long time without any apparent ill effects. It is not even true with regard to the attitude of some Communist countries vis-à-vis the Soviet Union. There is, of course, much more freedom in Finland than in even the most liberal Communist regimes. But its foreign political freedom seems to be more restricted. It is unlikely, to put it cautiously, that the Finnish government could invite Chinese leaders for a state visit as Yugoslavia and Rumania did in 1978.

Given Finland's geographical location and its small size (it has less than five million inhabitants), it is obvious that to survive as an independent nation, it has to take Soviet foreign policy interests into account and that it has to act with great circumspection: "So far from NATO—so near to the Soviet Union" to paraphrase the famous saying of a Mexican president. Finland had to be silent when other, more distant nations could speak up without fear. But when all these circumstances have been taken into account, it is still true that it was a fatal mistake to legitimize Soviet interference in Finnish domestic affairs, and now to deny that such legitimization has taken place. Nor is it likely that the Soviet Union would have invaded Finland if during the last decade there had been a little less fawning. It is easier to voice such criticism from a safe distance, but distance, on the other hand, does not invalidate an argument. To admire the resilience and courage shown by many Finns is one thing, to accept at face value the virtues of the "Finnish model" is another. And even if, for argument's sake, there was no alternative to both surrender in 1958, and the Kekkonen line in the two decades since, the consequences are only too obvious. While it is admirable that

[6] The Finns did have, in fact, for long periods under Tsarist rule a great deal of freedom. Russian subjects in Finland, on the other hand, could not practice medicine, teach history, serve in the army, or vote in local elections—to provide but a few examples. Finland not only had a parliament, but also was one of the very few countries in which women had the right to vote before 1914.

so much freedom has been preserved, Finland is not independent in the accepted sense of the term, and it is quite beside the point to argue that no country in the modern world is "altogether independent." There is a growing feeling in Europe that the Soviet leaders are correct in considering Finland a country in a category apart—neither satellite nor neutral. Hence the debate about Finlandization—*Suomettuminen* in Finnish.

The term "Finlandization" has entered the political dictionary despite the protests of the advocates of the Kekkonen line, their Western well-wishers, the Russians and some American neo-isolationists. There is an element of injustice whenever geographical terms acquire a political meaning—not everything in Byzantium was Byzantine, not everything in the Levant was Levantine, not everyone in Shanghai is shanghaied, and if the Balkans were balkanized, it was largely the fault of outside powers. "Finlandization" in any case is here to stay. It has become the subject of articles, books, and even doctoral dissertations.[7] Though the term is of recent date, its origins are by no means certain. The phenomenon was allegedly first described in 1953 by the Austrian foreign minister Karl Gruber warning his government not to follow the Finnish example. He did not, however, actually coin the term. Richard Lowenthal said in an interview with *Time* magazine (December 1974) that he may have been the first to use the term sometime in 1966, when the Warsaw Pact countries suggested the dissolution of all military blocs at their meeting in Bucharest. (According to some Finnish writers Lowenthal's memory was at fault, he had actually used the term four years earlier.[8]) Subsequently the term was used by Pierre Hassner, the present writer and many other authors. It was usually interpreted as a process or a state of affairs in which under the cloak of friendly and good neighborly

---

[7] J. M. Lafond "Finlandization" (Dijon, 1974); Harto Hakovirta's *Suomettuminen, Kaukokontrollia vai rauhanomaista rianakkaiseloa?* ("Finlandization, remote control or peaceful coexistence?") (Tyvaskyla, 1975), is largely a reply to Nils Ørvik, *Sicherheit auf Finnisch* (Stuttgart, 1972), one of the few critical studies of the Kekkonen line which gave much offence in Helsinki.

[8] "After Cuba—Berlin?", *Encounter* (December 1962). I have not found the term in this article.

relations the sovereignty of a country is reduced. While retaining its traditional institutional forms, the country concerned adapts both the personnel of its governments and its foreign policy "either to the dictates of the Soviet Union or to what it feels Russia really wishes."[9] This process of "adaptation" gradually saps the energy of the nation, which is no longer able or willing to resist further pressures. Interpreted in this light the term is, of course, considered highly offensive and detrimental to national prestige in Finland. But outside observers too have warned against the use of the term. Some have argued that Finlandization conveys a wrong picture about Finland's real situation; others have maintained that Finland is anyway a unique case and the application of the term with regard to other countries is misleading. Yet others have claimed that Finlandization, far from being a danger, is a positive phenomenon, worthy of emulation. And lastly, there have been a few optimists expressing the belief that Russia's East European satellites are far more likely to be Finlandized than Western Europe.

President Kekkonen and Prime Minister Sorsa belong to the first group. In their view "Finlandization" is the favorite term of those in the West who wish to lay Finland open to suspicion; it is used by scholars, journalists and politicians who have difficulty in understanding or lack the will to understand the position of Finland and her foreign policy. It is an expression of prejudice and ignorance—a symptom of the feeling of insecurity in those who find it hard to accept the political development towards detente and increasing West-East cooperation such as pioneered by Finland. It is "not meaningful and it is neither descriptive nor analytically useful. Its use is based on ignorance, biased or normative statements, misuse of analogies, poor understanding of internal developments and their relationship to external conditions in Finland and other European countries, and on a failure to analyze psychological factors" (Maentakanen). In short, it is an invention of the cold warriors, the opponents of detente, a horrible word to be disposed of once and forever.

These are quotations from speeches and interviews given by Finnish statesmen and a reaction of this kind is psychologically quite understandable; perhaps, to placate the Finns, the term should no longer be used. But even if the offensive word disappeared, the substance

[9] G. Maude, *The Finnish Dilemma* (London, 1976).

would remain; for the precariousness of the Finnish situation cannot just be removed by official denials. With this in mind, President Kekkonen in two famous speeches on April 4, 1973, and October 15, 1974, has argued that there is indeed such a thing as Finlandization but that it should be interpreted in a positive way. The same line has been taken by lesser commentators. Far from being a subject of pity, Finland has been getting the best of both worlds. It has excellent relations with both West and East, its security is guaranteed as a result of the defense pact with the Soviet Union, it has economic ties with West and East, and it has done more than its share of working for detente and closer cooperation between the power blocs.

One of the sharpest denunciations of the term "Finlandization" has come from George Kennan ("No greater injustice has been done to any European people. . . .") According to him, Finlandization means some sort of helpless and humiliating situation, a spineless acceptance of Soviet domination and willingness to accept Soviet dictation in all essential aspects of political life.[10] This as Mr. Kennan sees it is a gross distortion of the truth, for while Finnish policy towards the Soviet Union has been prudent and restrained, it has been conducted with remarkable dignity, with cool nerves and composure, with quiet but firm and successful insistence on the right to lead their own lives.

These are fine sentiments but they have little in common with the realities of the Finnish dilemma. No one has argued that Finnish behavior has been spineless or that they have been willing to accept Soviet dictation in *all* essential aspects. The point is surely that they have accepted (or had to accept) Soviet domination in *some* essential aspects. A fatal mistake was committed in 1958 when under Soviet pressure Kekkonen brought about the resignation of the Fagerholm government. Once this precedent was established, the Russian right of veto, or to be precise, the Finnish assumption, that the Russians had such a right, became a permanent feature of Finnish political life. Finnish resistance to Soviet interference in their internal affairs would of course have entailed risks. The Finns preferred prudence and caution; it is a disservice to historical truth (or the cause of Finland) to pretend that they behaved otherwise. The speeches and articles of Messrs. Kekkonen, Leskinen,

[10] G. F. Kennan, *The Cloud of Danger* (New York, 1977), p. 145.

and Sorsa, and of the younger generation of Finnish policy-makers and publicists may or may not, be necessary exercises in *Realpolitik* but there is nothing particularly dignified about them. One suspects, in fact, that some of these politicians may by now sincerely believe in the truth of their own statements—great are the powers of repetition and self-hypnosis. Much pious humbug has been written about the Kekkonen line, and there has been an effort to draw a veil of silence over its less pleasant aspects. As far as Soviet-Finnish relations are concerned, the golden rule is to call a spade an agricultural implement; not to observe this rule is to be branded an enemy of Finland, of the Soviet Union, and of course of detente.

Lastly there are those in the West who, quite independently of Mr. Kekkonen, have reached the conclusion that Finlandization has much to recommend itself as a model for other countries. Thus a *Washington Post* columnist writing in December 1972 maintained that Finland was "where most of Europe wanted to be," an independent and neutral country, not dependent on the presence of foreign troops, having both security and more real freedom than the countries in fear of being Finlandized. On the scholarly level, Professor David Vital, in a book on the *Survival of Small States* [11] proclaimed Finland a paradigm for the future—a solution for the problem facing an isolated minor state pitted against a great military power. Mr. Vital, in contrast to the *Washington Post* columnist, did not have Europe in mind but above all the Middle East which he saw as likely "to fall slowly under the preponderance of a single power—in this case the Soviet Union." In the circumstances the survival of a minor (Middle Eastern) state depended first and foremost on its ability to manipulate or maneuver within a "balance of restraint and pressure between it and the preponderant power in whose sphere of interest it falls, as does Finland." While Mr. Vital did not specify what minor state he had in mind, it is unlikely that he meant Libya.

Mr. Vital expected a similar process in Southeast Asia, under China. But since neither events in the Middle East nor in South East Asia proceeded as he envisaged, he may well have modified his views about the need for other nations to emulate the Finnish example. A diametrically opposite view has been taken by Dr. Vloyantes, an American

---

[11] (London, 1971).

political scientist and author of a book on Soviet-Finnish relations.[12] According to him it is nonsense even to talk about Finlandization, because Finland's situation is altogether different from that of other countries. Mr. Vloyantes wrote that it is "fantastic" to assume that Russian influence could possibly replace American influence, referring to (among other factors) a "European revival" and French, Italian, and British political and economic power as pillars of West European strength. He, too, has been a little unlucky with his examples. Mr. Vloyantes quotes with approval an earlier article by Mr. Kennan in which it had been argued that the analogy applied to the term Finlandization turns out to be absurdly overdrawn and unsuitable because the Soviet Union is most unlikely to make specific demands on Europe under threats of force: "The smaller and weaker a country the more sensitive its government to any hint of military pressure being applied against it and the more ready its resistance to anything that smacks of pressure or blackmail from the stronger power."[13]

Such arguments against "Finlandization" rest on certain assumptions with regard to the stability, the strength, and the political will of Western Europe. That a strong Europe need not fear Finlandization goes without saying, but how strong is Europe? Writing in 1977, Mr. Kennan was somewhat less optimistic than three years earlier, "One may have one's opinions as to the likelihood or necessity of Western Europe's ever accepting such a position" (Finlandization). It may well be that the Soviet Union will not make specific demands on Europe under threats of force. But there were no Soviet threats of force in 1958 either and yet the Finns caved in despite dignity, persistence, strong nerves, fearlessness, and other qualities which they no doubt have, which have been rightly praised, and which, to put it cautiously, are not found in equal measure in all other European countries.

The case of Finland is in some respects quite unique, be it only because it is a small country of less than five million inhabitants. The country was defeated in the Second World War, it was clearly within the Soviet sphere of influence, and the West never indicated that it would be able or willing to extend support to Finland in the case of a con-

[12] John P. Vloyantes, *Silk Glove Hegemony* (Kent State University, 1975).
[13] "Europe's Problems, Europe's Choices," *Foreign Policy* (Spring 1974).

flict with its eastern neighbor. The other European countries either belonged to NATO or had no common border with the Soviet Union. Austria was the one exception, but it was in a more fortunate position as the Soviet Union was not the only occupying power—there was also a Western presence.

It could be argued furthermore that there is no evidence so far for regarding "Finlandization" as an ongoing process leading towards total loss of freedom. Perhaps it is a stationary condition, a symptom of a state of affairs in which a country can no longer exert full sovereignty. Such a condition might deteriorate following, for instance, a radical change in the global or regional balance of power, or if the country concerned was no longer able to muster the strength to resist foreign encroachments.[14] On the other hand, it is at least conceivable that the degree of dependence may be frozen or that it may even decrease a little following some favorable development in the international constellation. Some countries which initially only accepted self-censorship ended up with censorship, *tout court*, but there have also been cases in which greater freedom was attained.

The Finnish analogy, like all analogies or parallels, has its limits, but it is certainly not a "myth," as some Finnish spokesmen have claimed.[15] At the present time it is, unfortunately, as real as Finland. For when all allowances for the uniqueness of the Finnish case have been made, it is still true that Finland is something of a model and that the Soviet leaders regard it as such. If Poland or Hungary constitute one example of a close relationship between the Soviet Union and its smaller neighbours, Finland provides another. 'Finlandization' is the assumption that in certain conditions this kind of relationship might spread to other parts of the globe.

[14] Finland in 1978 is slightly less free than ten or twenty years ago, but since the deterioration was not dramatic some observers may argue that the process is not irreversible.

[15] "[it includes perhaps] . . . a certain doubt or mistrust on the part of the Americans towards a possible accommodation of or alternative for the neutrality of Western Europe . . ." (E. Maentakanen, "The Myth of Finlandization" in *Yearbook of Finnish Foreign Policy*, 1974.) The doubts and mistrust are more widespread in Europe than in America. The effects of Finlandization on Finnish policy are so obvious as to make the official denials ineffectual. When a struggle for power took place for the leadership of the Center Party, the argument used against Virolainen, was precisely that he could not be trusted because his identification with the Kekkonen line was not above suspicion.

FINLAND'S NORDIC NEIGHBORS

The countries most vulnerable, most open to pressure, are Finland's Scandinavian neighbors. They are thinly populated, they cover a vast area, and they face a massive Soviet military build-up, on land and sea, extending from Schleswig-Holstein and the Baltic approaches to the Kola peninsula. Nevertheless, Sweden adopted a plan according to which the total effectiveness of Sweden's defense organization was to be halved up to 1980. Danish defense spending, which was 3 per cent in 1963, declined to 2 per cent in the mid-1970's; in Norway the decrease has been less. What a Swedish authority wrote in a spirit of understatement about his country's new departure in defence politics is certainly true with regard to all Scandinavian countries: "It is based on optimistic notions about the future." [16]

These optimistic notions were based on the assumption that the overall military balance in Europe would remain static, and that therefore to put it somewhat crudely, Scandinavia would get a free ride. It was expected that detente would deepen, that there would be a further relaxation of tension, and that major conflicts would be virtually ruled out in the forseeable future. Some Scandinavians argued that their countries could make a special contribution towards improving West-East relations. Misconceptions about the essence of detente are quite widespread in Scandinavia, so is the belief that the position of the Nordic countries would not be affected even if the European balance changed in favor of the Soviet Union. Many Scandinavians seem genuinely to believe that the Soviet leaders share their conviction that military power is of no political use.

Scandinavian isolationism constitutes something of a riddle to outside observers. There is no doubt about the attachment of these peoples to their traditional values, their deeply cherished way of life and to in-

---

[16] Nils Andren, *Sweden's Security Policy* in *Cooperation and Conflict*, 3/4, 1972, 145. It should be noted however, that this process reached its climax in 1973/4; since then there have been increases in defense spending in Norway. For a more recent review of Scandinavian defense, Nils Andren, *The Future of the Nordic Balance* (Stockholm, 1977). It is still argued occasionally that Swedish neutrality is credible because the country spends a higher percentage of its GNP on defense than some NATO members. But such comparisons are quite meaningless, for Sweden is not threatened by Luxemburg or by Denmark, and its defense spending should be compared with potential attackers.

dependence. Yet at the same time there is strong opposition to any collaboration with outside forces defending their independence. Usually, at decisive moments, this policy has failed to work; Denmark in the First World War was compelled to collaborate militarily with the Germans. The fact that it was again willing to do so in 1938/9 did not prevent the German occupation in 1940. Finland was attacked by the Soviet Union in 1939, and Norway was occupied in 1940. Sweden alone escaped occupation, but Swedish neutrality too, was deeply compromised by its collaboration with Germany between 1939 and 1942. This very briefly has been the price that had to be paid for military unpreparedness and isolationism. But since both in 1918 and in 1945 the setbacks were followed by (relatively) happy endings, there was a strong temptation to ignore the lessons of the past.

In the 1930's the Norwegians spent the equivalent of $3 per head on defence; in Sweden and Denmark it was a little more—$5. Norway had conscription, but it lasted eight weeks only, which was an all-time world record, and the prime minister of the day, Nygaardsvold, was saddened because he failed to reduce it even further. The Norway Year Book of 1938 stated flatly: "The country is easy to defend." This might have been true if there had been soldiers to defend it, but when the invasion came only 13,000 Norwegian soldiers were under arms, and these forces were, of course, insufficient to offer more than token resistance. The Danish army was even less prepared.

In Sweden there had been a great deal of self-satisfaction since the First World War. As Herbert Tingsten noted, neutrality for Sweden seemed natural, it was a morally superior attitude, it showed that the Swedes were a wiser and less aggressive nation than the others. They, for one, had realized that the conflicts in the world at large were the result of ill will and of a culpable failure to establish a lasting order.[17] There was a rude awakening in 1939, but once the Second World War was over, Sweden quickly reverted to the old pattern of behavior. Forgotten were the inconvenient facts—the passage of German troops through Sweden, the delivery of vital war supplies, the political efforts to adjust Swedish policy to Hitler's New Order in Europe. What remained was the memory that Sweden alone among the Nordic countries had es-

[17] H. Tingsten, *The Debate on the Foreign Policy of Sweden* (London, 1949), pp. 295–96.

caped occupation. Forgotten also was the fact that the Swedish defense budget had been increased almost twentyfold from $28 million in 1935 to $527 million in 1944 and that the country had not gone bankrupt as a result. When in the late 1940's Norway and in its wake Denmark decided to join NATO, Sweden opted for staying out, firmly convinced that this was the best way of safeguarding the country's independence. It is true that during the subsequent two decades Sweden made an effort to make its neutrality credible; its per capita defense spending was among the highest in Europe; in the middle 1960's Sweden had as many fighter aircraft as the British airforce. After that date Sweden and the other Northern countries decided that the time had come for drastic defense cuts. The reasons officially given were that the danger of conflict in Europe had passed, that the superpowers were not that much interested in Scandinavia anyway, that Soviet policy in this region was defensive, and that in any case, a continuation of the defense effort on the previous level would ruin the economy of the Nordic countries. That both hopes and fears were without foundation was quite immaterial; what mattered was, their perception of them not reality, and seen in this light the decisions taken were intelligible—the less money spent on defense, the more there would be for social services. That these decisions would erode the credibility of Swedish neutrality and make Norway and Denmark even more vulnerable was not accepted. Scandinavian policy-makers, in any case, were concerned with immediate problems, not with the more distant future. Mogans Glistrup, the leader of the Danish Progress party, suggested the abolition of defense forces altogether and instead that a record ("We surrender") be played in the case of a (Soviet) attack. Glistrup's proposal certainly had the advantage of consistency, for defense spending below a certain minimum level is a waste of resources; it will provoke a potential enemy, not deter him. The various "inexpensive" defense schemes (territorial defenses and guerrilla warfare) on the other hand, that were suggested to justify the cuts in defense did not have much to recommend themselves.[18]

Would Denmark and Norway have been invaded if they had made a greater effort in the late 1930's? This is a question of more than histori-

---

[18] Scandinavian high ranking officers had few illusions about the efficacity of guerilla warfare except in coordination with regular forces. See, for instance, Per Hjalmar Baner, *Gerilla och svenskt Forsvar* (Stockholm, 1969).

cal interest. In the light of the German documents that have become available the answer is fairly clear. The commanders of the *Wehrmacht* and their intelligence officers were quite familiar with the lack of Danish and Norwegian military preparedness; in their secret memoranda they stressed moreover that pacifism and even defeatism were deeply rooted and widespread, that neither Danes nor Norwegians would offer any determined resistance. But they also noted that the Norwegians could have mobilized 90,000 men and the Danes eight divisions; in these circumstances an invasion would have been a high risk operation for the *Wehrmacht*—not because Germany could not have occupied these countries, but they had not enough troops to spare before the fall of France. After that date, time would have been running short for the *Wehrmacht,* since everything was subordinated to the preparation of the invasion of the Soviet Union.[19] Switzerland was not invaded because it kept 125,000 men under arms at the time—and many more in 1941/2; again from the German point of view it was a question of twenty German divisions that were not available. Sweden was not attacked, partly because it was militarily stronger than Norway or Denmark. But help for the Swedes came from unexpected quarters. The Soviets made it clear that they wanted Sweden to remain neutral, and Hitler could not afford to antagonize his ally at the time. Furthermore, it was assumed in Hitler's headquarters that with the occupation of Denmark and Norway, Sweden would have to cooperate with Germany in any case. Thus the lessons of the Second World War are that lack of military preparedness was an open invitation to the aggressor. If these lessons were not sufficiently heeded, the reasons were the same as before 1939; deep-seated pacifism coupled with the belief that the storms of the world would somehow bypass the Far North and that the West could in any case not provide effective military help.[20] Opposition to a defense effort was particularly strong among the radical (new) left which, though numerically

[19] *Neutrale Kleinstaaten im zweiten Weltkrieg* (Munsingen, 1973), p. 16.

[20] This refers, above all, to Sweden, and to a lesser extent to Denmark where there has been traditionally substantial opposition to NATO. It is much less true with regard to Norway, where support for NATO has in fact increased over the last decade, even among the left and the circles bitterly opposing Norway's entry into the EEC. This may be connected with the fact that Norway felt itself and its oilfields particularly vulnerable to the Soviet build-up in the Far North. For details see Henry Valen and Willy Martinussen in Karl H. Cerny (ed.), *Scandinavia at the Polls* (Washington, 1977), p. 61.

small, was exceedingly influential in university circles, and, more important yet, in the mass media:

> When the sons and daughters of the managerial and administrative elite return from their universities convinced Marxists, this is likely to have some impact on their parents, too; a certain radicalization of some parts of the bourgeoisie appears to have taken place over the dinner table. But other channels have also been important. The influx of socialists into the journalistic profession has left its mark on the handling of news, and it is likely that the Scandinavian image of the world has changed considerably in recent years.[21]

The average Swedish newspaper reader was bound to gain the impression in the 1970's that an aggressive American foreign policy constituted the main danger to world peace, that Sweden should not get entangled in European affairs; events in the East were largely ignored. There was a constant stream of criticism against oppression and the violation of human rights in distant parts, from Chile to Vietnam, from Franco's Spain to South Korea. Similar manifestations much nearer home were belittled or altogether ignored. Offending General Pinochet was not particularly risky whereas criticism of the Soviet bloc countries was much more subdued because it might have had unpleasant consequences. Practices like these were freely admitted by spokesmen of the extreme left in Sweden such as Jan Myrdal who noted that though the Swedish government had reduced its aid to Cuba following its intervention in Angola, it continued nevertheless to support Castro "for one must not displease our mighty Soviet neighbor." And he added: "The Finlandization of Sweden is not impossible; this will be terrible and not only for us. . . ."[22] There is nothing specifically "Marxist" about Scandinavian pacifism. It would have been intelligible if the radical left, second to none in its enthusiasm for national independence, opted for neutrality or perhaps a Scandinavian defense community. But neutrality, to be credible, involved a heavy defense effort and this was not acceptable either. It was pacifism rather than Marxism that inspired the belief that

[21] D. Tarschys, "The Changing Basis of Radical Socialism in Scandinavia," in Cerny, op. cit., p. 150.

[22] Claude Glayman (ed.), *Suède la reforme permanente* (Paris, 1977), pp. 250, 260.

even a moderate defense outlay would result in the bankruptcy of the welfare state. The foreign and defense policies of Sweden and Denmark, and, to a lesser extent, of Norway were based on the belief that Soviet interest in Scandinavia was limited and in any case purely defensive in character, that other European countries would anyway maintain strong armies, that the U.S. engagement in Europe would continue, and that as a result the balance of power in Europe would not substantially change. The philosophy of the free ride, while not morally superior, made some sense as long as these assumptions remained intact; but they were always questionable. Other countries might be tempted to emulate the Swedish example; in this case the American presence in Europe is bound to be eroded or perhaps disappear altogether. If this happened, Scandinavia would find itself within the sphere of influence of the superpower next to it; the question of what would remain of its neutrality and independence in such circumstances was not widely debated in the Nordic countries.

Much has been written about the mixed blessings of the modern welfare state in Scandinavia; yet with all their shortcomings, these societies were and are, among the most civilized societies in existence. The absence of fanaticism and brutality is striking; standards of democratic behavior, of social justice, of honesty and decency, the lack of corruption in public and private life are unparalleled. In some respects these societies have been luckier than others—protected for a long time from war and similar such convulsions, these countries benefitted from the cohesion inherent in smallness, there was less anonymity than in the mass societies, community ties and solidarity were more strongly developed. How then explain that peoples who had shown so much maturity in arranging their domestic affairs, failed to show similar responsibility and far-sightedness in their foreign policies. It would appear that the qualities which have made for maturity at home are not necessarily the same that make for a better understanding of the outside world. Parochialism breeds both isolationism and the belief that preoccupation with foreign affairs is unnecessary and unhealthy, since the traditional way of life is likely to suffer as the result of too close an involvement with the outside world. This instinctive reaction may well be part of the strong rural heritage of Scandinavia, and it was inherited, above all, by the socialist parties and the trade unions. Wishful thinking in Scandinavian perceptions about the outside world manifested itself in the deep belief in the League of Nations in the 1920's, the trust in Germany's peaceful intentions in the 1930's, the bridge building between West and East in the late 1940's, the faith in the United Nations in the 1950's and 60's. A high Norwegian diplomat declared as late as 1970 that activities in the U.N. are of "central importance" for Norwegian foreign policy.[23] By 1978 the conviction had gained ground that events in Spitzbergen were of central importance too. There is a clear and consistent historical pattern broken only when an outside threat has grown to major proportions.

[23] T. K. Derry, *A History of Modern Norway* (Oxford, 1973), p. 420.

9

EUROPEAN PERSPECTIVES

Towards the end of his *magnum opus,* Gibbon relates how, nine hundred years after the fall of the Roman Empire, in the last days of Pope Eugenius the Fourth, the learned Poggius and a friend ascended the Capitoline Hill, reposed among the ruins, and viewed from this commanding spot the wide and various prospect of desolation:[1] "The place and the object gave ample scope for moralizing on the vicissitudes of fortune which spare neither man nor the proudest of his works, which bury empires and cities in a common grave and it was agreed that in proportion to her former greatness, the fall of Rome was the more awful and deplorable."

Decline and Fall has been referred to frequently in recent years and not only in view of its bicentenary. As a quarry for speculations about the decline of Europe it has been as rich as was the Forum Romanum in providing stones for medieval Roman masons. But this much seems to be certain: if indeed Europe one day presents a similar picture of desolation it will not just have been the vicissitudes of fortune that have caused it. The doctrine of predestination is no longer often invoked in theological discussions; it should not be permitted to establish itself in political thought.

The question of decline and decadence has preoccupied historians, philosophers, and poets since time immemorial and the most frequent explanation has been the one given by Cicero—*O Tempora, O Mores!* But the mores have allegedly deteriorated since the Fall. Hans Delbrueck, in an amusing essay, has shown that for many centuries each new generation was led to believe that life had been infinitely better in

---

[1] Poggius is Gian Francisco Poggio Bracciolini (1386–1459), the famous Renaissance scholar and historian.

the past.[2] Reflecting on the decadence of the Romans, a favorite theme of nineteenth-century Romantics and twentieth-century historical systems builders, Montesquieu reached the conclusion that depravity set in with the improvement of material conditions and the spread of the Epicurean school. What follows from this is not entirely clear; material conditions have improved for a long time all over the world and what we now know about the savage life makes it appear less noble than commonly thought in the eighteenth century.

It is with reluctance that one uses the term "crisis" with regard to the present state of Europe, for it has been debased by constant overuse. Just as "progress" was the watchword of Europe during the second third of the last century—a fact reflected, among other things, in the names of newspapers and political parties—so in the recent past "crisis" became the key concept in European thought. Countless books and articles focussed on the "crisis"—in culture, economics, education, theology, and, for all one knows, in philately and beekeeping. This was the period in which it became fashionable to reflect on the causes of human misery, to complain about coercion, enslavement, degradation, dehumanization, conformism, manipulation of mind and sentiment; and to despair about the suppression of creativeness, about limiting man's self-expression, about the sins of mass society and the evils of mass culture—to recall only some of the catchphrases of a time in which hyperbole reigned supreme. The last three decades, meaning the period after 1945, were in the words of one of these critics, nothing but a "grotesque record of unbridled genocide." But even less shrill complaints betrayed a striking lack of perspective. The critics protested against the lack of freedom and equality in their societies and while the facts they quoted were not necessarily wrong, they forgot to add that there had been enormous progress in recent decades and that these societies were considerably freer and more equal than ever before. Complaints about a "quasi-totalitarian" system, about "fascism," Gestapo brutality, genocide, were bandied about at the slightest provocation and sometimes even without provocation. In conditions such as these, words lost all meaning, a feel-

---

[2] "Die gute alte Zeit." The idealization of primitive, remote tribes, who had escaped the evils of civilization was, of course, quite common in ancient Greece. Thus Pindar describes the Hyperboreans as free from disease and old age, free from work and fighting. John Ferguson, *Utopias of the Classical World* (London, 1975), pp. 16 ff.

ing of apocalyptic crisis was engendered, and future generations may well be at a loss to understand how so much commotion was created in an age of almost idyllic peace, progress, and high standards of civilization.

The complaints, the feeling of malaise, were to a large extent a concomitant of the great material progress that had been achieved; people who suffer from acute starvation or have no shelter, seldom, if ever, reflect on the philosophical causes of human misery nor do they complain about missing opportunities for self-expression. "The only cause of depression is prosperity"—what Clement Juglar wrote in 1862 about the business cycle may or may not be true in economics, it certainly applies to most cultural crises. The prosperity of the 1960's made it possible to concentrate on the problems of the future rather than the problems of the present moment. Unfortunately, the opportunities for a sober assessment of the dangers and the possibilities facing mankind all too often caused hysterical outbursts. Thus, when a real deterioration occurred in the situation in the 1970's, all the superlatives had already been used to decry the state of society; once the impending end of the world had been announced it obviously made no sense to say that the situation was "critical." The "crisis" literature of the 1960's and early 1970's reflecting a mood of cosmic despair makes fascinating reading in retrospect. It was perhaps not altogether useless except in its most absurd manifestations, but, in any case, it was overtaken by events. As a real deterioration in the situation set in, the preoccupation with the issues that had figured so high on the scale of priorities while the going had been good all but ceased. And yet, one cannot but regard the European situation as critical in view of the coincidence of several threatening trends: structural difficulties in the European economies, the domestic weakness of governments and their inability to take unpopular decisions, weakness in European defense, as well as the more general problems of the ecological imbalance and *Kulturpessimismus*.[3]

---

[3] J. Habermas in an essay on "What does a crisis mean today?" discusses three developing crises (the ecological balance, the anthropological balance, and the international balance) before turning his attention to "legitimation problems in late capitalism." Yet there is a curious inconsistency: While noting that these problems cannot be regarded as "crisis phenomena specific to the system," he says later on that these are "three global consequences of late-capitalist growth." Some Marxists may argue, not altogether convincingly,

About the cultural crisis little need be said except perhaps that it is not a specific European phenomenon, that there have been many precedents in history, and that it is felt much more intensely by intellectuals than by other members of the society, which of course, is not to say that it is either unreal or unimportant. Whether and to what extent man was born to be happy and to feel secure is a theological and philosophical question that has been the subject of earnest and unending debate; there certainly have been happier and less happy periods in history. But it is always much easier to say what prevents happiness than to point out the conditions conducive to this blessed state. The assumption, already referred to, that mankind was happier in its more primitive stage seems to be largely mythical, a fact that was known even to some of Rousseau's contemporaries.[4]

The cultural crisis is usually explained with reference to the loss of faith and the loss of ties which have occurred since religion began to go out of fashion and since traditional communities began to dissolve. The process was, of course, a little more complicated, because some of the secular religions, such as the belief in progress, nationalism, and socialism in its more extreme forms, provided a quasi-religious faith at least as powerful as that experienced by seventeenth and eighteenth century intellectuals who no longer believed in a personal god. On the other hand the weakening of social ties was caused not just by the general dislocation which resulted from the development of modern industrial societies, but equally from the spread of individual liberty. A heavy price had to be paid for the security and the rootedness of pre-modern times in terms of obedience and conformism. New remedies may emerge for the discontent felt about the loss of ties; there are no known cures for the loss of a transcendent faith except, of course, through a return to religion or a similar faith which cannot be achieved by an act of will. All that matters in the present context is that the cultural crisis of the West is neither the cause nor the result of the current political and social crises of Western societies and will not disappear once these crises are

that alienation is a specific problem of late capitalism, but it can hardly be made responsible for the Sino-Soviet conflict nor for all pollution. (*Social Research,* Winter 1973, 649 ff. Originally published in *Merkur,* April/May 1973.)

[4] The Chevalier de Chastelux noted in 1772 (*On Public Felicity*) that the great age of Hellas was a time of pain and torture for humanity.

overcome. Perhaps, for reasons mentioned more than once in this study, the cultural crisis will be even more acutely felt when political, economic, and social difficulties no longer figure as prominently as they do at this moment in history.

Nor should the ecological crisis preoccupy us here, because the problems are worldwide. The pessimists argue that given growth at a constant percentage rate per year ("exponential growth"), many mineral resources will soon be exhausted, whereas the optimists believe that most of these resources will be available for a long time to come, admittedly at a higher price, and that, given human adaptability and ingenuity, new technologies will sooner or later replace the finite resources. Seen in this light, problems such as the unequal distribution of resources are not intractable.[5] The optimists do not deny, of course, that there are considerable difficulties ahead and that relative scarcity quite apart, other issues will have to be tackled, such as pollution and the security risks connected with the growing use of nuclear energy.

Most of the debate has centered around the social and economic implications of the crisis, and these aspects are in many ways specifically European. In recent years there has been a revival of Marxist criticism culminating in the argument that the inherent contradictions in the system make a lasting recovery of the economy impossible. Little need be said about the importance of Marxist analysis; no intelligent discussion of modern history is possible without a knowledge of the Marxist method. But Marxist scholars labor under a triple handicap; the first is the undisputed fact that societies established on Marxist (or quasi-Marxist) principles are not very attractive. The Marxist case would no doubt be much stronger if there were no communist societies in existence. It has been argued that the shortcomings of these societies are the result of the unfortunate fact that communism has so far prevailed only in backward countries, and that communism in a developed society would work infinitely better and would not inevitably lead to political repression. But this is no more than a hope; has it been by accident that communism has come to power in backward countries? Sec-

---

[5] The best-known statement of the dangers of resource depletion is, of course, Dennis Meadows (ed.), *The Limits to Growth* (N.Y., 1972). The political and economic implications are studied in Philip Connely and Robert Perlman, *The Politics of Scarcity* (London, 1975).

ondly, Marx and Engels under-rated or ignored certain factors in their analysis which have not only changed the character of capitalism but are bound to affect any modern society quite irrespective of its structure. Thirdly, the impending ruin of capitalism has been announced with great confidence countless times for more than a hundred years, and since it has not happened yet, the more enlightened Marxists have become more cautious. Few of them will now argue that capitalism is already at the end of its tether—they are concerned with the long-term perspectives, not with events likely to happen tomorrow or the day after.

At the time of the great depression, around 1930, it was said in Marxist circles—and in many other circles as well—that capitalism was finished, and capitalist economic theory bankrupt. This was unfair to Mr. Keynes and his school, but on the whole there was little optimism at the time. There were only a few who dared to envisage, as Schumpeter did, that the "capitalist engine" would repeat its previous performance for another half century. He calculated that in this case by 1978 per capita income in the United States would rise to some $1300 in terms of 1928 purchasing power: "This would do away with anything that according to present standards could be called poverty, even in the lower strata of the population, pathological cases alone excepted."[6]

Schumpeter thought that there was no economic reason that made such doubling of income impossible even though he believed it unlikely for political reasons. We can now examine this prediction with the benefit of hindsight. The capitalist textbooks were perhaps deficient, but there was nothing essentially wrong with the "capitalist engine." Schumpeter's optimistic prediction actually underrated the growth of the American G.N.P. by some 65%. Progress in every European country has been at least of a similar magnitude, and in some it has been far greater; if nevertheless dissatisfaction with capitalism has spread, this is not because it has failed but because our perception of poverty has changed; what was thought tolerable in 1928 is no longer acceptable today.

According to the Marxists' interpretation of the crisis, it is quite mistaken to see its roots in the ungovernability of democratic societies or the quality of political leadership. For them the cause of the present

[6] Schumpeter, *Capitalism, Socialism and Democracy,* fifth ed. (London, 1976), p. 66.

crisis is the inherently unstable character of capitalist growth, the fact that wealth is concentrated in a few hands, that the economy is based on the profit motive, the market and competition, that capitalism has to accumulate and to expand in order to survive. Thus it is self-destructive, doomed to recurring and ever sharpening crises of underconsumption, of ineffective demand. The only way out of this dilemma is the nationalization of the means of production and centralized planning in the interest of a classless society. At the same time many contemporary Marxists are quite willing to admit that capitalism has profoundly changed since Marx's time, and that some of the basic tenets of Marxism have to be discarded, or at the very least to be modified in the age of "monopoly capitalism" on one hand, and growing state intervention on the other.

Growing state intervention in the economy is one of the most difficult theoretical problems facing Marxists today. Public expenditure which was about 13 per cent in Britain before the First World War is now approaching the 60 per cent mark, and taxation has risen to 40 per cent of the G.N.P. The state, in short, directly controls about half of the gross national product in the United Kingdom and the trend in all other European countries (and the United States) is similar. In these circumstances the role of the state is of course of the greatest importance; it can intervene at any time in the economy and it has a great many stabilizing (or destabilizing) devices at its disposal. These devices may not work, but if they fail to have the desired effect the reason could well be political rather than economic. Perhaps state intervention is half-hearted, not radical enough? One of the main Marxist arguments against the monetarists is, of course, that their policy is incompatible with political democracy, that a political party advocating mass unemployment would have to suppress not only the trade unions but also free elections. For it could not possibly hope to gain sufficient electoral support for a policy from which a great many people are likely to suffer even if only temporarily. This argument may or may not be correct, but it applies, *mutatis mutandis* to any party envisaging radical cures for economic illnesses. A state in which the means of production have been nationalized may well announce the existence of a classless society, but there would still be no agreement over the distribution of the national wealth. If such a state stuck to the democratic system, it would have to face the same old questions concerning income differentials, accumulation of capital and allocations for social welfare. In the past it was argued that a totally socialist, planned economy in contrast to capitalism would provide steady growth. But the more enlightened Marxists now freely concede that the basic weakness of capitalism is not inefficient production of goods—Marx clearly underrated the capacity still left in capitalism to produce; he was, of course, quite enthusiastic about its past performance. And on the other hand it now appears that Marx's concept of man's unlimited mastery of nature, the vision of everlasting progress and abundance was a dream, at least for the forseeable future.[7] In short, no miracles should be expected as far as the economic performance of fully nationalized economies are concerned. The Marxist case against capitalism has to be based not so much on its inefficiency as on its injustice. Nor is planning the central issue; a mixed economy is, in principle, perfectly capable of engaging in rational planning; even state capitalism can do so with great ease as wartime experience has shown; it is not an economic but a political problem. Thus the Marxist critique of capitalism is based, in the final analysis, on the political weakness of the contemporary democratic system, its incapacity to resolve conflicts. The question as to whether this can be achieved by any economic and social system within a democratic framework is left open.

The historical origins of this debate are usually overlooked. The antecedents of the theory of state intervention in the economy leading to state socialism are not to be found in Marx. But there were other economists, who dealt with the subject and whose works viewed in retrospect are again today of considerable interest. The most important among them was Simonde de Sismondi, the Swiss historian and political economist, who did not share the general optimism about the natural harmony of social interests prevailing among his contemporaries. Sismondi felt that the capitalist mode of production was likely to cause a great deal of unnecessary suffering; unfettered competition would result in overproduction and in crises. Hence his conclusion that it was the task of the state to intervene; growth and accumulation should not become a

---

[7] See, for instance, Andrew Gamble and Paul Walton, *Capitalism in Crisis* (London, 1976), *passim*.

fetish—the decisive criterion was the well-being of society. If necessary, growth should be limited in its interest.[8]

This, of course, was anathema to the classical economists, who ridiculed Sismondi as a hopeless romantic; as J. B. Say commented in his copy of Sismondi's book: "To arrest the growth of industry so as to help society . . . Good God!"[9] The writings of some outsiders apart, such as Rodbertus and Dupont-White, Sismondi's ideas were not taken up and some fifty years were to pass until the idea re-emerged that state intervention was necessary not just to solve the problems created by capitalism but to establish a more rational economic system. It figured prominently in the writings of the German *Kathedersozialisten*. Adolf Wagner established something akin to a law about the ever-expanding role of the state in the economy (*Gesetz der zunehmenden Staatstaetigkeit*); Schmoller and others pointed to the crucial role of the bureaucracy in a socialist society. The idea of state socialism brought about by the Hohenzollern family with the help of an army of bureaucrats was unlikely to appeal either to conservatives or to the working class. Thus, except for their proposals for practical social reform, the *Kathedersozialisten* were not taken very seriously. But with all the weaknesses in their analysis they realized more clearly than the Marxists, or anyone else at the time, that the question of administration, rather than production, was likely to be the crucial one in a socialist society. They also had a better appreciation of the staying power of nationalism, and its likely impact on the future of socialism.

The role of Sismondi and the *Kathedersozialisten* as predecessors of state socialism is now too obvious to be ignored any longer. But "statism," the central role of state sovereignty in a socialist society, also had its enemies on the left from the very beginning. The Anarchists argued that little would be gained if the tyranny of capitalism and militarism were replaced by the despotism of some other central authority which, even if claiming to act on behalf of the common good, would in fact con-

[8] Sismondi, *Nouveaux principes d'economie politique* (Paris, 1818), vol. 1, p. 76 ff. Sismondi's influence on Marx was greater than that of any other economist, yet his works have been neglected, the *Nouveaux principes* have not been translated, and there is no biography of Sismondi in English.

[9] Quoted in Eric Roll, *A History of Economic Thought* (London, 1973), p. 240. But what if growth had been arrested in 1820? Good God indeed.

stitute a new and probably more severe form of repression. Bertrand Russell, not a dyed-in-the-wool anarchist, realized that there was much to this argument. In 1918, making the case for socialism as the only sensible political order, he wrote: "There are various forms of Socialism; the form in which the State is the employer and all who work receive wages from it, involves dangers of tyranny and interference with progress which would make it, if possible, even worse than the present regime."[10] Various remedies were suggested to find a way out of the dilemma: Syndicalism in France, Industrial Democracy in the United States, Guild Socialism in Britain. Underlying these blueprints was the belief that the means of production should be owned and controlled not by the state but by the producers; such pluralism was to combine social and political democracy. More recently workers' control and *autogestion* have preoccupied socialists, and Yugoslavia has tried decentralization and workers' councils. Orthodox Communists have been opposed to such experiments for two reasons. The first, that there is already full freedom in Soviet society, need not be seriously discussed. The second, that no modern industrialized society can function on the basis of decentralization such as proposed by the advocates of *autogestion,* for all important decisions have to be taken by a central authority, cannot be so easily dismissed.

The pessimism about the future of the mixed economies and of democratic institutions is shared by some non-Marxist economists. It is based on the belief that freedom will not survive much longer because the pressures for government intervention in an overcrowded world are becoming overwhelming. Other economists argue, on the contrary, that there is no sound *economic* reason for this to happen, because the mixed economies of the West have shown more adaptability in coping with new conditions and emergencies than the rigid and centralized structures of the Soviet system.[11]

Lastly there are those who, starting from a different set of propositions, have also reached pessimistic conclusions with regard to the survival of liberal democracy. They refer to the generation of excessive ex-

---

[10] Bertrand Russell, *Roads to Freedom* (London, 1918), p. 209.

[11] Andrew Shonfield, "Can Capitalism Survive Till 1999?" *Encounter* (January 1977), and the ensuing discussion between Shonfield and Heilbroner.

pectations on one hand and the disruptive effects of the pursuit of group interests in the market place.[12] Following the writings of Hayek and others, they believe that the progress of statism endangers human freedom. Politicians making unreal promises compete in the market place for the votes of an electorate, the majority of whom has made no great effort to acquaint itself with the complexity of the issues involved. In contemporary conditions governments are torn into opposite directions by the need to combat inflation on the one hand and by the pressure for inflationary policies from trade unions which have now become far more powerful than at any time in the past. This school sees the root of the evil in the ever-increasing hold of the idea of egalitarianism over the intelligentsia and the working class.[13] For excessive egalitarianism creates conflicts which are insoluble in a democratic society. If disparities in income are reduced this does not necessarily affect the outrage felt about those that remain. And even if there were no differentials at all, there would still be complaints that it is unjust to give equal pay for unequal efforts. The conclusions reached by the pessimists have been summarized in a statement by Peter Jay—that free collective bargaining by trade unions, full employment, and usable currency are not in the long run compatible, and that on the other hand a liberal democracy cannot abandon any of these principles. Something will have to give, and most likely it will be the political system.

All these arguments rest on the weakness of the political system. The ills noted by the neo-Marxist school could be tackled by a state capitalist dictatorship, which would freeze wages and prices and somehow maintain full employment, drilling holes in the ground, if necessary, or distributing mail ten times a day. The old assumption that capitalism is bound to collapse once accumulation falters is questionable; capitalism, let alone a mixed economy, could coexist with limited economic growth at the rate of, say, 3 to 4 per cent. There still would be conflict and discontent but their expression would be suppressed by an authoritarian regime. At the same time such a regime could take those long term

[12] The argument has been put most ably by Samuel Brittan, in *British Journal of Political Science* V (1975): 129 ff.

[13] According to a frequently quoted public opinion poll, 80 per cent of those questioned in Britain said they would rather receive an extra £4 a week in common with every one else than receive £5 if everyone else's income were to rise by £6.

decisions that affect society as a whole and that cannot be left to the market mechanism. Under "state capitalism" part of the economy would still be in private hands, but if wages and profits as well as prices are regulated by the state, political power is, of course, far more important than economic power. In these circumstances the differences between state capitalism and state socialism increasingly tend to disappear and are of little practical consequence.

But there are legitimate doubts too, with regard to the arguments of the liberal school. Their predictions on the impending end of the liberal age in Europe seem to rest on the assumption that political democracy can exist only on the basis of a high degree of *laissez faire* capitalism; if so, democracy in Scandinavia and in Britain should have disappeared long ago. It can be taken for granted that for various objective reasons statism will make further progress and that individual freedom will have to be somewhat limited. But this does not *a priori* rule out a compromise between the rights of the individual and the interest of society, it does not imply that fascism or communism are the only possible alternatives. Political freedom pre-dates economic freedom in history. The maturity and rationality of the individual members of society and the altruism of groups should not be over-rated, but nor is it true that conflicting interests cannot be reconciled. Excessive expectations, after all, are not an invention of the 1960's, and there have been class struggles throughout history. This alone is insufficient ground for a mood of despondency. Conflict in society has admittedly become less tractable than in the past, precisely because it is no longer a clear-cut confrontation between classes, but between many interest groups, with one union sometimes turning against another insisting on greater differentials. The polarization anticipated by Marx has not taken place. Instead of a clear-cut confrontation between the bourgeoisie and the proletariat the general trend has been towards fragmentation and conflict within the classes. The problem, paradoxically, is not working-class solidarity but its absence, except on rare occasions, and the same is true for other classes.

All this leads us back to the weakening of the authority of the state as the core of the problem. The question is not whether a strong authority imposing strict controls on society could cope with the economic challenges. It could, and it will, if necessary. The crux of the matter is that such a system of government, while possibly beneficial for the

economy, may be harmful for the well-being of society in most other respects.

EUROPE—HALF FREE?

The question of Europe's political future will come up again, but
Europe's domestic problems cannot be discussed in isolation from the
foreign political environment.

What makes Europe's foreign policy problems so difficult to tackle
is not the enormity of the military threat, but the lack of a sense of
urgency when facing a clear threat to survival. Some Americans have
advised their European friends, echoing President Roosevelt, that they
have little to fear but fear itself. Such reassurance has its value in international relations, as in psychotherapy, though it should be accepted
that not everything is a matter of perception. If, for instance, a patient
happens to have a broken leg, psychological assurance alone will not
make him walk. Given West European proclivities, the advice of benign
neglect with regard to its defense is the worst possible advice that
Europe could receive at the present time, with the possible exception of
the counsel not to save energy. To select at random two of the voices
against magnifying the dangers: Mr. G. Kennan has admonished his
European friends that "the assumptions with relations to Soviet
strength are as exaggerated as are those that relate to Western European weakness. The belief that stronger powers dominate weaker ones
and dictate terms to them simply by the possession of superior military
force, or by demands placed under threat of the use of such force, has
extremely slender support in historical experience."[14] A similar message
has been conveyed by Mr. Leslie Gelb: "If you paint the Russians as ten
feet tall, you have accomplished the basic purpose of Soviet foreign policy without her having to lift a finger."[15] It is useful, no doubt, to be
reminded from time to time that the Russians are not ten feet tall, but
they still have a lot of tanks and other hardware and continue their build

---

[14] G. F. Kennan, *The Cloud of Danger* (Boston, 1977), p. 124.
[15] *Parameters*, No. 3 (1977). Mr. Gelb is Director of Politico-Military Affairs in the State
Department.

up at a considerably faster rate than NATO. Or, to put it differently, the core of the problem is not Soviet power, but Europe's lack of it; the Russians may be only six feet tall, the Europeans are even smaller.

However, concerning the danger of Finlandization it might be argued with some justification that as long as there is NATO, and as long as the United States do not fall too far behind the Soviet Union, Western Europe will not be subjected to strong Soviet pressure, nor will it lose its freedom and independence. As for the "slender historical evidence"—that stronger powers do not dominate weaker ones—it would be wise not to put it to a test. It is, of course, perfectly true that the United States have not dominated Cuba for the last twenty years. But then Cuba had a determined leadership and a reliable and powerful protector, and they faced a weak, confused, and irresolute America. It is unlikely, to provide an illustration, that a *Soviet* minister would have welcomed European military intervention in Angola as a positive contribution to stabilizing the situation.

It could be argued furthermore that even a neutral Europe would remain free and independent, provided its neutrality is credible and based on strength rather than weakness. But this would involve much closer cooperation between the countries of Europe and also a much greater defense effort. The problem again is not the magnitude of the threat but the mixture of lethargy and hypochondria which has afflicted Europe in the 1970's, the centrifugal pressures, the constant emphasis on national interest narrowly interpreted which has its corollary in a lack of courage and moral fiber. In recent years whenever Europe has had to face a challenge or an external threat there has been impotent handwringing—but little action. To put it mildly and not to use the ugly term "appeasement," there are many signs of a mood of accommodation in Europe. The incidents may have been trivial, such as Soviet attempts to change the program of the Venice Biennale, or the Soviet displeasure about the size of the French and Italian defense effort, modest as that is. Other examples come to mind, including the pressure brought on Spain not to join NATO; the advice given to the Turks not to be too fussy about violations of their airspace and to the Austrians not to modernize their army; the pressure on Scandinavia exerted by Soviet leaders (November 1977) who pretended to regard the small defense effort made by Norway as a threat to the massive Soviet build-up on the Kola

peninsula; Mr. Brezhnev's warnings in January 1978 about the consequences if the European members of NATO were to adopt new
weapons' systems—it is easy to imagine how the Soviet leaders would
have reacted if the Europeans had issued similar warnings with regard
to the deployment of the Russian SS 20; the attempts to erode the status
of Berlin; the pressure on all European countries not to provide facilities
to Radio Free Europe and Radio Liberty, and not to broadcast material
critical of the Soviet bloc countries, and not to complain when Soviet
and Eastern bloc countries beamed far more virulent attacks on the
West.

There is nothing startling about these and other Soviet initiatives
which in one form or another have been going on for a long time. They
would not even be worth mentioning but for the signs of an increasing
Western readiness not to give offense. European reactions to President
Carter's early human rights initiatives are of considerable interest in this
context. While this policy was (and is) popular among many Europeans
of all political shades, leading newspapers have reacted with concern
and anger. If President Giscard d'Estaing was the only European statesman to express his disapproval openly, others are known to have privately uttered similar opinions. It was not, of course, that they opposed
human rights, but they feared both domestic and international compli-
cations as a result of annoying the Russians. According to this line of
reasoning, it is legitimate for the Soviet Union to receive and support
foreign Communist leaders, whereas it is in bad taste for Western
leaders to receive Soviet dissidents or to express support for their activities. But moral obligations quite apart, Western protests against in-
fringements at human rights would only be a logical and quite effective
reply to the Soviet ideological offensive, which, it has been proclaimed,
time and time again, will continue detente or no detente.

It may be said that while such behavior is not very courageous, the
policy of "accommodation," of taking a low profile, is applied by European governments towards the OPEC countries not less than vis-à-vis
the Eastern bloc; the motive is certainly not ideological. When issues of
principle facing British or French foreign policy are discussed, the argument that recurs, all too often, is that countries whose economic survival depends on the good will of others, have to adjust their policies accordingly; they have to be morally neutral and should not wait for a

threat or an ultimatum, but rather shape their policies in such a way as to prevent the occurrence of these situations. Such behavior has occurred at all times among many people, and it would perhaps be easier to accept if the fear of angering a powerful neighbor or a wealthy client did not appear behind a mask of superior political wisdom and even self-righteousness.

What has been said about European attitudes vis-à-vis the Soviet Union and the danger of Finlandization also applies, of course, *mutatis mutandis* to Europe's position vis-à-vis the United States and to its dependence on the oil-producing countries. A detailed review of United States–European relations and Europe's policy towards the OPEC countries and the third world would lead beyond the confines of this study. Certain political facts are so obvious that to restate them is only to repeat what everyone knows anyway. There is no good reason why European foreign policy should be made in the White House and the State Department, or why European defense policy should depend on the Pentagon. There is something profoundly unhealthy in such a relationship. Even if Europe is not able to defend itself entirely without American help, the extent of Europe's dependence could be substantially reduced. Such dependence was, of course, inevitable in the immediate post-war period when much of Europe was in ruins. More than three decades after the end of the war, with more manpower at its disposal than the United States and greater industrial production, there is no objective reason why Europe should be so vulnerable to pressure from outside and so dependent on America, except, of course, the belief in Europe that the continent's constitution is not robust enough to undergo such intolerable exertions. Alternatively, it has been argued that it should not even try, for Europe's mission is not in the field of power politics, rather it is to be a great "civilian power." If it tried to emulate the two super-powers Europe would lose its soul; if, on the other hand, it works for peace and greater social justice, it can be a beacon of hope for all mankind.[16] These are noble sentiments but out of place in a sinful world in which political and military power is still decisive. For unless Europe can defend itself and regain a greater degree of independence it will never be in a position to carry out its mission. All past experience

[16] See, for instance, F. Duchene in M. Kohnstamm and W. Hager (ed.), *A Nation Writ Large?* (London, 1973). The title of the German translation is *Zivilmacht Europa*.

shows that dynamic, self-confident societies are capable of coping with their domestic and foreign problems at one and the same time. Those on the other hand who claim that they would collapse under the burden, that domestic reform programs can be undertaken or expanded only if defense spending is radically cut, are either looking for an alibi for inaction or want to reduce defense spending for political reasons. No striking social reforms, no selfless help for poor third world countries should be expected from them.

These manifestations of weakness, it has been argued, are unpleasant, but how dangerous are they? At the present time direct foreign interference in the domestic affairs of any European country would not be tolerated. European political parties and their leaders do not need the stamp of Soviet approval and seen in this light Europe has not been Finlandized yet, nor has it been bought by the owners of the new wealth.[17] But time does not stand still and what is true today will not necessarily be true some years hence. If Europe's decline continues, the tendency towards accommodation may turn into fully-fledged appeasement, or worse. Optimists will argue that since a military attack on Europe is highly improbable, and the imposition of direct political control not much more likely, all that can be expected is more of the same—an even lower European profile, and frequent professions of friendship towards those threatening it. Such optimism rests on the assumption that the disintegration of Europe will not proceed beyond a certain point, and that in any case, there will still be the American safety net on which to fall back. And if such a state of affairs lasts long enough perhaps the threats may diminish or disappear altogether, for those threatening it from the outside are not immune to political and economic upheaval.

These suppositions may be borne out by future events, but not one of them can be taken for granted. At the very least, such speculation is dangerous. Only professional gamblers would bet on their own survival against such odds. Most human beings would make every possible exertion to reduce the risks. Yet what is true of Europeans as individuals,

---

[17] King Jugurtha, upon leaving Rome: "Rome is a venal city and doomed to quick ruin if there will only be a buyer" (Sallust, *Bellum Jugurthinum*, ch. 35, 10). Jugurtha's downfall preceded Rome's by several centuries, but in our time his North African descendants have appeared as very active buyers in the markets of Italy and elsewhere in Europe.

does not apparently apply to them collectively. The laws of individual psychology are not those of crowd psychology; hence the willingness to take unacceptable risks, the willingness to let things slide instead of making the effort to reduce the risks to the survival of free institutions in Europe.

THE YEARS AHEAD

Little is known about the origins of *abulia* and while there are remissions, and while the disease may indeed disappear altogether, this seems to be spontaneous and there is no known cure. While the origins of the disease are shrouded in mystery, there are no secrets about its symptoms and likely effects. It manifests itself, *inter alia,* at one and the same time in the belief that democracy cannot show us the way out of the crisis and complaints about the unsatisfactory state of the democratic system and its institutions. It is not that these complaints are imaginary, but they are frequently based on the unrealistic assumption that society and its institutions can be more perfect than the human beings which constitute it. It is unrealistic to demand a further reduction of authority at a time when the decline of authority in democratic societies endangers their survival in any case; more of the same medicine will neither alleviate the symptoms of the malaise nor affect their causes. Sometimes the blame is put on "blockages" of various kinds in societies. But such descriptions are of limited help; the blockage may well be inherent in the system, and therefore irremovable without changing large parts of the system. Bureaucracy has no more friends than capitalism, and centralized planning has grave disadvantages, but modern society cannot function without rational planning. A radically different life-style has been proposed as an alternative: small, decentralized societies in which bureaucratic interference into the life of the individual would be reduced to a minimum, in which much of our food would be grown in our backyards, and following William Morris, many necessities of daily life produced in our homes. Thus, according to one group of social forecasters the typical family of the year 2000 may live in a converted farmhouse on the edge of a hill between 70 and 150 kilometers from a major city:

> This farm is one of a group forming a small rural hamlet. . . . to speak of families, though gives a wrong impression. Many of the children have broken away during adolescence and have joined other groupings, sometimes with other adults, sometimes with each other. . . . People do not follow life time careers. Instead, people mix different roles. They may be postmen or milkmen in the mornings, students in the afternoon and entertainers in the evenings. Similarly they may be managers at 25, students at 35 and craftsmen at 45.[18]

The temptation to ridicule such visions should be resisted; similar ideas can be found, after all, in the writings of the Utopian Socialists, and it may be useful to recall that the most important of them, Saint-Simon, was also a pioneer of the European idea and one of the first to develop the concept of crisis in modern political thought. If Marx poked fun at their fantasies, later generations are not quite convinced of the superiority of "scientific" over "utopian" socialism, and the idea of a more variegated human existence (postmen or milkmen in the morning, students in the afternoon, and so on) can be found, after all, also in a famous passage in the work of Marx. He wrote in his *Deutsche Ideologie* that in a communist society people would hunt in the morning, go fishing in the afternoon, raise cattle in the evening and be critics after dinner. It has been pointed out that the idea of "raising cattle in the evening" was a little far-fetched, but then Marx was not an agriculturist, and, in any case, the lapse does not affect the basic thrust of his argument.

It could well be that without the utopians of other times as Anatole France once noted, men would still live in caves, miserable and naked. But the great problem of freedom in utopian society apart (which need not concern us in the present context), there has always been the vexing question of how the transition from the present unsatisfactory state of affairs to utopia will come about. Several generations of utopians based their optimism on an evolutionary process, on a belief in reason, progress, and above all scientific discovery. Others, even before the First World War, were less optimistic and solved the problem by means of some cosmic disaster, or at least in a nine years' period of destructive warfare or total economic collapse.

[18] Peter Hall (ed.), *Europe 2000* (London, 1977), p. 258.

The blueprints for a radical change in life style are not inherently unfeasible; settlements of the kind mentioned above have existed and some of them continue to flourish even now.[19] But the Israeli Kibbutzim, to chose the most obvious example, consist of a small elite and they came into being, furthermore, in a specific historical situation unlikely to repeat itself on a broad scale. Thus we are back to the old question concerning the willingness to undergo radical change. The European record of making voluntary sacrifices is not impressive.

Those nowadays engaged in social planning of the utopian kind are usually geographers, technocrats, or sometimes economists. Insofar as they deal with politics, the issue of transition is either relegated to a minor place or ignored altogether.[20] But this is surely the crucial issue; what will bring about the move to the small rural hamlet—enlightened self-interest, a sudden conversion, or perhaps the advent of a new generation with different social values and priorities?

The planners are likely to answer that if rational behavior will not do it, dire necessity will, *volentem fata ducunt nolentem trahunt*. The question of energy is bound to be brought up at this point as well as the problem of other finite resources. At the present time, large-scale oil production in Alaska and from the North Sea makes the situation relatively tolerable, but in a few years hence production from these sources will level off and then decrease, and the availability of oil will fall below requirements. This will happen in the early 1990's, according to optimistic forecasts and around 1985, according to pessimists. But well before that most European countries will face grave difficulties in paying for their oil imports. Since non-oil energy supplies will not substantially relieve the situation, and since the lead time of new technology is

---

[19] But is it still far-fetched to predict that the "typical family of the years 2000" will live and work in a small rural hamlet. William Morris in a review of Bellamy's famous book (*Looking Backward*) rightly pointed out that this utopia was based on the presence of a huge, well-drilled industrial conscript army, in short on urban existence and regimentation. But Morris never provided a convincing answer to the question of how densely populated countries could survive without industrialism.

[20] See for instance Wayland Kennet, *The Futures of Europe* (Cambridge, 1977). The chapter on "Politics and Institutions" is the seventeenth and last. "The literature of futurology," Victor Ferkiss writes, "is filled with predictions about long range social, cultural and economic prospects. There is however a remarkable sparseness of predictions about politics." Victor C. Ferkiss, *Futurology* (Beverly Hills, 1977), p. 41.

measured in decades rather than years, the crisis is quite literally around the corner. And while the question of energy is the most acute and dramatic of all the shortages, in view of its implications for economic growth and its political repercussions, it is only one of the harbingers of the new era of scarcity.

Warnings of this kind have been faulted in detail, but there is little controversy about the general thrust of the argument. To cope with limits and scarcity, some planning and order are needed; the more vulnerable a continent or a country, the greater the need for it, and it is of course quite obvious that Europe, poor in raw materials, is in a weaker position in this respect than the United States. The instruments for rational planning exist in Europe, but not the authority to impose it. Societies can live with a certain amount of anarchy, some admittedly, less happily than others. Yet a minimum of regulation is needed even when the going is good, and when difficulties arise it is usually only a question of time until the belief gains ground that a "new order" is needed. This could well happen under the guise of revolutions which are notoriously hard taskmasters and strict disciplinarians.

Europe has to face a period of entrenchment and as one of the wisest of the futurists, Dennis Gabor, has noted, an ordered retreat is the most difficult of military operations.[21] A political retreat is even more complicated in a free society; even if it is temporary and its consequences need not greatly affect our well-being. Diderot was aware of the dilemma when he wrote that there was a limit in civilization, a limit more comfortable to the felicity of man, "but how to return to it having left it, or how to remain in it, if we were there—I don't know." The main problem is the lack of psychological preparation for the implications of slower economic growth. Again to quote Dennis Gabor:

> An important fraction of university youth has become very impatient, but their movements are conspicuously lacking in constructive ideas. There are many thinking people, politicians not excepted, who are longing for a vision, but are overwhelmed by day-to-day work and by a feeling of impotence. Many feel that we are on collision courses, but do not know

[21] Dennis Gabor, *The Mature Society* (London, 1972), p. 168.

how to alter them. Stopping the machinery is not enough, any fool can do it, and there are enough fools busy doing it.[22]

The kind of ideological guidance that has been provided by Marcuse and others was based on the mistaken assumption that the age of scarcity was over. Keynes, to be sure, once had a similar vision, but he was writing about "Economic possibilities for our grandchildren," and he stressed that at least another hundred years would be needed to lead us out of the tunnel of economic necessity into daylight. Most orthodox Marxists still dismiss the idea that uninterrupted and unlimited economic growth may be impossible (or undesirable) as a capitalist fairy tale.[23] Others have shown their awareness that a problem does indeed exist which industrialized societies will have to face in the near future quite irrespective of their social structure and political orientation.[24] But these are for the time being a minority, and their message has not yet percolated to the politicians and the official communist ideologists.

In the absence of preparations for the changes that may well become necessary in our economies and our politics in the not-too-distant future, there is a danger that the pendulum will swing back too far from the present state of semi-anarchy in some democratic societies to a new authoritarian order. This is not, of course, a foregone conclusion; there will probably be no uniform pattern and the number of semi-, pseudo-, and anti-democratic possibilities seems almost unlimited. They range from relatively mild authoritarian regimes in which repression is kept to a minimum, to something akin to a second coming of fascism. Such a new fascism would have nothing in common with the still existing small European movements of the extreme right which derive their inspiration from the age of Hitler, Mussolini, and the lesser *fuehrers* of the

---

[22] Gabor, 168/9. There is a tendency to overrate the extent of the "retreat," for there is no sound economic and technological reason that growth at the rate of 3%–4% should not continue. For social and political reasons such growth is imperative, and it will be small only in comparison with the stormy economic development of the 1950's and 1960's. It will still be larger than it was during most periods in history.

[23] cf. E. Mandel, W. Wolf, *Ende der Krise oder Krise ohne Ende* (Berlin, 1977), p. 109.

[24] This refers, for instance, to Wolfgang Harich, André Gorz and Johano Strasser (*Die Zukunft der Demokratie* [Hamburg, 1977]).

twenties and thirties. Historical fascism is not only dead and buried, but also discredited, and no political party, drawing water from this poisoned well, would have any prospect of success. But this still leaves the field wide open for sundry populist or national socialist regimes which have important features in common with "classical" fascism, such as the aspiration towards a one party, dictatorial regime.

Communism, to repeat once again, has become as nationalist in Eastern Europe as it has in the West; thus, one of the main distinguishing marks between the communism of the pre-war period and fascism has almost disappeared; one would be hard pressed to point to the basic differences in foreign policy between the Gaullists and the French Communists. The new nationalism may be less aggressive in character; racialism is no longer in fashion. But Italian fascism, was not racialist for a long time and became so only under the pressure of Nazism. Nor is it of paramount importance that the new dictatorships may be headed by a small group of people rather than by a single fuehrer.

The new dictatorships may well be less brutal than those of the 1930's, perhaps, with luck, "fascism with a human face." Nevertheless, perspectives of this kind are highly unpleasant, and for that reason there is a strong inclination to ignore them or to dismiss them as alarmist. It will be said that fascism and totalitarianism, having caused so much destruction and suffering in the recent past, still provoke so much revulsion that most men and women will go to almost any length to prevent their resurgence. It is, of course, quite true that anti-fascist slogans are still quite popular. But no one under the age of forty in Europe today actually remembers fascism; those who were not deprived of freedom are unlikely to cherish it as much as those who lived through that period. They take freedom for granted and they are less sensitive to the threats to freedom. The new dictatorships, in any case, are unlikely to reappear under the sign of the swastika or the *fasci*, nor will their leaders be named Hitler and Mussolini. The old fascism is dead, but the "totalitarian [or authoritarian] temptation" continues to exist under different guises. The Pasok party in Greece preaching "Mediterranean Socialism" such as practised in some North African and Middle Eastern countries may be a portent of the future: a mixture of socialist and nationalist demagoguery, anti-liberal views, and the "revolt against the West" which was so typical for fascism—all this under impeccable "progressive," "anti-fascist" auspices.[25] Whether this is "Mediterranean Socialism," or as less kind observers may claim, Levantine Fascism, is beside the point—it is not an attractive political system in any case. One Volk, one party, one Fuehrer—Theodorakis summarized it. The danger of a second coming of fascism could be ignored if it were indeed, as some still claim, an essentially conservative movement and "the tool of monopoly capitalism." But in its more radical and more effective form it is nothing of the kind, but on the contrary anti-bourgeois, which is precisely what gave it its appeal to people cast adrift by the disintegration of their customary way of life.[26] The time may have come to eliminate the term "fascism" from our political dictionary with regard to any contemporary political movement, be it only in view of the indiscriminate and mostly misleading use that is made of it. But national socialist movements of various provenance with sundry populist slogans still have a magnetic power which may increase as conditions deteriorate. At the present time it is not fashionable in Europe to advocate dictatorship openly. But is is certain that the fate of an opposition would not be enviable following the victory of a movement of this kind.

There are powerful pressures in the direction of totalitarian rule and these may become even stronger in future. For once the road to dictatorship has been chosen, it becomes more and more difficult to arrest the movement midway and to turn back. The measures taken by an authoritarian government are bound to be unpopular. Inflation can be tackled, but usually at the price of shortages. Unemployment can be cut in a command economy, but what if those ordered to work as milkmen and postmen do not like their new jobs? Resistance from below leads to more pressure from above, emergency measures become permanent, partial control becomes total, and the return to a democratic order may be blocked for a long time.

The real problem is, of course, that dictatorship is not just the result of mass hysteria but is in many ways better equiped to deal with difficult problems than parliamentary democracy. Democracy is impossible without debate, but what if the debate does not lead to action in

---

[25] A. Papandreou, *Il socialismo mediterraneo, Intervista a cura di Enrica Lucarelli* (Cosenza, 1977).

[26] G. Lichtheim, "The European Civil War," in *The Concept of Ideology and Other Essays* (New York, 1967), p. 237.

the end? Democracy has shown great flexibility and has triumphantly emerged from grave tests and trials. But there have also been situations in which the leaders have thought that democracies cannot bear to hear the truth, situations in which the consensus has broken down and with it the democratic regime. The more sophisticated advocates of dictatorships have usually regarded it as a temporary expedient to cope with a state of emergency. Unfortunately experience has shown time and again that once the emergency passes the dictatorship remains, that freedom is easily surrendered but regained only with the greatest difficulty. In ancient Rome, at least up to Sulla's days, dictators were elected for a period not exceeding six months and their powers were still limited by law. In modern times dictators are usually not elected and once in power some of them want their rule to be established for a thousand years.

But the totalitarian response to the crisis is, of course, not the only one possible and in some countries certainly not the most likely one. The capacity of many societies to live with a certain amount of anarchy should not be under-rated; we have witnessed a state of affairs in some places in which strikes and absenteeism are a frequent occurrence, in which trains do not depart on time, in which the collection of garbage and the distribution of mail is no longer carried out on a regular basis, in which public order is only partly safeguarded. Such a situation will be considered intolerable in some societies but not in others, nor does the economy immediately grind to a halt as a result. A situation of this kind will be more readily accepted in Italy or Spain than in Germany. But it will not last forever. Societies have descended into anarchy; reference is usually made to the fate of the late Roman empire. But such disintegration has happened only rarely in modern times. Societies, like individuals, may have suicidal tendencies but they rarely commit suicide. Eventually, they recover, but the price paid for the "restoration of order" can be very heavy indeed. Men and women can exist without voting; they cannot survive without eating.

Democracy, to be sure, rests on certain preconditions. The most obvious need hardly be mentioned, that there can be no democracy without democrats. If there is no agreement on fundamentals, if conflicting economic or other interests of sections of the society cannot be reconciled, if there is no tolerance for diverging views, democracy will not survive. The syndrome is well known. The conviction spreads that the political leadership is no longer up to its job, that the political parties are either "corrupt" or inefficient and no longer representative of the will of the people, that the law is not consistently applied or not obeyed, that real power no longer rests with the parliament, that minority groups successfully defy the will of the majority.[27] Government is no longer in command; it has become an arbiter, and not a very efficient one, among various pressure groups. If no important and urgent decisions need be taken, such a system may work, but in a critical situation and under pressure its weakness will be obvious. Next the search begins for new forms of government. Even in free societies there are provisions for a constitutional dictatorship; there was, to give but two examples, a clause to that effect in the Weimar constitution (paragraph 48), and article 16 in the constitution of the French Fifth Republic is also open to such interpretation. Military dictatorship is another possibility, but a somewhat unlikely one in contemporary Europe, for present-day armies are both too small and unsuitable for other reasons to serve as the main pillar of an authoritarian regime for any length of time.

In previous ages the transition to authoritarian rule was smoothed by the appearance on the scene of a charismatic leader ("the saviour"), to whom the believers felt tied by a bond of personal loyalty. Alternatively, enthusiasm was generated through some powerful new myth. But people have become distrustful of great leaders and myths alike; soldiers went to their death with the name of Hitler and Stalin on their lips; the Central Committee of the party or the Supreme Control Commission cannot possibly inspire similar enthusiasm. The psychological attraction of strong leadership is certainly not what it used to be. And yet, once the conviction has gained ground that the old system no

---

[27] "The entire world found itself in a crisis of disbelief. Disbelief in the established social order . . . disbelief in the economic order of individualistic capitalism . . . disbelief in "middle class" moral standards, especially in matters of sex; disbelief in older values such as thriftiness, diligence, respectability, even property-owning; disbelief in any absolute scale of values whatsoever, disbelief in real progress; and finally disbelief in the ability of human reason to make anything coherent out of the muddle that is life. Such a wholesale collapse of established values produced an unbreathable atmosphere, a crisis of civilization." These observations sound quite familiar. They were made by a contemporary observer of the Nazi rise to power, Edgar Mowrer, *Germany Puts the Clock Back* (London, 1937), p. 34.

longer functions, some form of authoritarian rule is likely to emerge whatever its specific features and manifestations.

But there are political systems other than full-scale dictatorships and there are indications that in some European countries these may be tried once parliamentary democracy breaks down. This refers, for instance, to a pluralism reminiscent of the social order of the Middle Ages. There is no effective opposition in such a system and not that many human rights. But a pluralist regime of this kind, providing checks and balances of sorts, is still preferable to totalitarian rule. It is conceivable that Italy's two strongest parties will base their rule on a compact of this kind; the same may happen in Spain, and elsewhere the trade unions may enter a coalition with other forces and constitute the *de facto* government. It will be said that such conditions may be short term expedients, unlikely to last, but this is by no means certain. The fight for power between Church and monarchy or between the monarchy and the nobility in the Middle Ages lasted for a long time, but so did cooperation between them. A greater problem is trade union leadership in Western Europe; while union power has become very strong, its internal divisions and conflicts make it just a giant pressure group, not a political factor able to offer a coherent policy and leadership.

A system of this kind would be quite compatible with the old concept of the corporate state. It was advocated by German conservatives of the nineteenth century, by the French solidarists, by Professor Spann and his "universalists," and it could be argued that the idea of the Soviets and of Workers Councils in some ways also belong to the same tradition. The corporate state officially existed in Italy after 1926 but in practice hardly amounted to anything at all. The Nazis after playing with the idea for a little while rejected it, because they wanted a monolithic *Führerstaat,* not a pluralistic *Ständestaat.* Equally, in Russia after a year or two of experimentation the Soviets lost whatever importance they initially had. In view of its unfortunate history, the *Ständestaat* is likely to reappear, if at all, under a very different label—perhaps as "Producers Councils" and "Consumers Councils."

It is still unlikely that a new, refurbished kind of corporatism will be a decisive factor in politics, for in the absence of a consensus the important, the difficult, and the unpopular decisions can only be taken by a strong executive. But a vertical, functional kind of popular representation, suitably dressed up in a populist garb would no doubt be attractive to believers in participatory democracy and it would certainly make it easier for them to swallow the bitter pill of authoritarian government.

When democracy was first conceived there were no political parties, and it is, of course, also true that political parties have a great many defects such as the tendency towards bureaucratization and elite rule. But on the other hand democracy is meaningless without an opposition and the possibility of change. Democracy is compatible, in principle, with both capitalism and socialism; it is the politics of the capitalists and the socialists that counts, not their economics. It cannot survive if the majority of the population gives its votes to anti-democratic parties as was the case during the last years of the Weimar Republic. But the present crisis of democracy is different in character. Anti-democratic parties nowhere constitute a majority, neither is the intensity of the class struggle nor the aspirations of separatist movements the main reason for the failure of the democratic system. Together with a lack of government authority and of identification with the state it is the wide variety of conflicting interests (and interest groups), which were once thought to be one of the best guarantees of democracy, which now threaten to paralyze the political system.

The dangers confronting Europe may soon be comparable to those threatening a country at war, yet the societies respond as if they are facing one of the usual cabinet crises. The dangers of granting emergency powers to the executive are well known. Germany in 1933 is an excellent example of a "Constitutional dictatorship" turning into totalitarian rule. But a feeble response at a time of danger is courting disaster; a Brüning equipped with dictatorial powers would not have been an inviting prospect, but he would certainly have been preferable to Hitler. Europe in 1979 is of course very different in most respects from 1932; but one of the few constant features is the weakness of democracies when faced with the dangers threatening their existence, which is reflected in their inability to act forcefully and in time. This weakness is part of the price a democratic society pays for its freedom. The problem is that in certain conditions the price of inaction becomes intolerably high.

A great deal will of course depend on the character of the political attitudes of the younger generation in Europe; freedom is defended, after
all, not by manifestoes issued by parties and their leaders but by people
willing to fight for it. The desire for freedom seems to be the over-riding
passion of a younger generation opposing the present state and society
precisely for its repressive character. The form and the intensity of this
opposition vary from country to country; at its most extreme it manifests
itself in terrorism; more widespread is an emotional rejection, an unwillingness to identify with the state, let alone to support it, because of its
unfulfilled promises and other imperfections.

The phenomenon is not, of course, a new one. Since time immemorial the politics of younger generations have been radical in character;
young people have attacked their elders for their failures, and older people have been horrified by the extremism of youth. If German or French
students gravitated towards fascism in the inter-war period, a subsequent generation has tended towards the extreme left or has opted out
of politics altogether, concentrating (or dissipating) its energies in the
various counter-cultures.

There has always been a generation gap manifesting itself in the
call to replace the old and corrupt compromisers by a new generation of
pure revolutionary leaders who have the courage of their conviction.
Youth politics have frequently been wrong, sometimes dangerously so,
but it is also true that the world could not have dispensed with the idealism of the younger generation, for what great things have ever been accomplished without the enthusiasm of youth? Such enthusiasm has seldom been lacking among the younger generation, very much in contrast
to the tiredness and scepticism of their elders who only saw difficulties
and obstacles whenever major new initiatives were needed.

But idealism and enthusiasm can be misdirected or even suicidal;
the younger generation of the 1930's turned their back not just on the
shortcomings of the parliamentary system but on tolerance, humanism,
and on the values of Western civilization *tout court*. There is, to put it
bluntly, a similar danger today. Extenuating circumstances can always
be found: the full value of political freedom is appreciated only by those
who have been deprived of it. For the children of the post-war period
fascism and the Second World War are abstractions. Nor are they likely
to be impressed by the argument that the European societies had never

been as free or that there has never been as much social justice. Their historical consciousness begins with Vietnam, and they can see only the wide discrepancies which still exist between the realities and their ideals. Even more disconcerting than specific political aberrations, such as regarding Russia and China, North Korea or Albania as examples worthy of emulation, is a negative attitude reminiscent of that onslaught on basic human values which took place in the 1930's.

Young revolutionaries of bygone ages had to struggle for their ideals; facing strong and self-confident authorities, they were soon made aware of the risk involved in challenging them. A new generation of radicals, the children of the permissive age, has had it much easier; positions were surrendered to them without a fight and the risks they ran were small or non-existent. Such conditions do not make for heroism and it remains to be seen how such a generation of radicals will behave if faced by an enemy made of sterner stuff. To put all the blame on them is, of course, unfair, for to a considerable extent the fault has been that of their elders who through guilt and the fear of being labeled authoritarian shied away from their responsibilities and failed to impose restrictions whenever such restrictions were in the interests of society. In the resulting vacuum the consumers' society was left as the only basic value, a situation bound to generate discontent and a longing for higher ideals. A surfeit of freedom, a world without duties and responsibilities, was bound to lead to the desire for a new order. And at this point the ideological confusion has made a generation of radicals an easy prey for charlatans of various sorts; their resistance is low because they thirst for a new message; the "critical approach" is skin deep and behind it lurks the eagerness to accept a new conformism.

What has been noted so far refers to a minority; to generalize about the character of an entire generation is as unfair as to praise or to condemn a whole nation. But this minority is highly vociferous; it includes large sections of the young intellectual elite, and like a few drops of oil on a large quantity of water, it covers a great deal of the surface. The *Zeitgeist* is always shaped not by the silent majority but by the most active and noisiest minority.

Seen in this light there is good reason for pessimism. Incapable of seeing the dangers ahead, having gone through a process of intellectual and psychological disarmament this radical generation will be unwilling and indeed unable to resist a new age of tyranny. But one should always bear in mind that the mood of younger generations tends to change quickly, and often quite radically: the life span of a generation in our age is seldom longer than five or ten years. Few contemporaries would have believed that the Oxford students who solemnly swore in the 1930's never again to fight for their country would have done exactly that with great valor only a few years later. Equally, no one can be certain what changes tomorrow's elite, the generation of the 1970's, will undergo in the years to come and what the ultimate outcome of their learning process is likely to be.

To list the possibilities and dangers facing Europe is to venture far into the unknown. If the definition of such terms as "authoritarian" and "totalitarian" has been in dispute when describing the past events there can be even less certainty as to what they will signify in future. It is commonly thought that authoritarian government refers to centralized power used without legal restraint to control political life, whereas totalitarian government imposes its rule on all aspects of social and individual life in an attempt to bring about a "revolution from above" culminating in the emergence of a "new man." But even these broad generalizations leave a great many questions open, such as whether Italy under Mussolini was really totalitarian and how to define Russia after Stalin. These debates are however of only limited importance in the present context, for Europe is not where Russia was in the 1920's and Germany in the 1930's, nor are comparisons with the state of affairs in the third world at all helpful. The question that concerns us is what may happen in Europe if its democratic institutions were no longer able to cope with the existing stresses.

To pose the question in this general way, the only way it can be put, implies that there cannot be an unambiguous answer, for the situation varies from country to country. What is true for Spain and Portugal does not apply to Sweden and Norway. In some countries the stresses may not be as acute, and the institutions stronger and more adaptable than some suspect. Nor is there any universal, objective yardstick to measure either the depth of a crisis or the effectiveness of democratic institutions since so much depends on subjective factors including, for example, the perception of the danger itself. But even if democracy is clearly in grave trouble, even if it is weak and almost defenseless it may not be supplanted by dictatorship, simply because there may be no dictators in the running or because they are too weak to assert themselves. In this case the state of semi-anarchy could continue for a long time. Alternatively, public opinion sufficiently alarmed by the seriousness of the situation may grant the ruling party, or parties, limited and temporary emergency powers and these may be sufficient to cope with the difficulties, with relatively minor restrictions of freedom.

Nor is there any certainty that authoritarian rule would follow previously established patterns. There is no demand for new Caesars; even the supporters of an authoritarian regime would expect no more than measures re-establishing some order and reforms that fall far short of the unlimited ambitions of past totalitarian dictatorships. There would be no enthusiasm for a regime with either a messianic ideology or an elaborate apparatus of indoctrination and terror. An authoritarian regime would be pragmatic perhaps like Pisistratus or Kemal Ataturk, to name but two predecessors distant from each other in time. It would be expected to provide a preparatory, educational dictatorship leading to the restoration of a democratic regime at some future date. It would be a developmental dictatorship, an *Entwicklungs-diktatur* carrying out economic and social reforms at a difficult stage of transition. But the aim of such dictatorships would have to be the very opposite of what it was in the communist countries or in the third world where the main target was rapid industrialization.

This, of course, is the best case scenario for authoritarian rule, based on the assumption of real or imaginary "objective need." But "objectively," the Nazi crimes were not what Germany needed in 1933, nor was Stalinism the cure for Russia's ills. Modern dictatorships, unlike those in past ages, need a popular base. The masses have to be mobilized, the opposition has to be liquidated not just rendered temporarily ineffective. Thus authoritarian rule is constantly tempted to turn itself into something far worse. An enlightened monarch of the eighteenth century could afford to pursue a relatively liberal policy, something which autocrats in the late twentieth century might regard as a dangerous luxury.

There are, to summarize, different possibilities as to how the countries of Europe might react to the crisis. The status quo in which representative, parliamentary government continues to function relatively smoothly; a state of semi-anarchy in which democratic institutions partly or wholly cease to function, but in which no alternative contender for power emerges; a democratically elected government with emergency powers suspending certain freedoms; an authoritarian-style government with absolute powers but limited ambitions exposed to and responding to pressures from below; and lastly fully fledged totalitarianism. If, as may happen, part of Europe should move one way and the other part in an opposite direction, Mao's "great disorder under heaven" will have finally arrived in Europe.

The threats that have been discussed are real enough, but this is not to say that we have been reduced to the role of spectators watching the unfolding of a Greek tragedy. Some observers have argued that modern economic growth makes society highly vulnerable, undermines the legitimacy of institutions, and leads to the disintegration of the social order; and that the instinct of survival will impel the Western democracies along the road to the totalitarian state.[28] But if modern society is highly vulnerable, it is also very resilient and if technology has created terrible dangers it can also provide the means to control some of them. Science, to be sure, will not provide the answer to political problems. But this still does not justify the concentration by the prophets of doom on the easily discernible self-destructive trends in modern society which may lead to tyranny, for it is also true that the spirit of freedom has never been quite extinguished. And it seems at the very least a little premature to announce that in this respect a decisive, historical turning point has been reached: the end of freedom.

It has been well known for a long time that it is much easier to predict economic or demographic trends or even scientific discovery than political developments, let alone the emergence of new creeds,

[28] I am paraphrasing E. J. Mishan, *The Economic Growth Debate* (London, 1977), p. 265, the most persuasive discussion of the case against economic growth. The arguments for growth are most succinctly stated in Wilfred Beckerman, *In Defence of Economic Growth* (London, 1974).

transcendental or secular religions. Even the professional futurists, it has been noted, usually shy away from such hazardous ventures.

But there are always probabilities, and about certain policies it can be said with a high degree of probability that they will lead a country or a society to ruin. Examining the prospects for Europe there is, as always, the temptation to project past and present experience into the future. Such experience can be a useful guide for the next step or two but is of very little assistance beyond that, except in a negative sense. It is safe to assume, for instance, that, come what may, Luxemburg will not become a superpower. Lenin was right in assuming that revolution in his native country was possible. However, his hypothesis developed in *State and Revolution* in 1916, of what Russia would be like after the revolution was as far off the mark as anyone else's. Pursuing this argument it is much easier to predict what is unlikely to happen in Europe in the years to come. That Europe will face grave dangers in the years to come goes without saying, and while there are many ways of coping with these dangers (or failing to do so) they all involve more restrictions of individual freedom than Europeans have known since the end of the Second World War. This is not a pleasant prospect, but nor is it sufficient reason for black despair. In his preface to *The American Commonwealth* Lord Bryce wrote that "a hundred times in writing this book have I been disheartened by the facts I was stating; a hundred times has the recollection of the abounding strength and vitality chased away these tremors." Similarly, the student of contemporary Europe is torn in opposite directions and while there is ground for pessimism, he cannot easily give up hope. Having passed through countless ordeals in their long history, having gone through many dark periods, the countries of Europe have never suffered ultimate defeat. One of the benefits of studying the tradition of historical pessimism, at the very least, is that it compels one to suspend judgment. Quite likely the crisis, some of whose components have been described in this study, will take longer to unfold than anticipated. In the rarified air of futurology both progress and disaster are usually more distant than they appear to the naked eye; as in the theatre there are almost always retarding factors. This, of course, does not offer much comfort, for the history of a continent is not measured in months or years, and disaster deferred is not disaster averted. But the uncertainty is compounded by the many unknown factors in the equation that is Europe's future. Perhaps the dangers threatening Europe from the outside will be less acute or formidable than they now appear. Perhaps the Soviet Union may not be in a position to exert much pressure. Perhaps the oil-producing countries will find it to be in their own interests to help Europe overcome its economic difficulties. It is not impossible that the destructive effects of the narrow-minded nationalism which has plagued Europe for too long will lessen under the coming shocks and that the separatist movements will be contained. It is by no means certain that the Communist parties in Italy or Spain will become more democratic in time, but the fact that such a process has not taken place so far in any country does not mean that it is *a priori* impossible. All these are slender hopes, and it is also true that even in the absence of such pressures from outside and from within, even if Europe remains relatively free and relatively independent, it will still be confronted with enormous domestic difficulties. But is equally possible that there may be resources of strength, civic spirit, and wisdom not visible today. In some European countries there have been encouraging signs of a new spirit of responsibility; it is too early, though, to sound the fanfares of victory, and what is true with regard to some countries does not, unfortunately, apply to others. Jean Monnet once said that the great crises are the great federators, and it is precisely at a time of adversity and acute danger that energies needed for a new awakening are released. Democratic societies do not always collapse in the face of grave dangers, they are capable of great effort and of subjecting themselves to a discipline unthinkable in normal conditions, if their survival is at stake. European history with all its sad stories of decline and fall is full of examples of regeneration and rebirth, and it shows that there are no limits to human ingenuity and perseverance. Periods of decadence and despair are quite frequently followed by eras of hope and a new confidence. One does not know what causes such regeneration; sometimes it occurs without a visible cause or reason, sometimes it happens as the result of a major challenge. Perhaps the body politic of Europe, weakened and corrupted, needs the present infection to produce the antibodies that may save it. Perhaps Europe is about to enter purgatory not for the first time in its history, a painful but necessary stage in its long pilgrimage. It would be foolish to deny that the present state of Europe inspires fear. But man is a creature of hope, of fantasy and imagination as well as of fear; without hope neither the great world religions nor the present-day political ideologies would have come into being. There is no need to leave hope to the theologians or to engineer it artificially even if it may be technically feasible by means of modern psycho-pharmacology. To the extent that hope is the passion for the possible (Kierkegaard) it is not a delusion, a weakness and an escape from reality. The possibilities for a recovery of Europe certainly exist and with them the hope for a new beginning out of the inertia and the present confusion. The next chapter of European history will probably not be a pleasant one, but nor will it be the last.

CONCLUSION

History continues oblivious of the time tables of authors and publishers. During the year it took to write this book some of the issues covered in it have become clearer, others have remained obscure. There are few doubts now with regard to the Helsinki conference and the Belgrade follow-up meeting; these were even more meaningless events than one had assumed at the time. There are few illusions left regarding detente. European unity is as distant and elusive as ever. Low-key Finlandization in all directions, *à tous azimuts* as the Gaullists would put it, continues slowly in various parts of Europe. But perhaps the very term "Finlandization" has outlived whatever usefulness it ever had; perhaps it should be replaced by self-censorship or adjustment; the Germans had that wonderful term *Gleichschaltung* in 1933. There have been no dramatic developments, only a further slight erosion of the political will. The limits of Eurocommunism are certainly more obvious now than a year or two ago; perhaps this term too should be discarded soon. On the credit side it could be argued that the worst has not happened in Britain and in Italy, and that inflation has substantially decreased. There has been a change for the better in Britain's fortunes, or at least an improvement in the national mood. Some long overdue measures have been taken to improve the defense of Europe. If the rise of the European currencies in comparison with the dollar were a true yardstick for their economic health, their political cohesion and stability, and their ability to defend themselves, there would be much ground for self-congratulation. But it is not a true yardstick at all. The various problems besetting the European societies described in this book have not disappeared, even if they have become less acutely felt here and there. The internal situation in Europe continues to be precarious and the military balance of power unfavorable. Europe could now no more defend itself alone than ten or twenty years ago, and these are the decisive issues, not the ups and downs of the money market.

Europe is as vulnerable as before with regard to its energy supply, yet no common energy policy has emerged. Production costs in Europe have risen so much that it has become increasingly difficult to compete in the world markets. There are many more manifestations of weakness, and they all show that the countries of Europe have come to resemble more and more the house built on sand by the foolish man in the Biblical parable: "And the rain descended, and the floods came, and the wind blew, and beat upon the house, and it fell, and great was the fall of it." The old houses have been comfortable, those living in them have grown fond of them, and moving house, everyone knows, always entails uncertainties and hardships. There is psychological resistance, and at this stage there is a strong urge to belittle the dangers ahead. Perhaps there will be only a little rain, perhaps the winds will not blow that hard, and perhaps the floods will sweep away only the neighbor's house? Perhaps, and perhaps not.

Most of the weaknesses of Europe are self-inflicted, and if this book were written all over again the criticism would be even harsher despite the fact that the European mood has improved a little of late. Criticism should be harsher because the problems facing Europe are not insurmountable, they do not involve rare wisdom and superhuman efforts. The difficulties are not that daunting; all that is needed is common sense and the will to cope with them. It is not that there are no mitigating circumstances for Europe's prostration—there always are. But in history, unlike in law, they never count nor is there a higher court of appeal. A compassionate historian writing the history of our times at some future date, long after our current preoccupations will have ceased to matter, may well find excuses. It is too much to expect such detachment and compassion from contemporaries, nor is it certain that it would make for better history.

INDEX

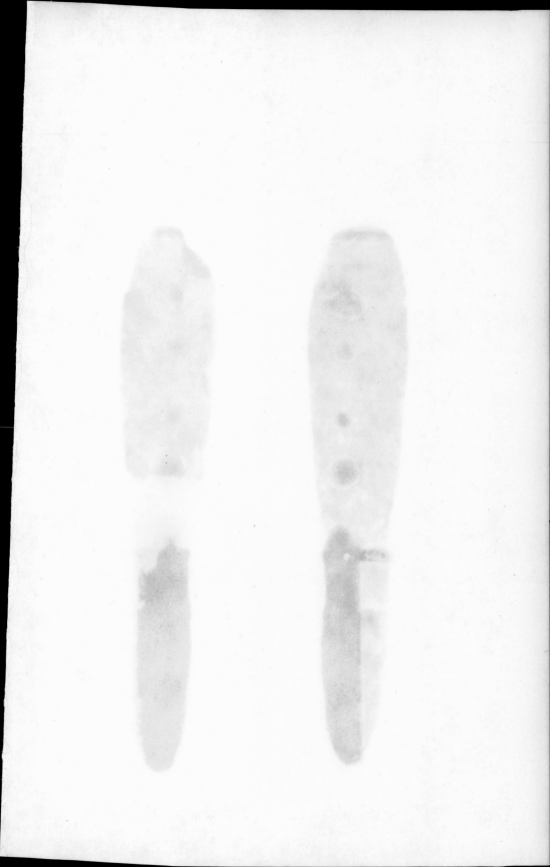

DATE DUE

GAYLORD   PRINTED IN U.S.A.